KOHN PEDERSEN FOX

KOHN PEDERSEN FOX

*Buildings and Projects
1976–1986*

*Edited by Sonia R. Cháo and
Trevor D. Abramson*

Introduction by Paul Goldberger

RIZZOLI
NEW YORK

To my family. S.C.

To Adéle and my family. T.A.

First published in the United States of America
in 1987 by Rizzoli International Publications, Inc.,
597 Fifth Avenue, New York, NY 10017

Library of Congress Cataloging-in-Publication Data

Kohn Pedersen Fox.

  Bibliography: p.
  1. Kohn Pedersen Fox (Firm)   2. Architecture,
Modern—20th century—United States.   I. Cháo, Sonia.
II. Abramson, Trevor.
NA737.K65K6   1987   720'.92'2   86-42707
ISBN 0-8478-0748-7
ISBN 0-8478-0749-5 (pbk.)

Designed by Alessandro Franchini Design, Inc.,
New York City

Set in type by David E. Seham Associates Inc., Metuchen, NJ
Printed and bound in Japan by Dai Nippon Printing

Cover illustration: Proctor & Gamble entry pavilion
night view
Title page illustration: General Re pavilion
Back cover illustration: Logan Hotel detail

CONTENTS

INTRODUCTION

by Paul Goldberger

There are few stories in architecture like that of Kohn Pedersen Fox. Other firms have achieved equal commercial success, and others have made as significant a mark in terms of design. But no other architectural firm in our time has succeeded in both realms so rapidly. Eleven years ago Kohn Pedersen Fox did not exist; today it comfortably occupies a position in the category defined by such eminent practitioners as Philip Johnson and John Burgee, I. M. Pei, Kevin Roche, and Skidmore, Owings & Merrill—the architectural firms that produce commercial work of consistent seriousness of intention. Kohn Pedersen Fox cannot claim to possess the historical depth of these other firms, of course, for it barely has a history at all. But if the firm's youth means it lacks the venerable record of its competitors, it more than makes up for this in the vitality of its work and the impact that its buildings are having on the current architectural scene.

What may be the most impressive thing of all about Kohn Pederson Fox—beyond even the obvious quality of the architecture itself—is the way in which the firm has restored to American architecture a sense that there is a meaningful and healthy center, a point of intersection between creative and innovative design and major commercial work. Such points have existed at many times in our history—H. H. Richardson represented one, surely, as did Daniel Burnham, and Louis Sullivan in his period of greatest activity; so did McKim, Mead & White, and in a much later period, Eero Saarinen. All of these architects were producing work that, if not all the way at the cutting edge, was at least consistent with the best design impulses of its time, and yet each was a highly active commercial architect as well. There seemed, in their practices, to be relatively little contradiction between esthetic innovation and commercial practice. The large-scale projects they made were generally the buildings by which their times were measured.

In the 1960s and 1970s, however, that kind of practice seemed to disappear. The fresher side of the profession seemed to divide between creative, design-oriented architects on the one hand and large-scale, commercial practitioners on the other. When the two worlds of serious esthetic intent and large-scale commercial practice did intersect, it seemed at the rear, not at the front, of the march of design. The most serious-minded of commercial architects in those years tended to be relatively conservative in terms of their designs— Skidmore, Owings & Merrill is perhaps the best example, a firm whose distinguished Miesian work in the early

1950s was the vanguard of commercial architecture. Skidmore's buildings in those days were truly the measure of their moment, but by the 1970s, Skidmore had barely changed, and it seemed not at the front but at the rear. So, too, with architects like Edward Larrabee Barnes or I.M. Pei—much of their work had high quality, but even the best of it was no longer setting esthetic directions. The profession could almost be described then as being like a backwards flying wedge— the firms leading the profession formed the two very separate flanks, and the middle, the place where esthetics and professional practice met, was at the rear.

The shift in emphasis in Philip Johnson and John Burgee's practice toward postmodernism can surely stand as the beginning of the reversal of that pattern, as the first time in recent years when an architect whose work was setting significant new directions was also building commercial projects on a large scale. But if Johnson and Burgee's work in the mid-to-late 1970s—late-modern buildings like the IDS Center and Pennzoil Place as well as postmodern ones like the A.T.&T. and Republic Bank buildings—could be said to have renewed the connection between esthetic innovation and the commercial mainstream, Kohn Pedersen Fox surely expanded and intensified that connection. And even now that the connection is secure, and architects like Cesar Pelli and Kevin Roche, not to mention the recent and significantly changed output of Skidmore, Owings & Merrill, all are doing large-scale commercial work that might be described as innovative esthetically, the practice of Kohn Pedersen Fox still stands out.

For it is Kohn Pedersen Fox that has forged the most natural and satisfying intersection between the esthetic intentions of postmodernism and the economic intentions of large-scale commercial development. It is no small achievement. In the last few years Kohn Pedersen Fox has managed to entice numerous real-estate developers into an acceptance of work that is no less serious and no less inventive than that which emerges from the drawing boards of any of the firm's competitors. That much of it is work that can be described as "postmodern," a term of opprobrium in many circles, makes the accomplishment all the more impressive.

The reasons for this success are several. One is surely the internal organization of the firm itself. There are not many relationships between a designer as creative as William Pedersen and a marketing man as persuasive as Eugene Kohn; strong designers like Pedersen most often work on their own, and high-powered salesmen like Kohn, sadly, are all too often paired with mediocre designers. But here, the two men obviously complement each other—William Pedersen is grateful that he has Gene Kohn stoking the fires of this office, while Kohn, far from unhappy about the level of creativity Pedersen has made KFP's trademark, has been a consistent booster of ambitious design, and serves not only as a supportive internal critic of Pedersen and the other design partners, but as a tireless advocate of their work on behalf of clients. And then behind both men is the third founding partner, Sheldon Fox, who might be described as the grease between these two wheels; his management skills are what keep the system operating smoothly. It is a combination that calls to mind some of the great partnerships of the past, such as that between Stanford White and Charles McKim, both designers themselves, and William Rutherford Mead, the stabilizer who kept that practice on an even keel.

As the firm has grown, this quality of balance has not been lost. Arthur May and William Louie now design numerous major projects, and Robert Cioppa manages many of them. Patricia Conway, who was with Kohn, Pedersen and Fox at the founding of the firm a decade ago, now has charge of a subsidiary, Kohn Pedersen Fox Conway, which has become a major presence in the field of commercial interiors.

But even the best internal organization and combination of personnel could not give an architectural firm the stature Kohn Pedersen Fox has earned. For this, only the work itself will suffice. In the first few years of the firm's practice, the buildings it produced were somewhat above the average for commercial firms, but beyond that were not exceptional, and it was difficult, eight or nine years ago, to predict that KPF would rise to its present position. Its architecture was obviously good and thoughtful, but so was that of many firms. KPF moved ahead of the pack, so to speak, somewhat gradually, if anything that happened in less than a decade can be referred to as gradual; the A.T.&T. Long Lines Building of 1980 in suburban Virginia marked a certain expansion of the firm's ambition, and the Hercules headquarters in Wilmington, Delaware, brought intentions to a higher level still.

But it was the completion of the 333 Wacker Drive building in Chicago in 1983 that forced the realization that this firm was a serious design presence. This sleek tower of greenish glass atop a granite and marble base was Kohn Pedersen Fox's first building of national significance. Built on a triangular site at a bend in the Chicago River that makes it one of the few skyscrapers in Chicago that stands alone, with no other building beside it, the building opens with a generous, gentle curve facing the river, and has a more linear, geometric face where it meets the city grid inside. At the top, the building flattens out, looking as if a flat plane had sliced into the curve, which serves at once to give the building a lively profile at its crown and to tie the sides together.

There is some awkwardness in the relationship of the polychromed granite base and the greenish glass tower: one senses here a late-modern tower atop a postmodern base. But the overall unity of form in a building that attempts to establish both a monumental presence on the river and a satisfactory relationship with an urban grid— two goals that might well yield a schizophrenic building— is impressive. That the form has considerable visual interest in its own right only compounds the achievement here.

The 333 Wacker Drive building represented Pedersen's belief that the design for an urban building must emerge out of the surrounding context—not in terms of reflecting it literally, which 333 Wacker Drive does not at all, but in terms of more subtle relationships of massing, street pattern, open space, materials, and presence on the skyline. The headquarters for Procter & Gamble in Cincinnati, perhaps KPF's most significant commercial building complete at this writing, makes the point well. It is a seven-story, L-shaped structure with a pair of 17-story octagonal towers set on either side of the corner of the L. The complex is all of limestone, and the tower roofs are pyramidal, giving the building significant impact on the Cincinnati skyline despite its modest height; the overall form, though it has no precise model, has the strong, spirited presence of the better eclectic skyscrapers of the 1920s, buildings like Raymond Hood's American Radiator Building and Carrère & Hastings's Standard Oil Building. The complex manages the difficult urbanistic gesture of relating comfortably to Procter & Gamble's old building, a low and bland box of limestone, by effectively extending the line of the old building and enclosing the space in front of it into a major urban forecourt. The old building, as banal a postwar structure as there is, is actually enhanced by being brought into a larger and more complex urban dialogue.

The call to design the Procter & Gamble building was in

itself confirmation of KPF's status; once that project was underway, the firm found itself ranked in a different peer group, and more and more requests to design major skyscrapers came its way. There have been times when KPF's eagerness to grow may have led it to accept certain commissions that might prudently have been rejected, such as the large building in New York that will rise behind fine small-scale commercial facades on Fifth Avenue, altering the scale of a venerable older block, or the immense tower designed for 383 Madison Avenue, one of Pedersen's more striking skyscrapers, but a problematic one given the intensity of mid-Manhattan congestion.

But by and large the recent list is a distinguished one—its most recent additions being 900 North Michigan Avenue in Chicago and major towers in New York, Pittsburgh, Boston, Dallas, Minneapolis, and Seattle, all of which are handsome structures that evoke the eclectic spirit of 1920s skyscrapers without either sentimentality or cute gestures. The problem of evoking the romantic spirit of the skyscrapers of half a century ago without appearing to be fawning in imitation is one that few architects have solved as comfortably and as consistently as Kohn Pedersen Fox. In New York, there is particular promise to a tower designed by Pedersen for the corner of Lexington Avenue and 57th Street that makes the gesture of a concave curve facing the corner, an unusual element that turns out to be entirely convincing thanks to a splendid little classical tempietto that fills the void of the corner and restores a sense of urban coherence. The same optimism can be felt about the apartment tower at 180 East 70th Street in New York, designed not by Pedersen but by Arthur May, one of the firm's other active design partners; a tower of brick with classical limestone detailing, it may come closer in sensibility to the apartment buildings of Park Avenue in the 1920s than anything else built in our time. So, too, with Arthur May's Hyatt Regency Hotel in Greenwich, Connecticut, a sprawling English country house that alludes to historical detail neatly enough to manage to appear sumptuous without seeming coy.

These are all recent projects, and they are stronger, by and large, than the work the firm was doing in its middle period, the years after its credibility was established but before it was set securely in the front rank. If Pedersen's designs had any flaw a few years ago, it was a tendency to make too much architecture—to fill each building with too many gestures, to use each and every design as an opportunity to flaunt his knowledge and his love of complex form. Thus there were such buildings as the tower proposed for the Bank of the Southwest in Houston, a highly complicated building that attempted to serve one role on the skyline and a different one at ground level—a laudable goal, but one that led Pedersen to a form that was so complicated it felt overwrought.

There is now in his work, and that of his partners, more of a sense that a building should be a coherent object—not a simplistic one, not one that denies the complex and often contradictory forces around it, but one that makes some effort to resolve these forces into a coherent and readable whole. One looks at his recent towers and thinks in terms of resolution, not of overdesign; like a talented writer whose sentences become simpler as he gets older, but no less subtle, Pedersen's work is taking on a quality of more natural, easy grace without sacrificing any of the concerns that have preoccupied the architect throughout his career.

At this point, the firm occupies a position in American architecture precisely like that of Skidmore, Owings & Merrill in the 1950s. As Skidmore managed to make Miesian architecture commercially viable without seriously compromising its integrity—and continued to innovate within the Miesian vocabulary as well—so has Kohn Pedersen Fox given postmodernism, the architecture that turns back toward historical form, a degree of commercial acceptability that it had heretofore not had. The values of Miesian architecture as practiced by Skidmore and of postmodernism as practiced by Kohn Pedersen Fox are not entirely the same, of course, any more than the 1950s are the same as the 1980s; the most urgent distinction is that architects of Kohn Pedersen Fox see their buildings not as minimalist abstractions plunked down in open space than they do as objects which exist as part of complicated urban environments and which are intended, by their very complexity, to support and enhance those environments. Kohn Pedersen Fox's buildings at their best enrich the cities of which they are a part, not merely by the addition of an exquisite object, but by the more subtle process of strengthening the overall urban fabric.

But these differences may still not be as important as the similarities. For in each case, Skidmore, Owings & Merrill in the 1950s and Kohn Pedersen Fox in the 1980s, the architects have stood as a beacon of serious intention in the commercial world, and as the maker of forms that historians will use as markers for their time.

INDEX OF SELECTED WORKS

First date is the design date;
second date is year of building completion.

SELECTED WORKS

WABC-TV–SEVEN LINCOLN SQUARE

New York, New York
1976/1979

The design for this news-broadcasting facility responds to a complex set of external and internal forces acting on and within the building. Its prominent corner location presents a context divergent in nature: a quiet residential neighborhood (West 67th Street) intersecting with a bustling commercial area (Columbus Avenue), requiring a massing sympathetic to both.

The solution is a rectangular steel structure, clad in a buff-colored brick curtain wall, toning with the color of the existing brick buildings in the neighborhood. On the upper levels, a two-story-high glass curtain wall echoes the rhythm of the two-story-high windows on the old studio apartment buildings which line the block. At the base of the building, the Columbus Avenue facade is glazed its full length, creating a strong visual interest for pedestrians.

The program dictates a two-part scheme: a large studio in a windowless "black box" with its attendant support facilities, and offices for the administrative, creative, and technical staff. Direct-loading access dictates the placement of the three-story-high studio on the ground floor. This requirement, together with the limited area of the site, results in the placement of the office functions on the upper floors. Expressed as a glass-enclosed void, carved into the solid mass of the building, is the three-story atrium which connects the upper floors. The focus of this communal space is a cantilevered stair which links the three office levels. This atrium concept is further developed in the AT&T Long Lines Eastern Regional Headquarters.

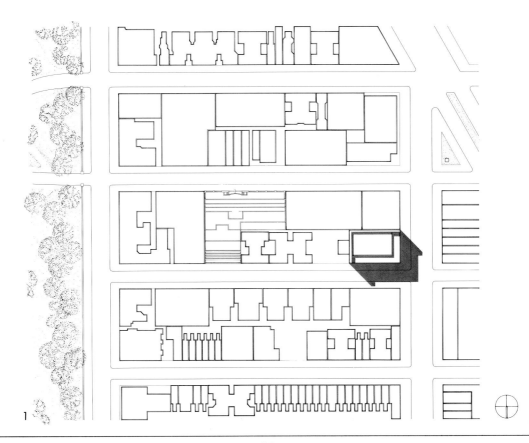

2

1. *Site plan*
2. *View from Columbus Avenue*

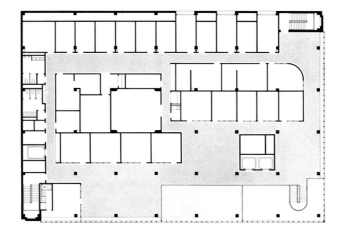

1

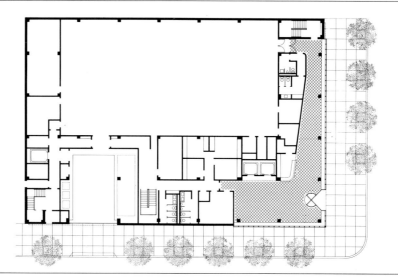

2

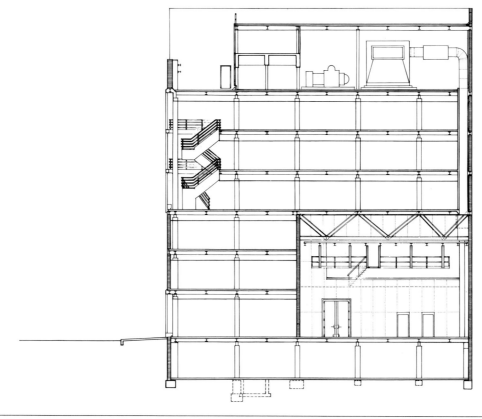

3

4

5

1. Sixth floor plan
2. First floor plan
3. Transverse section

4. Atrium
5. Entrance on Columbus
   Avenue

AT&T LONG LINES EASTERN REGIONAL HEADQUARTERS

Oakton, Virginia
1977/1980

Situated on 34 acres surrounded by small town houses, the three-story Long Lines building mediates the potentially awkward scale relationship between suburban housing and a large office complex. At the same time, the form of the building is a clear expression of program: blocks of flexible office space linked to fixed support facilities (cafeteria, training center, auditorium, and executive areas) by a linear spine, or galleria, that acts as an internal "street" for 2,000 employees.

Flexible office spaces are massed in three mechanically independent units, the height and width of which relate to town-house clusters across the street. Fixed facilities are grouped in a quarter-circle element, the shape of which declares its special function in supporting the rest of the complex. By simply extending the galleria, additional units of flexible office space can be plugged into the complex over time, expanding the initial 430,000 square feet to an ultimate size of 600,000 square feet.

The glass-vaulted galleria is an airy, active space lined with ficus trees and heavy wood benches, and overlooked by informal conference lounges at either end on the upper levels. The sculptural quality of the galleria vault, which arches one story above the roofline, reinforces the building's strong axial organization, both internally and when viewed from the highway or approached by foot from adjacent parking areas. This vaulted shape is repeated in the housings of mechanical units that occur perpendicular to the galleria on the roofs of each independently serviced block of flexible office space.

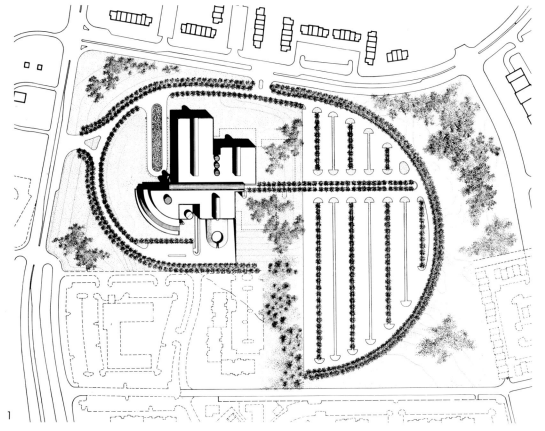

1

1. *Site plan*
2. *Informal conference lounge*

1

2

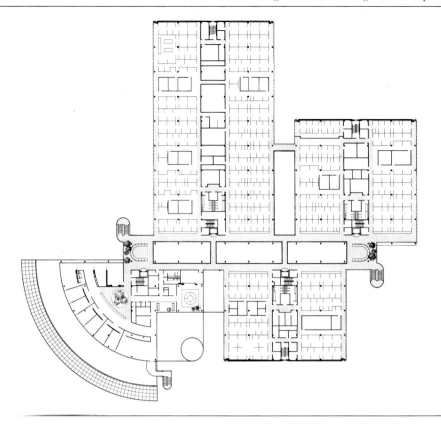

1.Third floor plan
2.First floor plan

3

4

5

6

3.Galleria
4.Galleria

5.Cafeteria
6.Staircase

1.Aerial view
2.View from main road

3

4

5

3. *View from neighboring*
residential area

4. *Visitors drop-off*
5. *Detail view of curtain wall*

EIGHT PENN CENTER

Philadelphia, Pennsylvania
1979/1981

In response to immediate contextual issues, Eight Penn Center is composed of two interlocking masses clad in contrasting materials. The southern and western faces are executed in a concrete wall with square punched windows, similar to those in the building across the street. The northern facade is a glass curtain wall which continues the grid established on the adjacent structure. The intersections of the glass and masonry elements are richly articulated to celebrate the juncture of the two contextual responses.

The composition is tied together at the base by a band of clear glass which introduces a human scale and transparency at street level. At the northwest corner, a rectangular concrete canopy over the bank entrance completes the streetline, allowing the curved glass wall to rise above. At the opposite corner, a cantilevered concrete frame demarks the office-building entrance and atrium beyond. The three-level lobby atrium is composed of travertine, glass, metal, and concrete with landscaping at its periphery. This space is activated by pedestrians moving along a large staircase connecting the lower-level public-transit system and its pedestrian concourse to the street level above. A concrete corner at the back of the building curves to admit light and air to the neighboring building. This curve houses a bank of six elevators, freeing the center of the small 10,000-square-foot floor plates for offices.

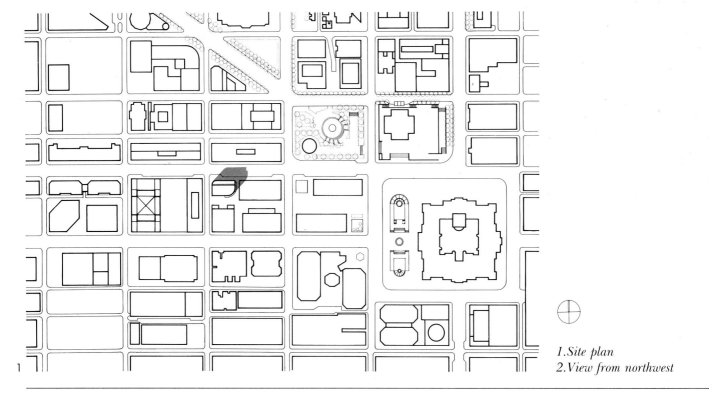

1. *Site plan*
2. *View from northwest*

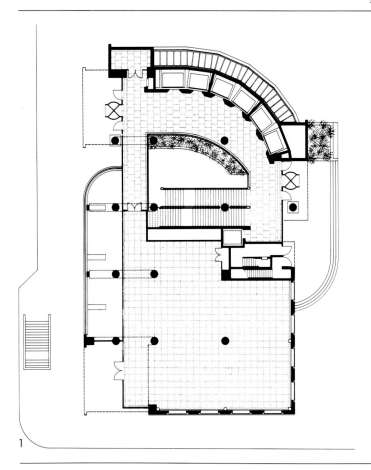

1

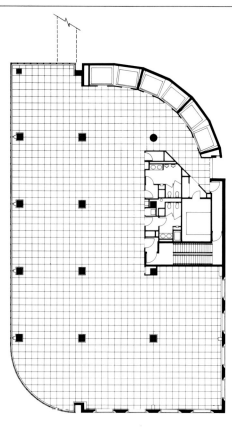

2

3

4

1.First floor plan
2.Typical floor plan

3.Bank entrance
4.Office building entrance
5.Atrium

5

ONE LOGAN SQUARE

Philadelphia, Pennsylvania
1979/1983

At the turn of this century, in the midst of the City Beautiful Movement, the Benjamin Franklin Parkway was superimposed on Philadelphia's grid, connecting City Hall and Fairmount Park. Logan Square is located at the midpoint of this diagonal thoroughfare and has become the institutional node of the city, home to the Public Library, Municipal Court, Academy of Natural Sciences, Benjamin Franklin Institute, and the Cathedral of Peter and Paul. The hotel and office buildings designed for One Logan Square fill the last vacant site on the square.

Completing the harmonious and classical setting of the square is the eight-story, 400-room hotel structure. The hotel streetwall is 273 feet of continuous facade. It presents a grand order of columns and niches that echo those of its neighbors. Its classical flavor and rich details result in a complex hybrid expression. The architectural elements—columns, capitals, cornices, and pergolas—create a symphonic rhythm. Alternating flamed- and polished-granite panels add to the depth of the facade. An arcaded pergola caps the building and reduces the apparent bulk of the hotel mass.

In compliance with zoning regulations, the 30-story office tower is set back 200 feet from the square. The granite and glass office tower blends in with the neighboring office buildings and is perceived as a backdrop to the hotel. The Logan Square buildings are a direct response to the plurality of their surroundings, resulting in the juxtaposition of two distinct building styles and scales on one site.

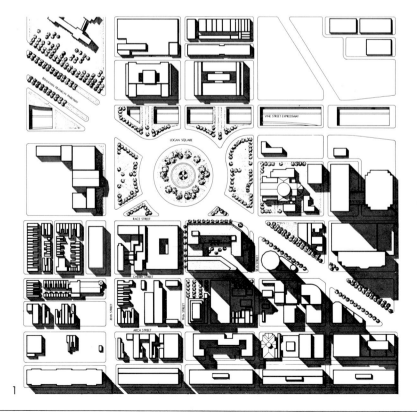

1. *Site plan*
2. *Aerial view*
3. *Building entrance*

1

2

3

31

3

4

5

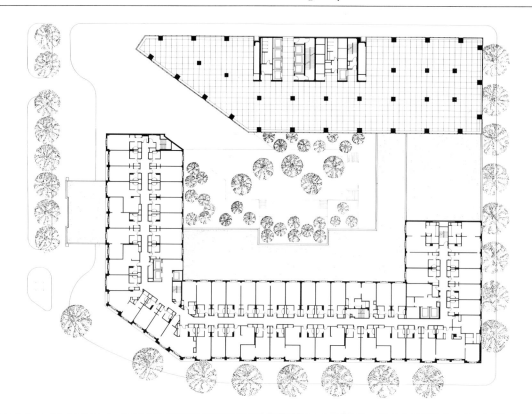

1

2

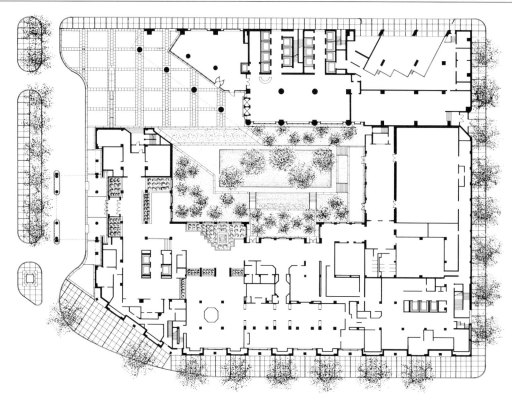

1.Typical floor plan
2.First floor plan

3

1

1. Hotel facade
2. Corner detail
3. Wall detail

2

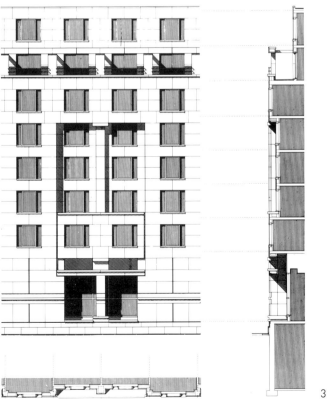

3

333 WACKER DRIVE

Chicago, Illinois
1979/1983

Located on a triangular site, the 333 Wacker Drive building marks a prime node where the rigid Chicago city grid meets the bend of the Chicago River. The mass of this 1,000,000-square-foot speculative office building responds directly to the external forces of the site: the junction of the dominant urban matrix and the flowing bend of the river.

The building's symbolic front is the taut curvilinear side, which acknowledges the neighboring waterway, and expresses the unique nature of the exposed facade. In order to emphasize the taut curve, the horizontal reading of the mullions is made primary by increasing their size and changing their color to contrast with the vertical mullions. Stainless-steel, half-round transoms are used on the horizontal, while the vertical aluminum mullions, tinted a gray green, blend in with the glass and downplay the definition of individual windows.

The segment of the building facing the elevated train tracks is truncated, thus giving the building four sides. This sliced side rises to address the city behind it, echoing the geometry of the downtown grid in its faceted silhouette.

Broad semicircular steps celebrate the formal entry from downtown. A pedestrian arcade of monumental proportions wraps the building's periphery. The arcade is anchored at the corners by enormous structural columns. The monumental base is justified by contextual and programmatic demands. The office floors are raised above the noisy elevated tracks, which cross the river and run directly alongside the building, by a large mechanical floor placed directly above the two-story lobby. The building thus gained a four-floor untenanted block at its base, free to be sculpted and allowing for grand-scale lobbies. The stone base of the tower, which keys into the glass shaft, is articulated with gray granite, horizontally banded by green marble. The stone has been detailed to express its non-load-bearing capacity and its intention to provide a lively pedestrian scale at street level. On the downtown facade, circular air-intake grilles set in black granite panels become grand decorative elements. The decorative stone-and-stainless-steel system of the base is continued into the two lobbies, integrating inside and outside and unifying the entire entry sequence. The base and lobbies evoke a classical flavor without literal references, owing to the well-defined, symmetrical, and sequential progression of spaces.

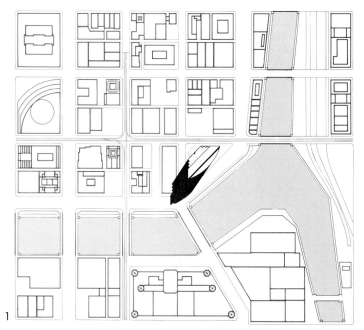

1

1. Site plan
2. View from Chicago River

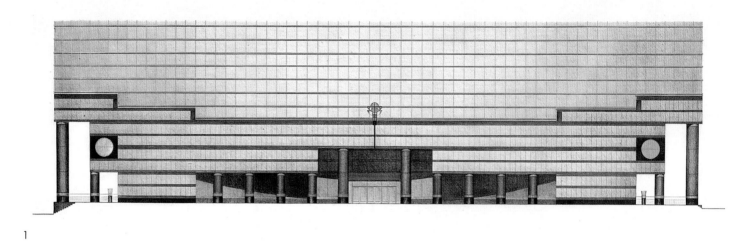

1

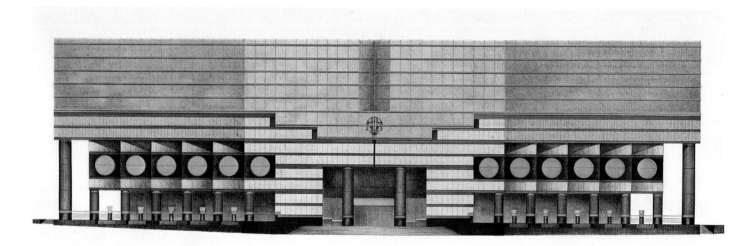

2

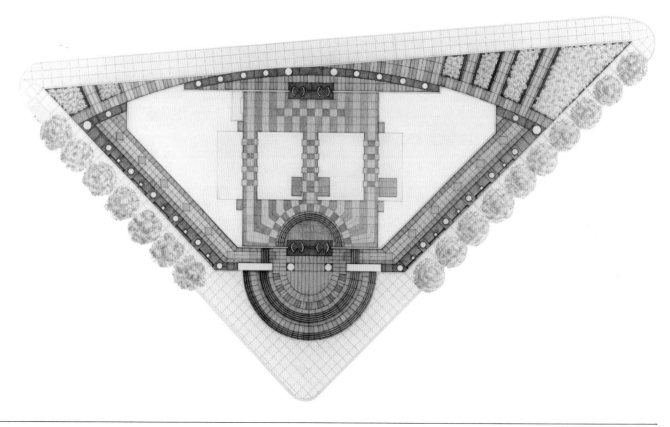

3

4

1. Base of building on Wacker
   Drive
2. Base of building on   3. First floor plan
   downtown side   4. Base, plan and elevation

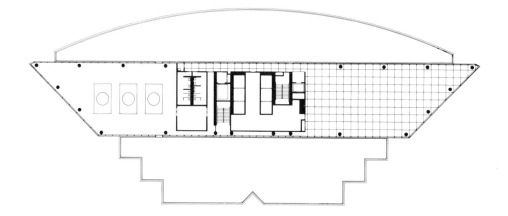

1

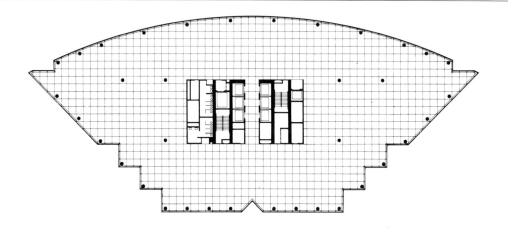

2

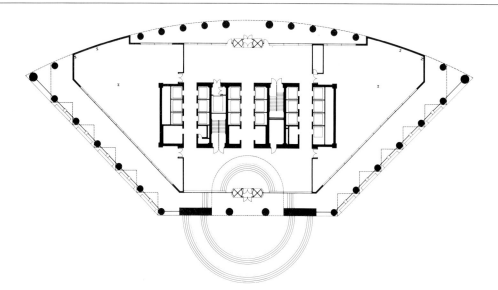

3

4

1.Thirty-fifth floor   3.First floor plan
2.Typical floor plan   4.Wacker Drive entrance

1. *View from across the Chicago River*

2

2.*View from elevated train tracks*

1

2

1. Stainless steel air grille at
   base
2. View of base along arcade

1

2

1.Lobby
2.Elevator lobby

HERCULES INCORPORATED HEADQUARTERS

Wilmington, Delaware
1979/1983

Majestically situated on the edge of downtown Wilmington, Delaware, on gently sloping terrain leading towards the Brandywine Creek, is a stout building, appropriately named Hercules.

This formidable twelve-story structure, despite its somewhat imposing bulk, is nonetheless a sensitive contextual neighbor, mediating between the scale of the city's historic center, two blocks away, and the scale of the adjacent residential district to the west and east. The prominent location, viewed not only from downtown and Brandywine Park, but also from the Interstate highway into Wilmington, makes Hercules the symbolic gateway to the city. As such, the building's form attempts to relate to each of these contextual scales.

The river facade is inflected, symbolically embracing the park and the views beyond. Projecting from these inflected planes and rising above its granite base is a vertical frontispiece which frames the atrium's north wall. The monumental two-story-high granite-framed panels of glass in the atrium north wall are imbued with classical overtones. The low granite base on Hercules recalls, in an abstracted manner, many of the nineteenth-century Beaux-Arts buildings on nearby Rodney Square, by using mannered sills and dentils, intricately detailed granite surfaces, and alternating cornice heights. The masonry base is sympathetically stepped down to the level of the adjacent lower-scaled residential neighborhood. The aluminum and glass cube above the base reduces the perceived bulk of the building. The base is punctured by seven-foot-square windows. These are subdivided into a wide central window, flush with the masonry wall, and two narrow recessed side windows. This manipulation of the glass plane reveals the depth of the granite facade.

Nestled into the building's U-shaped plan is a twelve-story atrium, which acts as the connective tissue linking the city's center to its picturesque outskirts. The cascading levels of the atrium enlivened by the presence of water and vegetation herald the park beyond. The atrium's geometric linear composition and detailing reveal Wrightian influences. The soaring piers and floating globe lighting fixtures are reminiscent of Frank Lloyd Wright's 1904 Larkin Building. Thus, a theoretical, compositional, and aesthetic correlation can be drawn between the Larkin and Hercules buildings. In both cases, the spatial openness has encouraged the interrelationship between all levels of the community in the building, breaking away from the more traditional hierarchical subdivision. Imposed on this composition is a Mondrianesque color-coded steel grid which adds to the richness and complexity of the space while giving a light and airy spatial reading. The two-story framework also adds a larger-scale reading to the atrium.

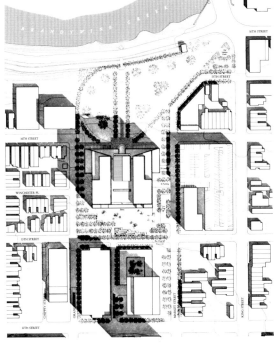

1. Site plan
2. View from Brandywine Creek

1

2

1.Entrance from park
2.View from downtown
3.Oblique view of park facade

4

6

5

4.Windows at corner
5.View from entry plaza
6.Entrance from downtown

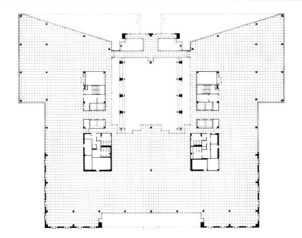

1

2

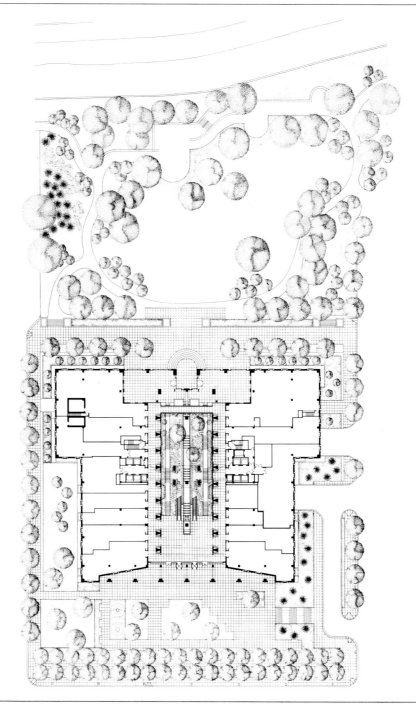

1. Typical floor plan
2. First floor plan

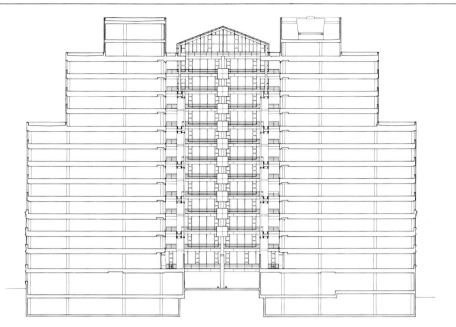

3

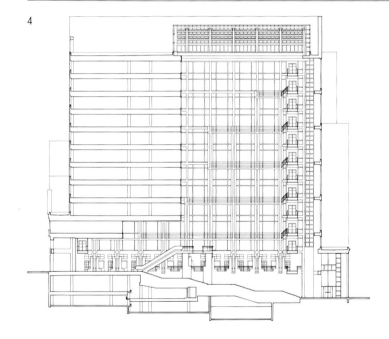

4

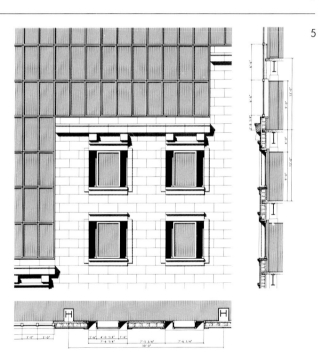

5

3. Transverse section looking
   north

4. Longitudinal section looking
   west
5. Wall detail

1

1.Atrium view looking north

2

3

4

5

2. *Entrance from park*
3. *Atrium view looking north*
4. *View from above*
5. *View of Mondrianesque grid*

GOLDOME BANK FOR SAVINGS

Buffalo, New York
1980/1985

On the northern edge of downtown Buffalo, sandwiched between a revitalized theater district to the north and the central business district to the south, is the Goldome Bank Building. The commission was to add a major phased expansion to an assemblage of structures built between 1901 and 1955. Encrusted in this assemblage is the orginal jewel-like 1901 Beaux Arts domed structure.

The solution frees the new-classical structure from its architecturally unsympathetic additions through a series of phased constructions, and introduces the massing of the new expansion parallel to Main Street, thereby reinforcing the City's pedestrian mall concept linking the adjacent districts. A formal mid-block court is interposed between the old and the new to mediate the stylistic difference and act as an urban vestibule providing entry to the complex. The streetwall is held by a new four-story rusticated podium carrying the scale and rhythm of the landmark building to the end of the block. The arcaded masonry base with its inlaid marble lunettes and projecting cornice echoes the composition and spirit of the domed building. The raised arcade further encourages pedestrian activity along the Main Street corridor. The new twelve-story office building rises above the masonry base as a taut reflective glass curtainwall, again, oriented in the north-south direction to reinforce the fragile urban fabric. By recessing the glass plane of the twelve-story mass, it acts as a backdrop for the rusticated podium. The taut glass expression is momentarily brought to ground as a curvilinear facade fronting on the urban vestibule to receive visitors and to pay homage to its mature neighbor.

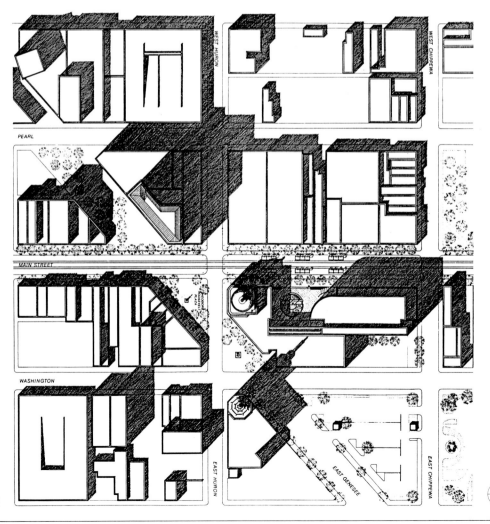

1

2

1.Site plan
2.View from business district

1.*Main street elevation*

2.Arcade
3.Arcade facade

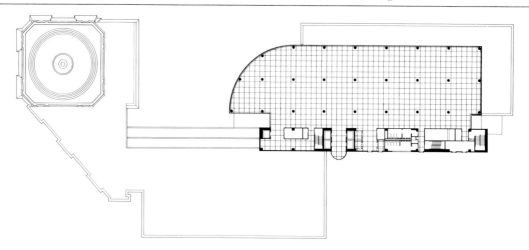

1

2

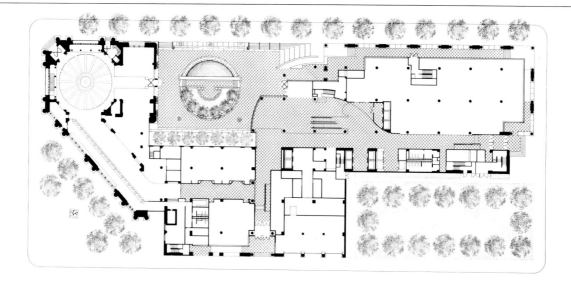

3

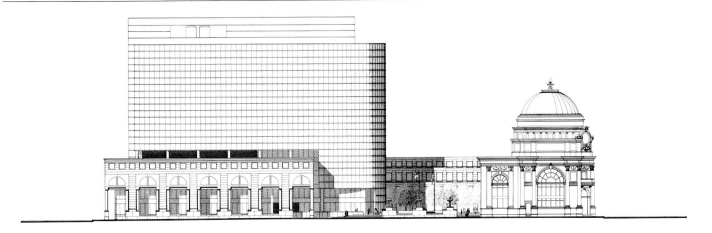

4

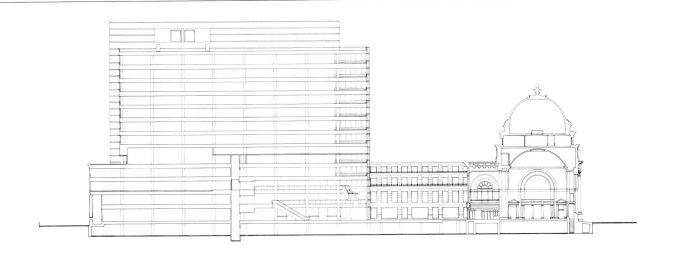

5

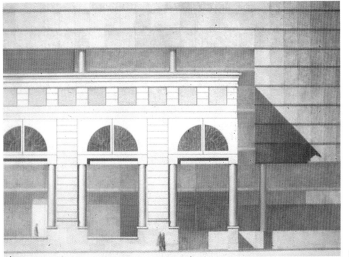

6

1. Typical floor plan   4. Main Street elevation
2. Third floor plan   5. Longitudinal section
3. First floor plan   6. Arcade elevation

BLOCK 265–HOUSTON OFFICE TOWER

Houston, Texas
1981

This proposal for an eighty-story office tower is an assemblage of contextual pieces that are fused together. The building's mass is a collision of forms which express the divergent nature of its surroundings. Located on the edge of Houston's downtown core and directly abutting a public park to the north, the building presents a park side and a city side and simultaneously establishes itself as both object and facade. A quarter-circle arc is drawn across the north face of the volume in a gesture that opens it up to the expanse of landscape beyond. The green reflective glass of this park face is a vertical extension of the park, and, unlike the smaller punched openings of the south sides, exposes the interior spaces to the favorable northern orientation and views. The south sides respond to the city's grid and urban fabric. Carnelian granite walls wrap two sides of the tower's square perimeter structural tube. Their solid compressed nature recalls the punctured-tube expression visible in many of the Houston towers. The base of the building projects beyond the towering mass. This painted steel-lattice structure interpolates the scale of the tower and the delicate two-story white framed houses that are preserved in the park.

1

2

1.Site plan
2.Photomontage

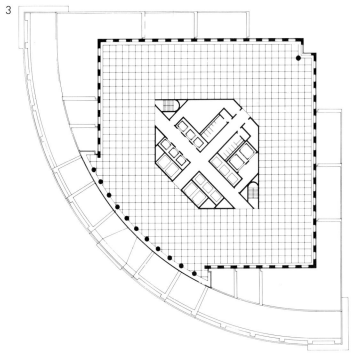

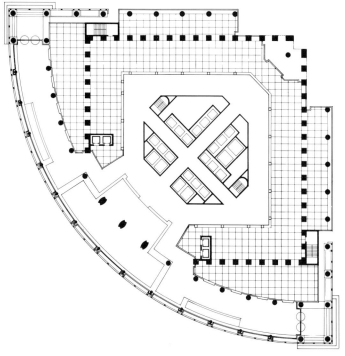

1.Site context model
2.Preliminary model study
3.Typical floor plan

4.Mezzanine floor plan
5.North elevation
6.Southeast elevation

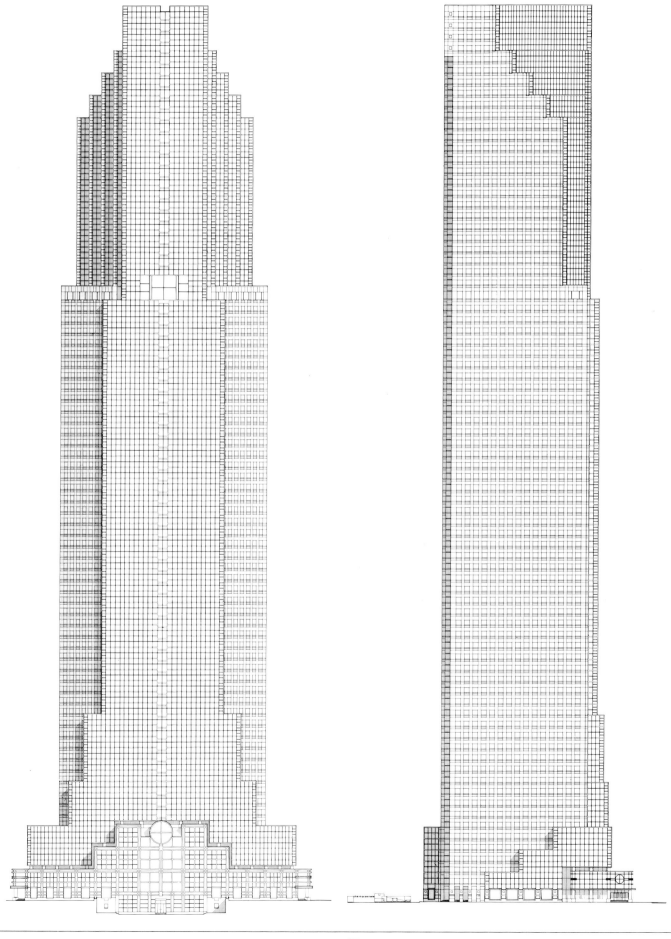

5

6

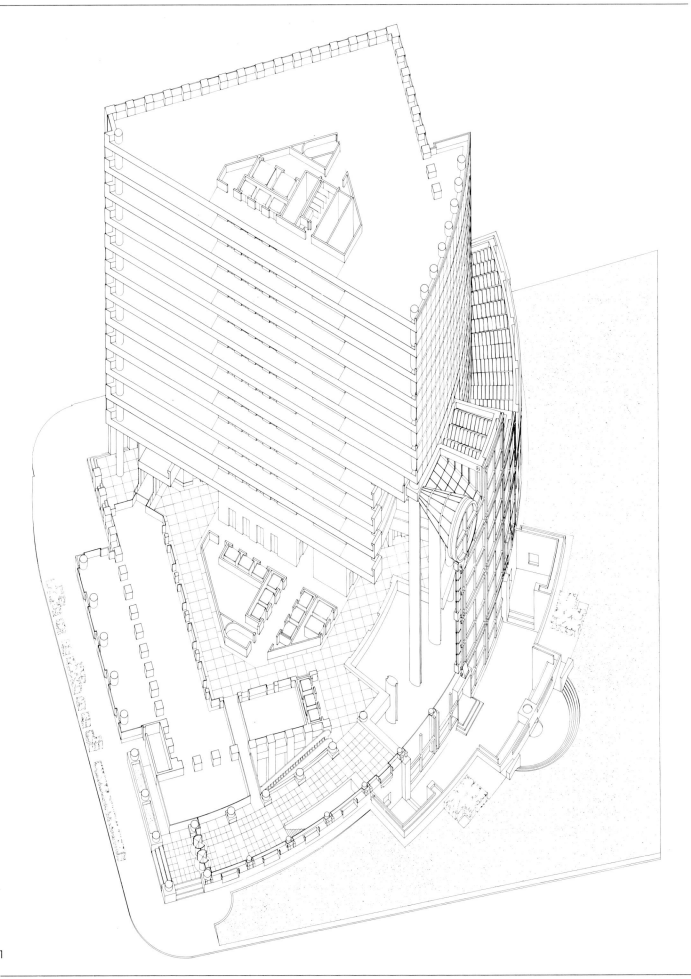

1

2

3

4

5

1. Cutaway axonometric view
   of base
2. North view of model
3. South view of model

4. View of model at park
   entrance
5. View of model at base

GENERAL RE HEADQUARTERS, SCHEME II

Stamford, Connecticut
1982/1985

The General Re corporate headquarters is located on the edge of an urban redevelopment area in Stamford, Connecticut. The building moderates a diversity of contextual forces which act upon it, while simultaneously facilitating very specific program requirements. The result is a massing composed of two distinct elements. The linear building mass is derived from a need to provide a maximum of perimeter offices for the user's predominantly managerial staff. The composition is anchored by an octagonal block which retains a separate identity for the company's executive group.

The linear building mass is bent away from a major highway which bounds the 7.4-acre site on the east. The effect is to focus the building internally away from the discordant context, onto a landscaped plaza. This space is enclosed further by the executive building and a natural rock outcrop to the west, cradling the circular cafeteria pavilion. A ceremonial staircase invites the public up to the landscaped courtyard, opening the complex towards downtown Stamford. The monumental clock tower which caps the octagonal block evokes an imagery of town center, and establishes an identity on the otherwise undifferentiated skyline.

At ground level a stone articulated base is established. Detailed in a small-scaled module, the tactile gray pink granite surface conceals the multilevel parking garage contained within the base. The blue-green reflective-glass curtain wall with its two-tone articulated mullion system is an exploration of a means of expression that conveys scale in this typically scaleless modern material. The major projecting mullion grid reflecting the floor heights is subdivided by a minor flush mullion grid which indicates the interior planning module. The building's gridded surface thus retains a readable scale, rendered to accentuate the surface depth and enliven it with varying shadows.

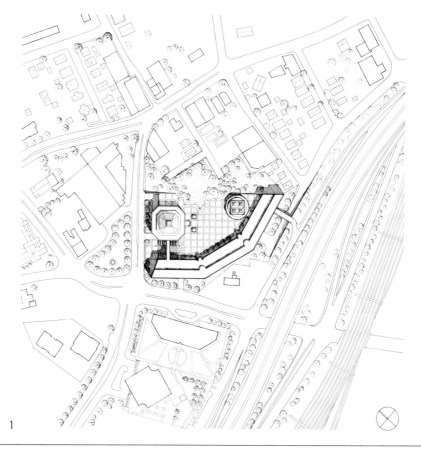

1

2

1. Site plan
2. View from downtown
   Stamford
3. Landscaped plaza

3

1.Monumental stair
2.Entrance from landscaped
  plaza

3

4

5

3.*Aerial view of complex*
4.*Clock tower*
5.*Stone articulated base*

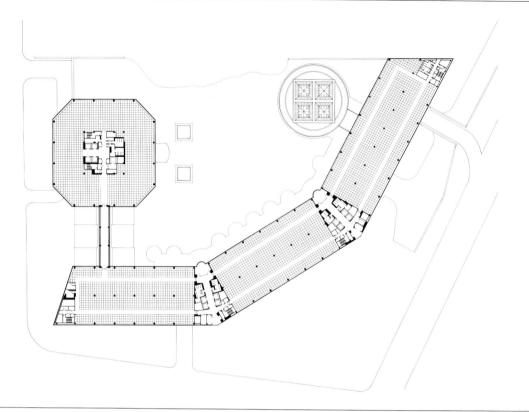

1

2

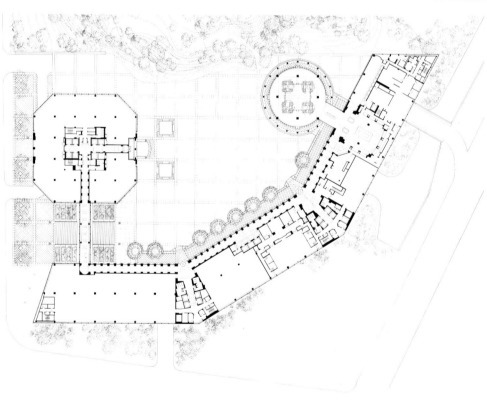

1.Typical floor plan
2.First floor plan

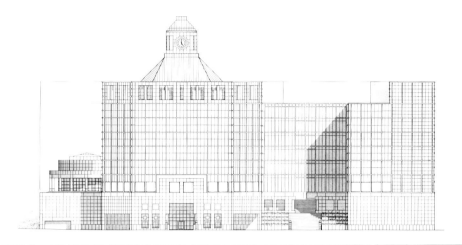

3

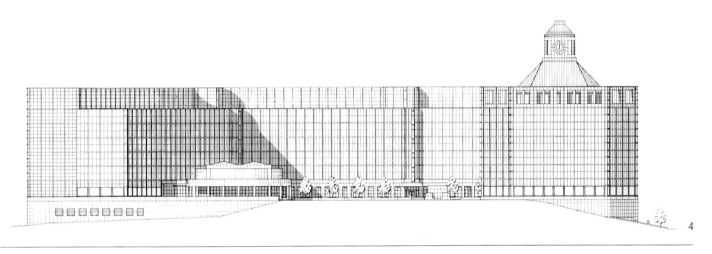

4

5

3.*West elevation*
4.*North elevation*
5.*Longitudinal section*

GENERAL RE HEADQUARTERS, SCHEME I

Stamford, Connecticut
1981

The building design is dominated by two key factors: a need to turn the building inward, away from the chaotic and visually undesirable context; and a necessity to provide a solution with a generous perimeter, in order to facilitate the large requirement for outside private offices. The crenellated U-shaped structure is focused internally, away from a residential community on the north and east, an intense development of commercial structures on the southwest, and the Connecticut Turnpike along the southern edge of the site. The building functions as an urban stabilizer in this context.

The U-shaped building forms a large courtyard into which is inserted a small office tower for the executive group. The crenellations of the surrounding U form additional courtyards which afford the facing offices pleasant views even on the outward sides of the structure. The large inner courtyard is surrounded on the lower level by a colonnade, off of which all functions of a public nature are located. This large inner courtyard is composed of two levels, the lowest of which cascades down a series of steps towards the public square. These steps constitute the "front door" of the structure and face towards the major axis back into Stamford. This front door is flanked by colonnades, off of which are small retail shops and a community room.

The building is sheathed in a combination of sandstone and limestone. The sandstone is confined to narrow horizontal bands within the limestone field. This palette is reversed in the central office pavilion. Each parapet is capped by a blue glazed terra-cotta frieze (the corporate color) and a projecting stainless-steel cornice. The pitched roofs over each of the mechanical penthouses are copper with a standing seam.

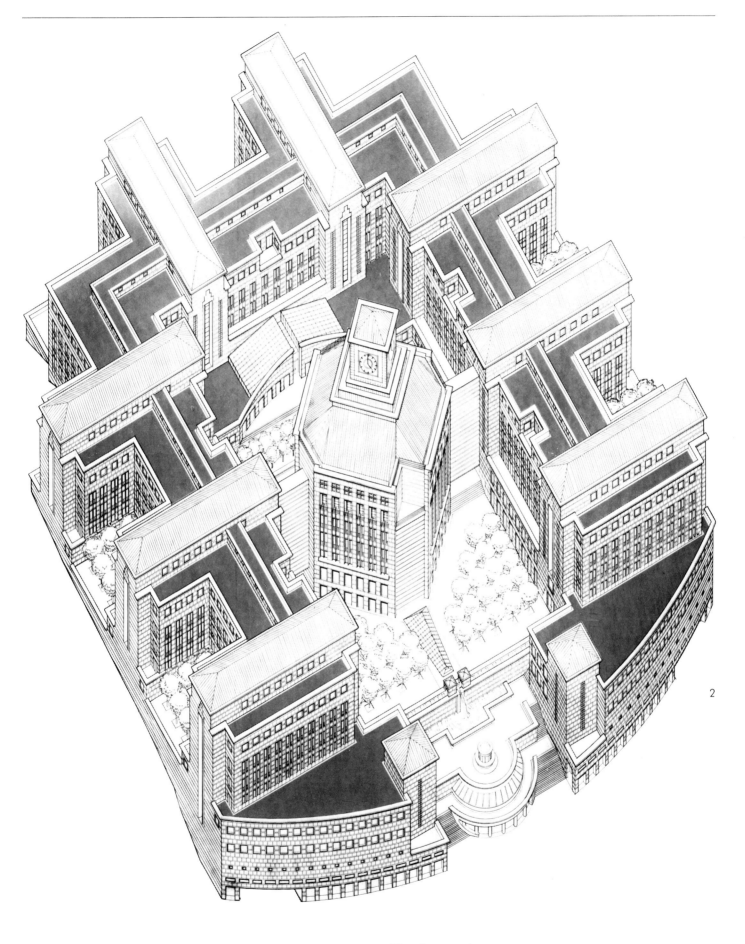

1.View from southwest
2.Axonometric view of complex

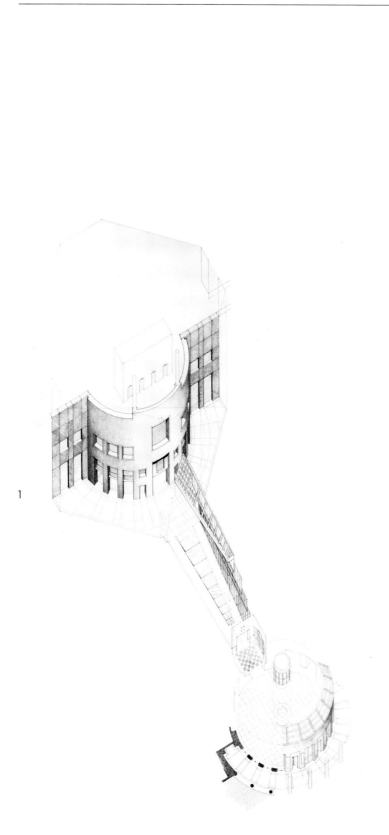

1

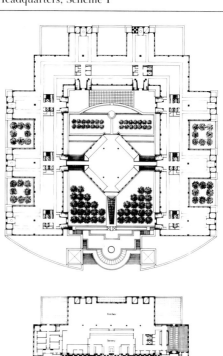

2

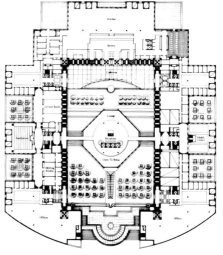

3

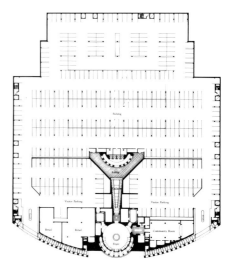

4

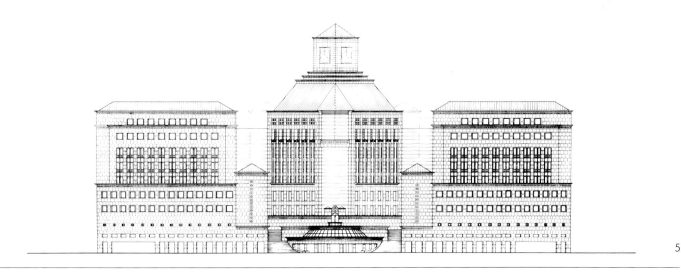

5

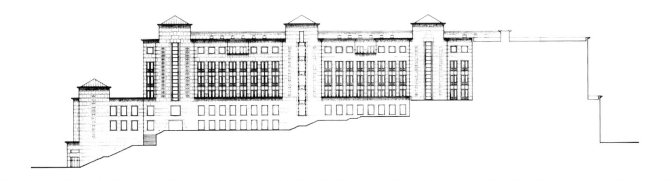

6

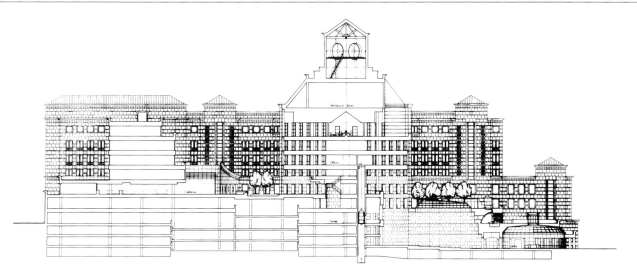

7

1. *Axonometric view of entry sequence*
2. *Typical floor plan*
3. *First floor plan*
4. *Garage floor plan*
5. *West elevation*
6. *Courtyard elevation*
7. *Longitudinal section*

PARK CENTRE

Calgary, Alberta, Canada
1982

This proposal for a mixed-use complex in downtown Calgary includes two 50-story office towers and a 25-story luxury hotel. It was the winning entrant in a developer-architect competition sponsored by the city of Calgary. The complex relates at its various setbacks and roof heights to a variety of scales reflecting the phases of Calgary's rapid growth. The 30-foot-high elliptical arcade relates to the area's lower-scale earlier commercial buildings. The 25-story hotel relates to nearby 1950s office buildings and the office towers to more current high-rise structures.

A hierarchy of detail in the treatment of the building masses, moving upward from the base to the top, attenuates the apparent bulk of the structures. The towers are a combination of glass with a superimposed granite grid in a large-scaled rhythm, evolving into a more prismatic imagery at the top, where they emerge as glass structures. The hotel is further articulated to express a more residential character. The richest detail has been used at the lowest levels in the arched arcades, gatehouses, entry portals, and in the multicolored array of the granite work itself.

At the center of the complex is a large plaza, defined by an arcade at ground level, and a skylit galleria at the Plus 15 level, integrating bridges required by the city for enclosed, above-the-street circulation. The plaza itself, inspired by many of the great European squares such as Bernini's St. Peter's and Michelangelo's Campidoglio, creates a sense of place for the pedestrian in the middle of an amorphous, traffic-oriented downtown. The focus of the plaza is a central pool with a pyramidal fountain surrounded by pergolas and a band-shell structure.

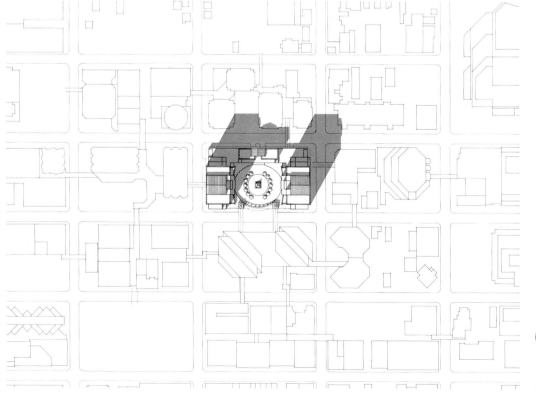

1. *Site plan*
2. *South view of model*

1.North view of model
2.Hotel entry and drop-off

3.Courtyard
4.First floor plan
5.Typical floor plan

3

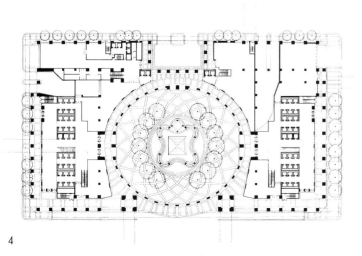

4

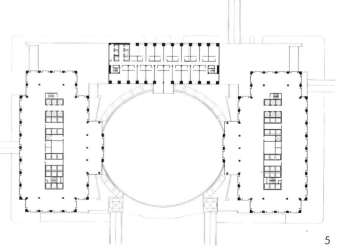

5

This solution embodies a combination of theoretical notions which have been pursued by the firm pertinent to the skyscraper. The base establishes a facade providing a continuity and cohesion to the public realm. The tower asserts its individuality as an object in the sky, at the same time ascribing itself to the classical tenets of a tripartite composition.

The symmetrical design of the building anchors the site and allows the tower to face equally in all directions. Capitalizing on the diagonal views between the large surrounding structures, the square plan of the rising shaft is rotated to sit diagonally upon its base. Thus the main shaft rises from the site on the diagonal to bracket a square glass shaft, which penetrates deep into its sides, announcing its presence geometrically and materially, long before it fully emerges at the top of the structure. As the building continues to rise vertically past its neighbors, the square glass upper shaft is reoriented to align, as does the base, with the urban grid. The primary materials are interwoven to reinforce the interconnection between base, shaft, and capital. On a figurative level, the material assemblage of stone, glass, and steel reflects the past, present, and future of Houston.

The arcaded stone base recalls the arcades of the city's past, which demonstrated a concern for the pedestrian in this climate, as exemplified by the Rice Hotel and the old Texaco Building. The base extends to the boundaries of the site, opening up as great portals at the corners. These portals clearly mark the building's entry, contributing elements of scale commensurate with the relationship of the building to the street facade. While the portals define the lateral boundaries of the base, the wall plane is articulated to provide a vertical termination of the surfaces. Contained within the base of the building is an urban room, concealed from the street by the enclosing facade. The void extends above the enclosing base structure, illuminated by natural light from the giant oculi in the upper walls. The boundaries of this room are defined by the internal exposure of the structural tube which supports the tower above. The shaft of the building, comprised of the two interlocking pieces, is capped by a white-painted, steel-trellis octagonal crown. Housing an observation deck and restaurant, the crown opens up as a *fioritura* in the sky, evocative of Houston's role in space research.

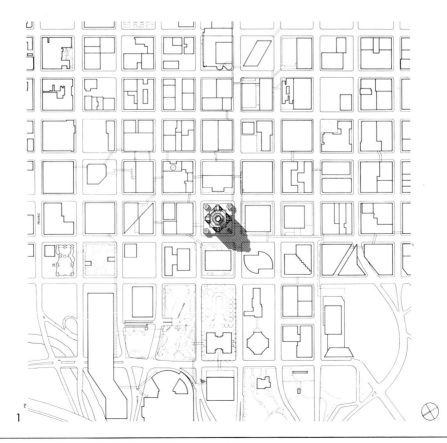

2

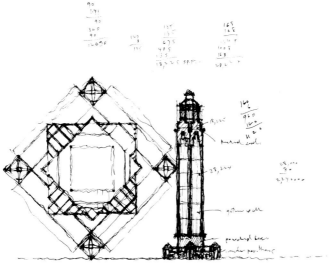

1.Site plan
2.Photomontage
3.Design sketch

3

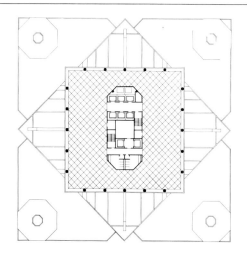

1

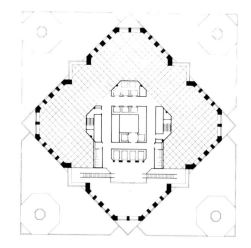

2

3

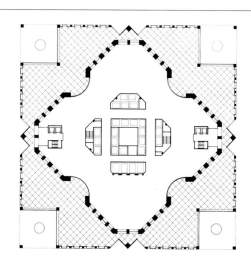

4

5

1. Typical floor plan, 79
   through 82
2. Skylobby floor plan, 60

3. Typical floor plan, 20
   through 32

4. Typical floor plan, 2
   through 4
5. First floor plan

6. Model
7. Section

6

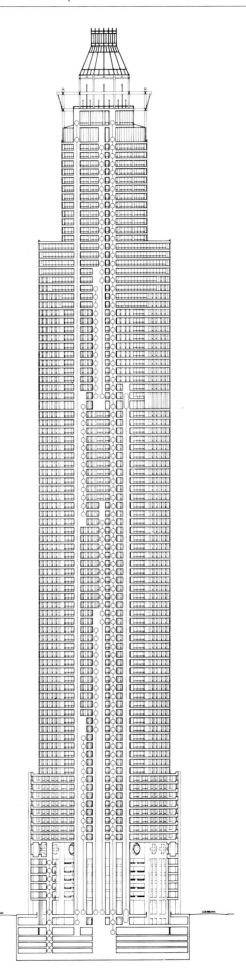

7

THE PROCTER & GAMBLE GENERAL OFFICES COMPLEX

Cincinnati, Ohio
1982/1985

This building is an expansion of the existing Procter & Gamble Headquarters office building in downtown Cincinnati. The intention was to unify new and old building elements and sites into a cohesive and clearly defined world headquarters complex. The site is located on the eastern edge of the central business district, flanking Fifth Street, one of the major east-west vehicular and pedestrian corridors. It is also a gateway to vehicular arrival into Cincinnati from the north and east along Interstate 71. The context of the site presents the challenge of a complex urban-edge condition.

The architectural resolution of the new structure takes on the form of twin seventeen-story octagonal towers, reinforcing the building's position as landmark and terminus. The dual-tower image has a visual strength which matches that of much taller buildings, while maintaining a sympathetically scaled profile rather than overwhelming the city with a ponderous mass. The towers have pyramidal roofs of terne-coated stainless steel and copper which make reference to the Art Deco towers on the Cincinnati skyline, such as the Post Times Star Building and the Cincinnati Gas and Electric Building.

The six-story L-shaped base of the building serves to enclose the new public gardens and to establish a dialogue between the existing eleven-story structure and the 830,000-square-foot addition. The surface treatment of the new building relates to that of the existing headquarters through a system of punched windows on a limestone facade. This surface is accentuated with an interplay of different glass types, planes, and silver-aluminum panels. This interplay achieves modulations in light, shadow, and tonality, within a subdued color range, on a sheer surface. Accent pieces of decorative white marble and dark gray granite appear at the base, cornices, and in the two towers, relating in scale and type to the existing building and other buildings in the city. A lengthy colonnade at the building's base, bordering the garden plaza on both new and old buildings, further unites the entire complex.

The garden is broken down into three individual rooms, each defined by perimeter pergolas. An elaborate progression is established through the trellised garden, into the lobby pavilion. A Piranesian sense of space is achieved in the lobby as ascending staircases and receding planes create a complexly orchestrated visual layering. A linear tectonic decorative system of Wrightian origins enhances the spatial reading. These stainless-steel members and suspended lighting fixtures unify the horizontal and vertical planes, drawing attention to their center, not their edges, and providing a dimensional quality absent in most modern structures.

On the second level, a spacious double-height circulation gallery runs above the exterior arcade, linking all the major spaces and connecting to the existing building. This space acts much like a city street, unifying the composition.

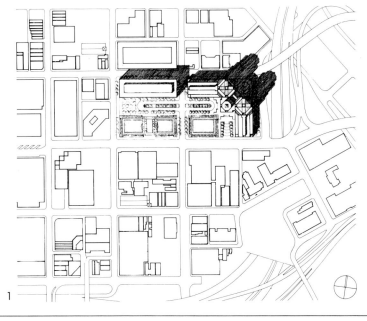

1. Site plan
2. Aerial view of complex from west

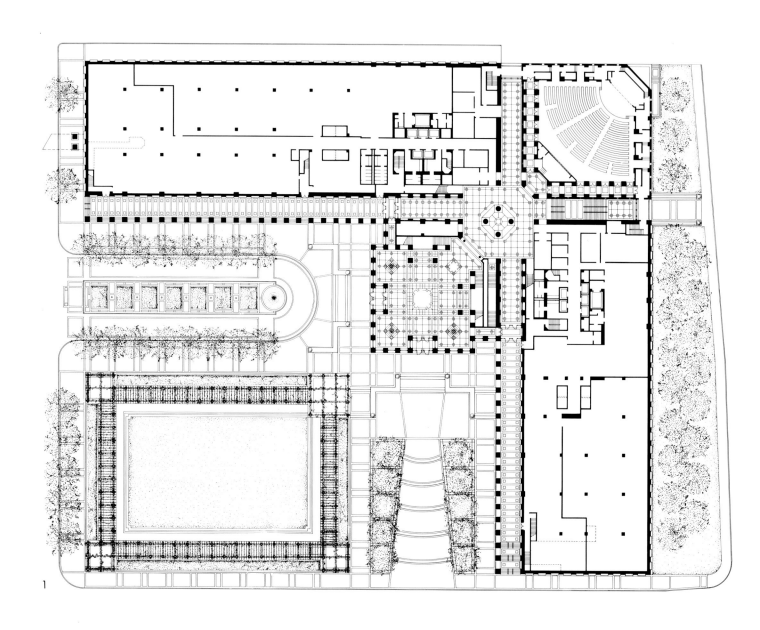

1

1.*First floor plan*
2.*Fifth floor plan*
3.*Second floor plan*

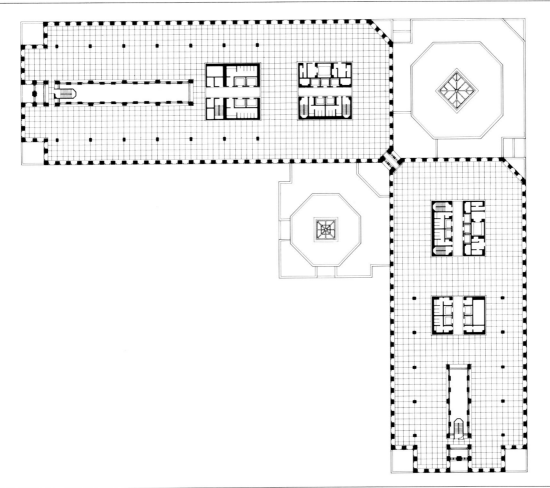

2

3

1. View from garden plaza
2. Study model

3.View from Interstate 71
4.Study model

3

4

1.Dining hall
2.Auditorium
3.Unity Temple—Frank Lloyd
  Wright

95

4

5

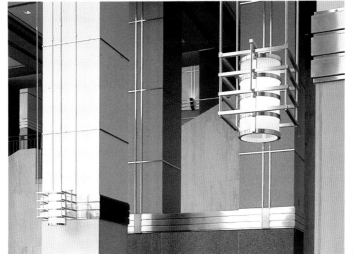

6

4. *Second floor galleria*
5. *Gallery lobby*
6. *Light fixtures*

1.Entrance pavilion
2.Lobby

3.View of lobby from galleria
  above

5

6

7

8

4.Lobby
5.Arcade
6.Garden trellis

7.Arcade
8.Bridge

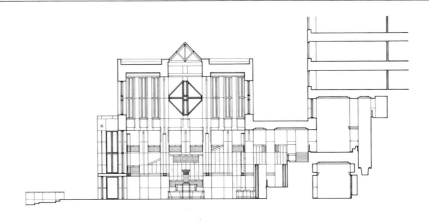

1

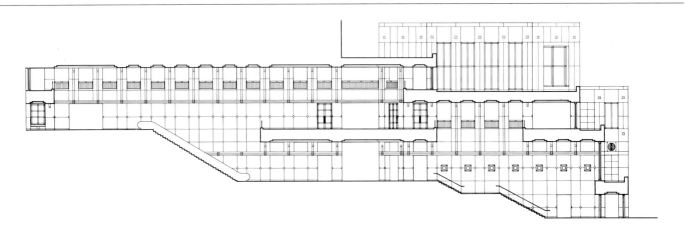

2

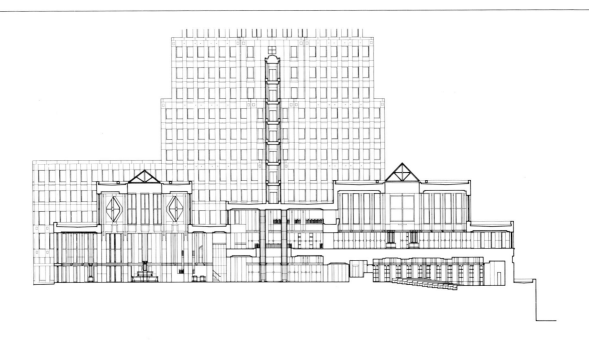

3

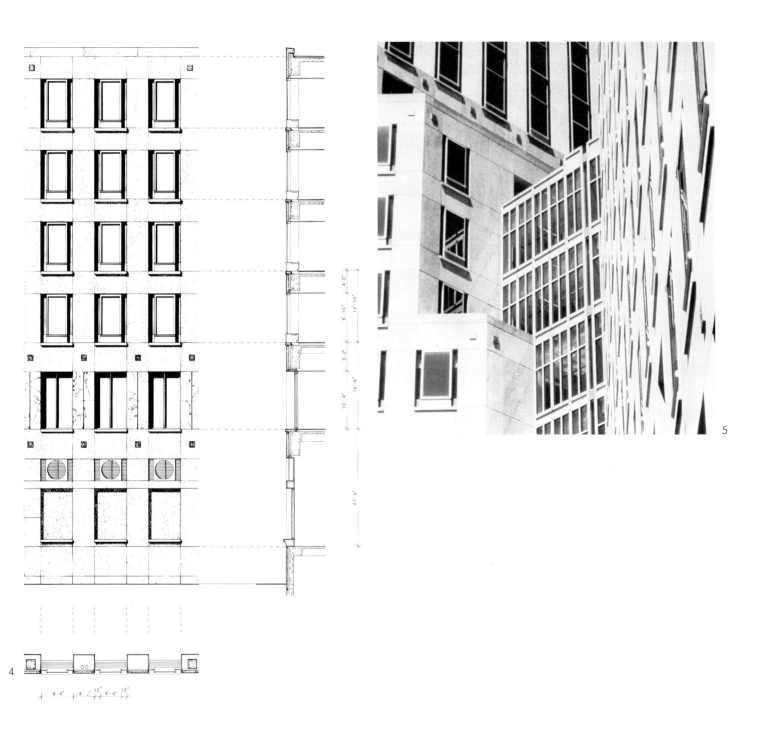

1.Entry pavilion and gallery
  section

2.East entrance and gallery
  section

3.Diagonal section looking
  northwest

4.Wall detail

5.Oblique view of bridge

1.Fountain detail
2.Fountain detail

3

*3. View from northeast towards
downtown Cincinnati*

UNIVERSITY PERFORMING ARTS CENTER

Lewisburg, Pennsylvania
1982

On the rolling hills of the university's picturesque campus are the proposed sites for the music school and performing-arts center. The master plan for this predominantly neo-Georgian campus was first laid out in 1840, in a traditional quadrangular organization. The two proposed schemes attempt to extend and reinforce the formal relationships established by the existing buildings.

The first scheme was placed on a steeply sloping site on the main axis of the campus, connecting the library at the top of the quad to the gymnasium below. Parallels can be drawn between the siting of this building and that of the McKim, Mead and White building at the University of Virginia, the difference here being the intention to extend the vista rather than to obstruct it. To achieve this, the U-shaped building is partially nestled in the ground, creating a garden terrace above the 1,500-seat concert hall and a sunken ceremonial entry court lined by the splayed colonnades of the two classroom wings. The ambulatory space connecting the two wings of the music school to the performance center is transformed from an open pergola structure to a glass-enclosed space. This space is animated by a myriad of

tunes escaping the adjacent practice rooms. At the corners, two glass-block structures rise to frame the garden-level view. These key circulation elements, set as objects in a landscape, are formally inspired by the siting of the buildings at the Villa Lante. In the relationship between object and landscape neither dominates, but a gentle opposition serves to reinforce and define one to the other.

As a result of economic restraints, a second scheme was developed. It was limited to a 1,200-seat performing-arts center and its support facilities. This proposal is sited on an axis parallel to the main axis of the campus, at a point where the grid of the stadium and the grid of the campus collide. The building's responsibilities here are, therefore, entirely different from those of the first scheme. Its facade becomes an extension of the existing facade of the quad and the entry hall becomes the pivot which absorbs and resolves the juncture of the two grids. In the process, a secondary quadrangle is created, spatially linking the adjacent structures. The Hellenistically inspired temple front establishes a relationship with the powerful architecture of the adjacent chapel's colonnaded Georgian portico.

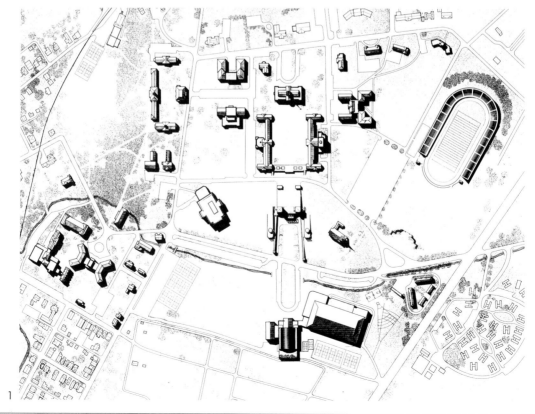

1

1.Site plan of Scheme I
2.View of campus model with
  Scheme I
3.Scheme I, model

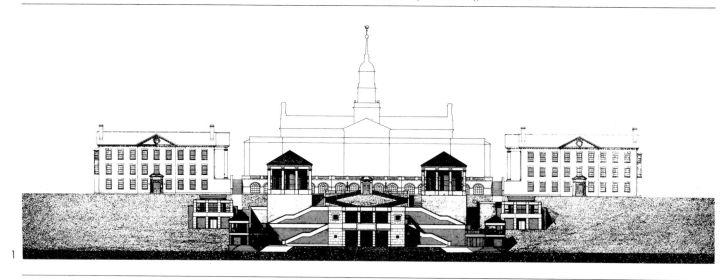

1

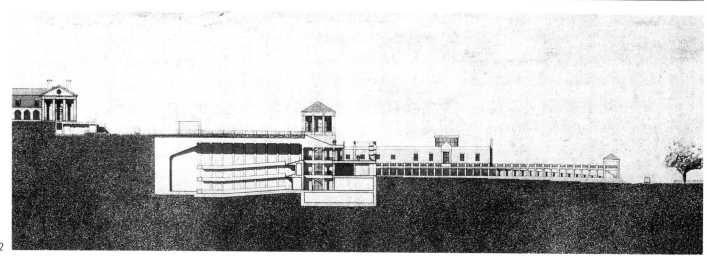

2

3

4

5

1.Elevation, Scheme I
2.Longitudinal section,
  Scheme I
3.First floor plan, Scheme I

4.View of campus model with
  Scheme II
5.Scheme II, model

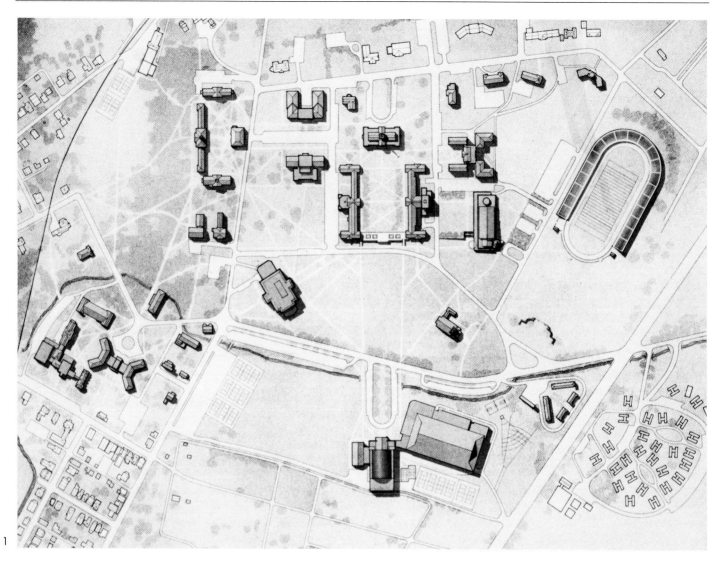

1

2

1.Site plan of Scheme II
2.Elevation, Scheme II

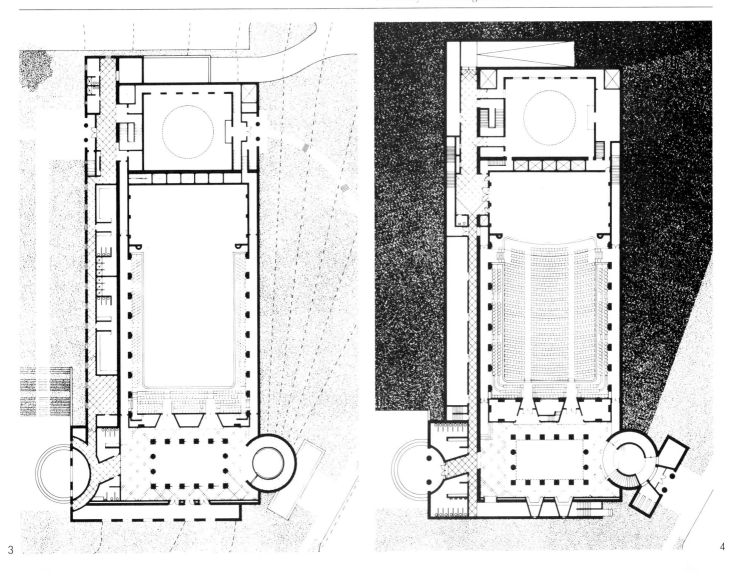

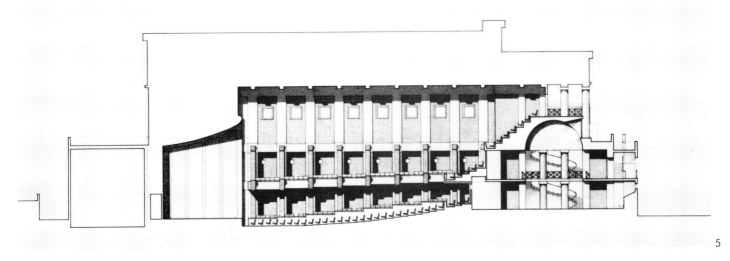

3. Mezzanine floor plan,
    Scheme II
4. First floor plan, Scheme II

5. Longitudinal section,
    Scheme II

GROUPE BOUYGUES CORPORATE HEADQUARTERS, COMPETITION

St. Quentin en Yvelines, France
1982

Located within the historic district of the Chateau de Versailles is the site for the proposed Groupe Bouygues corporate headquarters. It is a rural site 15 miles west of Paris near the town of Saint Quentin en Yveline. The site is bounded to the north, east, and south by the dense forests of the Bois Robert, a national park which extends to the southeast and which includes a series of recreational lakes. The competition proposal locates the corporate headquarters building on an axis parallel to the principle axis of the chateau and gardens of Versailles.

The ensemble is grouped around a man-made lake which becomes the centerpiece of the landscape plan. The scheme combines the principal building with a series of repetitive and expandable office modules. The principal building provides a focal point for the entire project and its grand entrance hall organizes the major spaces. These include all visitor functions, special program areas and executive offices and support facilities.

A rotunda and galleria join the principal building to the rest of the complex. This galleria serves as both a lining defining the major outdoor space and as an armature linking the repetitive office modules. These modules are constructed of long-span, precast, posttensioned concrete beams and are exposed on the interiors, showcasing the client's technological achievements in concrete construction.

The galleria is brought to the face of the building, allowing for views of the gardens and surrounding landscape. Garden courts between the modules in conjunction with internal atria complete the integration of the landscape with the working environment. A series of garden episodes link the ancillary facilities with the main building, allowing for a harmonious coexistence of the man-made environment and nature.

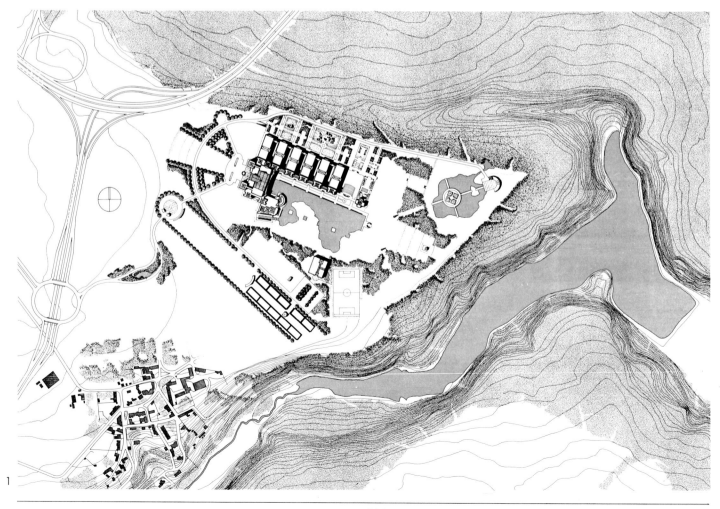

1

1.Site plan
2.Aerial view of model
3.Aerial view of model

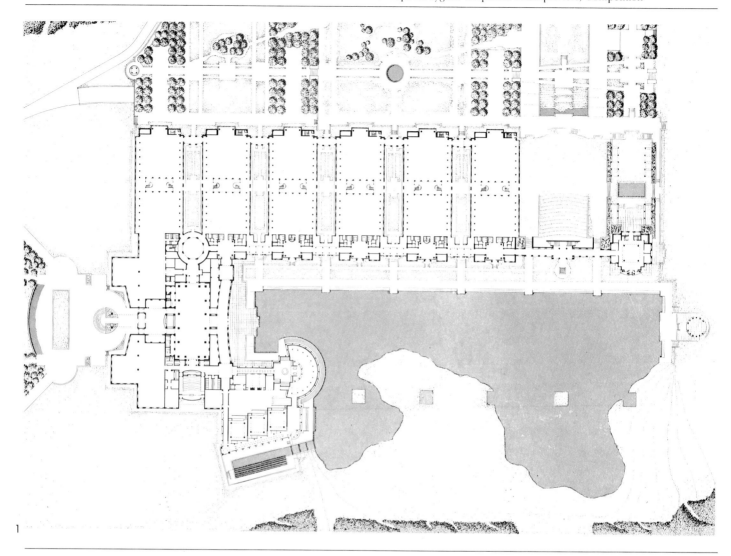

1

2

1.First floor plan
2.Galleria
3.Longitudinal section
   through office module

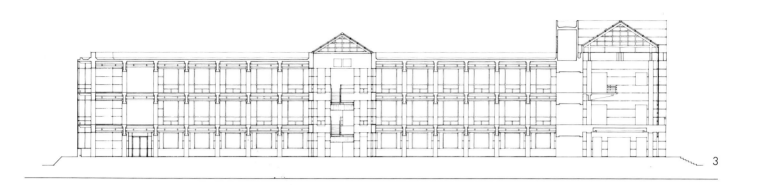

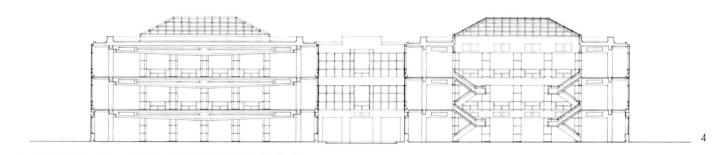

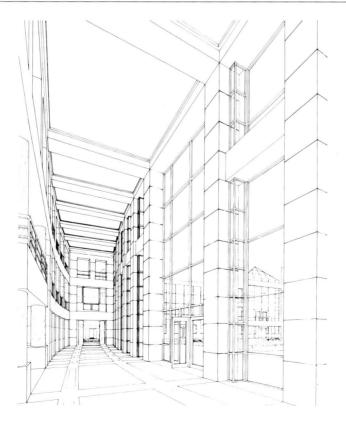

4.Transverse section through
  office modules
5.Commercial gallery

1

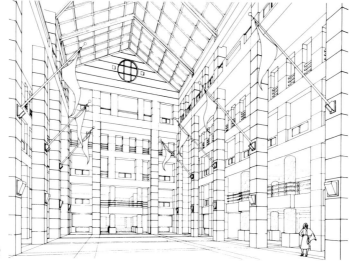

2

1. *View of complex, model*
2. *View of entrance hall*

3

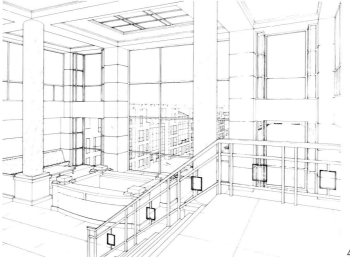

4

3. *View of cafeteria model*
4. *View of Le Club*

75 FEDERAL STREET

Boston, Massachusetts
1982

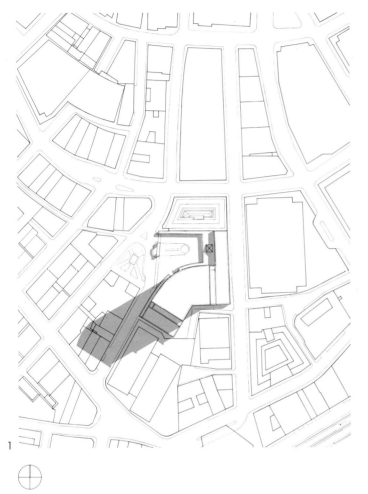

Sited adjacent to a pyramidal 21-story Art Deco building in Boston's financial district is this proposal for a 52-story tower. Conceptually, the envelope of this building is a traditional linear slab which is deformed to suit its context. The curved building establishes a localized order to the chaotic surroundings and allows for the creation of a cohesive U-shaped plaza with which the neighboring buildings share equal frontage. This plaza recalls in shape and scale the irregular street plan of the financial district.

The building's gridded-panel system, horizontal stone banding, and pronounced cornices recall the late-nineteenth-century landmarks in the district, and lend a time-honored presence to the structure. The front facade is divided horizontally by a progression of stone-framed panels which reduce in scale towards the edges, and a tripartite division is established, with heights of surrounding structures demarked by the stone cornices. The polychromatic curved face composed of granite, limestone, and marble is inspired by its colorful predecessors, extant in this area of Boston.

1.Site plan
2.North view of model

2

1

2

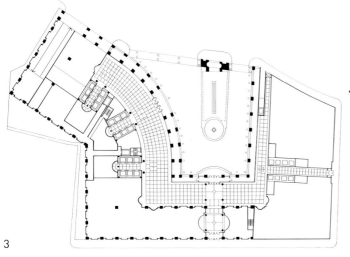

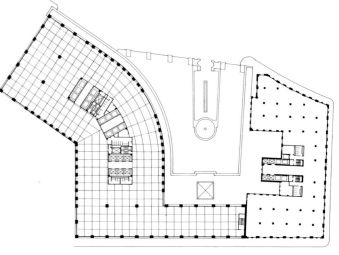

3

4

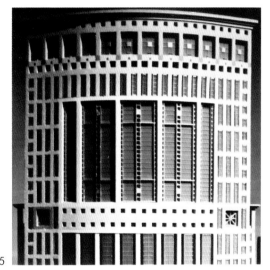

1.West view of model
2.East view of model
3.First floor plan
4.Typical floor plan

5.Top of building—front, model
6.Top of building—back, model
7.View of entrance, model
8.View of base, model

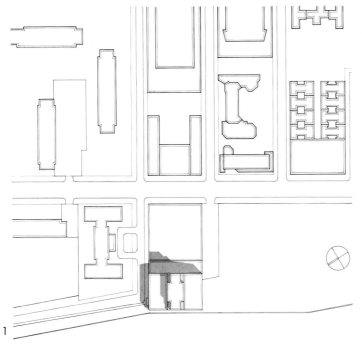

The Studio 23/24 building is a high-technology factory for the production of television shows. The program demands that all the functions be isolated in windowless "black box" environments. The density and highly specialized nature of the program result in a building form dictated primarily by the functional requirements, with creative latitude afforded exclusively in the design of the lobby sequence and the external skin. The building's symmetrical disposition is organized about a central spine. This spine is expressed in the mass of the building, projecting vertically above the cascading silhouette of the lower portion. The facades are a mannered interplay of standard industrial building materials: face brick, glass block, and industrial sash windows. The pure symmetry of the plan is broken at ground level in one instance. The entry and elevator lobbies are linked by a galleria space which hugs the western perimeter of the building. In order to animate this 100-foot-long space and to screen the undesirable neighboring views, openings at eye level are glass block with large clear glass windows above, resulting in a play of light and volumetric undulation.

1. *Site plan*
2. *View from west*

1.*West facade*
2.*North facade*

3

4

3.North facade
4.Galleria

1

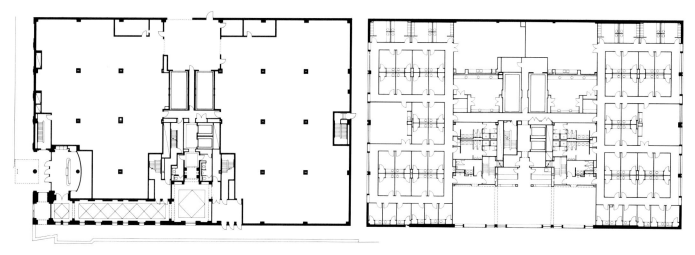

2

3

4

5

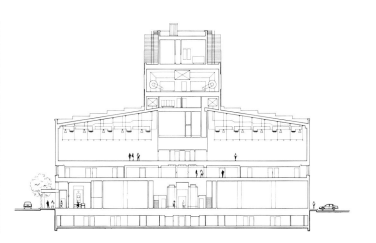

1.View from west
2.First floor plan

3.Dressing room level, floor
plan

4.Studio level, floor plan
5.Longitudinal section

THIRD NATIONAL BANK

Nashville, Tennessee
1982/1985

This 31-story office building owes much of its historical imagery to Nashville's heritage of Greek Revival buildings and its reputation as the "Athens of the South." Located in the heart of downtown Nashville, the building faces William Strickland's 1849 Downtown Presbyterian Church, designed in the Egyptian Revival style. This historic landmark is addressed by a spacious plaza that focuses upon an entry colonnade at the gray granite base of the building. The portico makes reference to the Greek Revival style of neighboring structures.

The U-shaped plan breaks up the exterior mass into vertical shafts of slender proportion. A large precast-concrete grid, infilled with reflective glass, further breaks down the scale of the building mass. A hierarchy of edge and center is established by the rotation of the center column in each grid bay. To reinforce the reading of depth adjacent to the columns, a gray glass is used in the reveals which separate them. The building is surmounted by a monumental pediment which makes a direct reference to the Parthenon, a full-size replica of which is a landmark in Nashville.

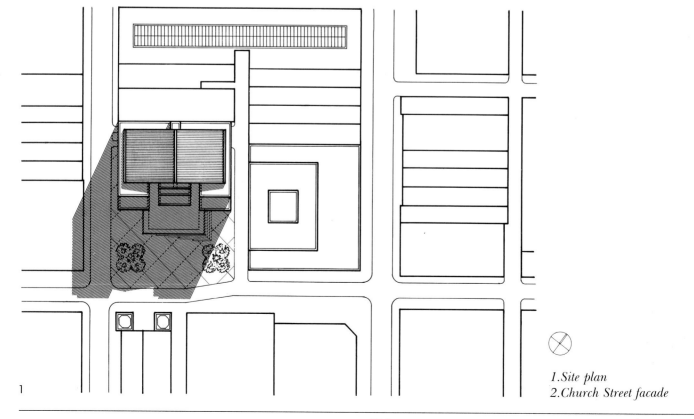

1

1.Site plan
2.Church Street facade

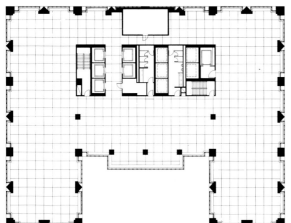

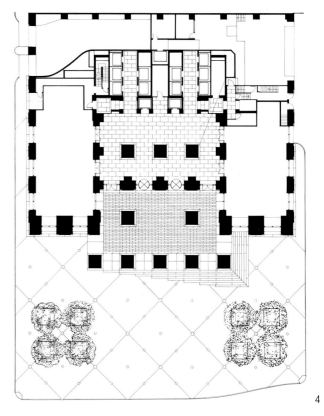

1. Entry portico from Church
   Street
2. Entry portico, looking west
3. Typical floor plan
4. First floor plan

5

6

7

8

5. *View of Strickland Church
   from entry portico*
6. *Tower view from Strickland
   Church*

7. *Lobby view, looking west*
8. *Tower view from West
   Church Street*

900 NORTH MICHIGAN AVENUE

Chicago, Illinois
1983/1988

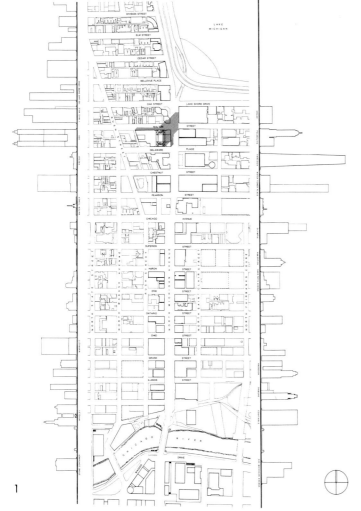

1

Unlike its predecessor at 333 Wacker Drive, which responded exclusively to the external exigencies of the site, 900 North Michigan's form is a result of both internal and external pressures. The 66-story building accommodates a complex mixed-use program within a traditional Chicago slab structure.

The design of 900 North Michigan honors the tradition of scale and enclosure of the city by placing volumes of low proportions directly along the avenue. The eight-level granite, marble, and limestone base of the building, housing retail space and a hotel lobby, is set at the height of the previously existing streetwall, filling the site to the building line. A great portal opens into an elaborate six-story atrium space surrounded by a shopping mall. Rising from the base and set back from North Michigan Avenue is a 58-story glass and limestone tower, containing office space, hotel guest rooms, and condominium residences. The massing of 900 North Michigan Avenue acts as a counterpoint to the 333 North Michigan Avenue building by Holabird and Roche, establishing an axial polarity between the two. The height and slenderness of this tower is enhanced by the volumetric stepping of its mass, reflecting the different programmatic changes, and culminates in a distinct tower at each of the building's corners. These gridded, translucent glass towers are lit at night to form lanterns.

The design also incorporates two major themes gleaned from Chicago architecture: the Chicago frame and the Chicago window. The building's frame is dense at the corners, establishing its boundaries, with vertical striations of taller proportions marking the building's centers. Within the frame, the tripartite design of the window, combining a wide center bay with narrow side bays, is a variation of the Chicago window.

1. Site plan
2. Aerial view of model

2

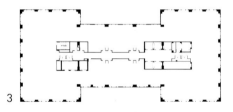

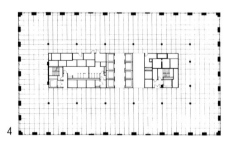

1.Contextual model
2.Top of building, model
3.Typical upper floor plan
4.Typical lower floor plan
5.View of entrance, model
6.Oblique view of model

7. Palmolive Building,
   Chicago, contextual reference
8. 333 North Michigan
   Avenue, Chicago—Holabird
   and Roche, contextual
   reference

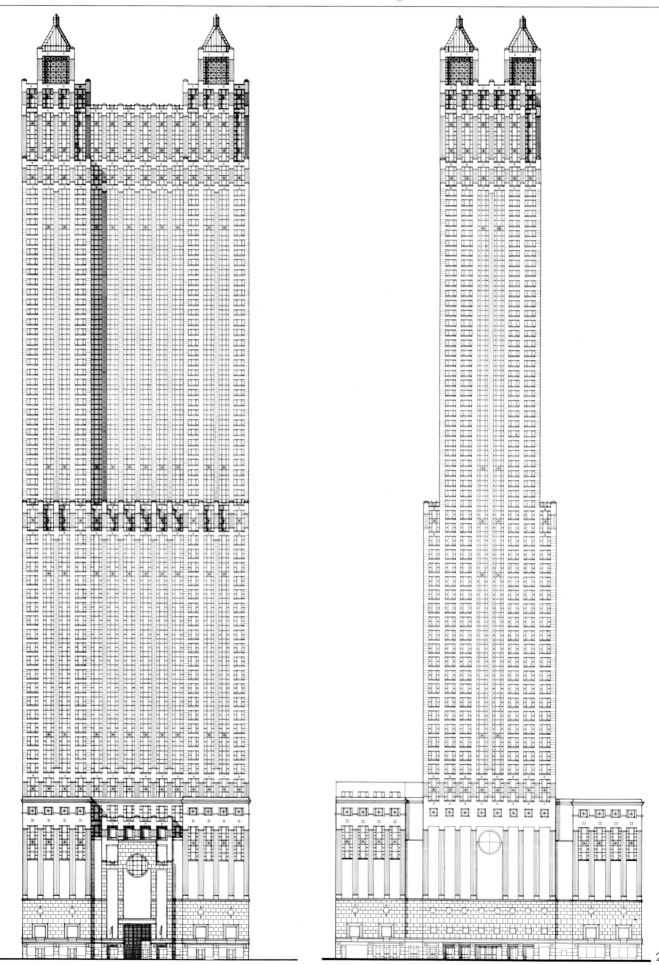

1

2

1.East elevation
2.South elevation
3.Axonometric

3

125 EAST 57 STREET

New York, New York
1983/1986

The complex massing of this building is a result of its direct adherence to the complicated zoning regulations which affect the site. The building draws on the principles of the two separate zoning districts which govern the different parts of the site. The task was to design an "as of right" building that would satisfy both the new midtown zoning's quest for compatibility with neighboring buildings on 57th Street and the old zoning's requirements for a plaza on Lexington Avenue.

The overall mass of the building is conceived as two structures, paired side by side, created as autonomous, individually centered entities, each with its own distinct and separate entrance. The division of the facade into two vertical elements gives the building a comprehensive scale, similar to that of the Fuller and Ritz buildings on 57th Street. Each of these vertical elements is capped by a stone cornice.

At the corner, the building envelope is carved away, providing a public plaza. A 33-foot-high pavilion of granite and marble denotes the formal entrance to the semicircular plaza, and sustains the streetline along Lexington Avenue.

On 57th Street, the base of the building conforms to the street grid, maintaining a unity with the existing buildings around it. The base accommodates the pedestrian scale by introducing finely detailed storefronts in combination of granites, glass, bronze, and stainless steel.

1

2

3

1.Site plan
2.Oblique view of model
3.East view of model

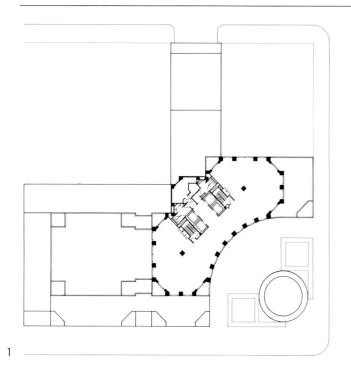

1

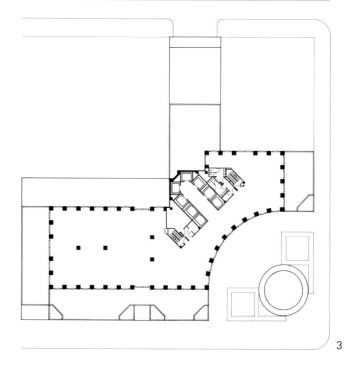

3

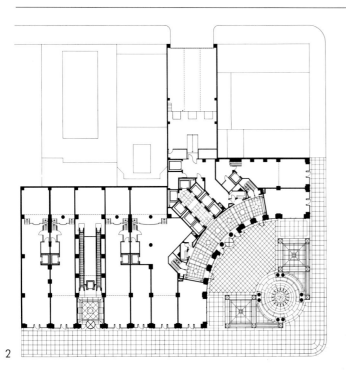

2

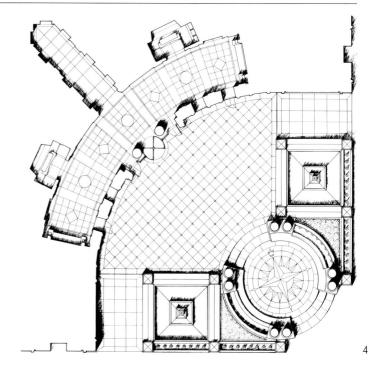

4

1. Typical floor plan, 29
   through 32
2. First floor plan

3. Typical floor plan, 8
   through 18
4. First floor plan, entry
5. South elevation

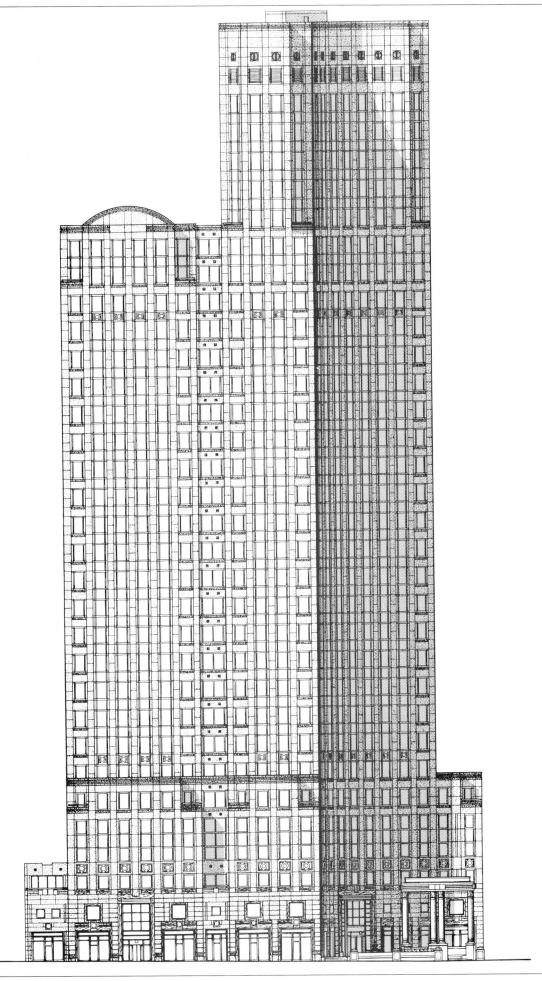

5

1. Corner pavilion
2. Entrance to shopping arcade
3. Photomontage

3

600 WHITE PLAINS ROAD

Greenburgh, New York
1983

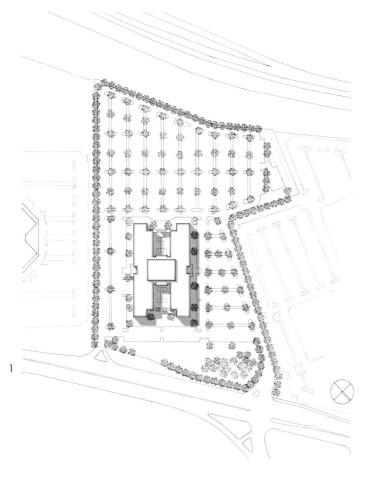

Set amid a strip of low-scaled speculative office buildings, this six-story office structure addresses the scale problems inherent in this building type.

The H-shaped configuration of the building and the tripartite division of its skin reduce the apparent bulk of the structure. The granite and limestone base engages the dark gray glass panels as they break through the bullnose cornice. A modulation of the surface plane is established by the contrasting silver and dark gray glass panels, which foreshortens the length of the building. The rhythm established by the dark glass figuration is similar in its intentions to the series of niches on One Logan Square.

Two entry courtyards lead to the main lobby, creating a unique context on an otherwise disassociated suburban site. At the centers of the elongated streetwall facades, projecting glass planes and limestone loggias demark the secondary entrances.

1

1. Site plan
2. Oblique view of model

2

1. *View of entrance, model*
2. *Lobby*

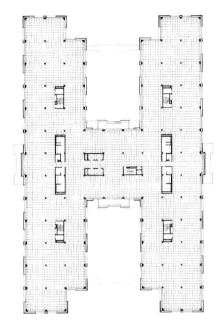

3

4

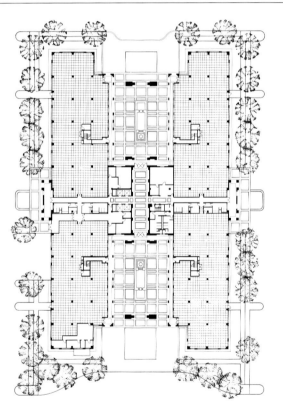

3.Typical floor plan
4.First floor plan

ARBOR CIRCLE

Parsippany, New Jersey
1983/86

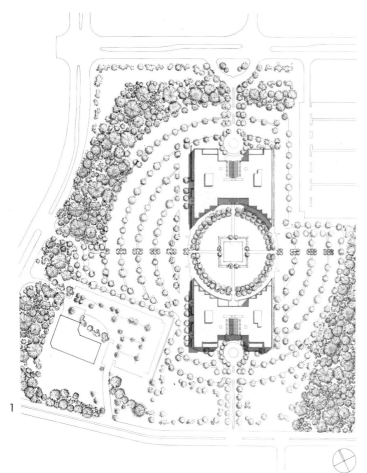

Located in a traditional, modern suburban office park, these two office buildings form a unifying node within the amorphous surroundings. The paired buildings create an inward focus, turning in on themselves to face onto a grand circular courtyard set between their masses. This formally landscaped room establishes a humanly scaled environment, offering visual relief from the asphalt surroundings. The form of the courtyard generates the radial parking pattern. From the parking areas, employees walk through this space to enter the two buildings.

The rectilinear perimeter of these buildings facing the adjacent motorways addresses the passing automobiles with grand entry gateways leading into a skylit interior garden space. This forecourt is given the character of a exterior entry court and is lined on all levels with loggias. As the larger circular exterior garden gives order and a sense of place to the complex, the entry court provides a similar sense of order and place to the interior. The dominance of the pedestrian over the vehicular is further reinforced by the axes that impose a clear movement through the complex.

The exterior is clad precast concrete panels and an aluminum and glass curtain wall. The taller precast mass is placed facing the motorways to give the complex a stately presence while the glass curtain wall steps down and opens onto the circular garden. The juxtaposition of these two primary materials and the manipulation of their mass reduces the otherwise imposing bulk of this large complex.

1.Site plan
2.Aerial view of model

2

1

1. *View from adjacent
motorway*

2

3

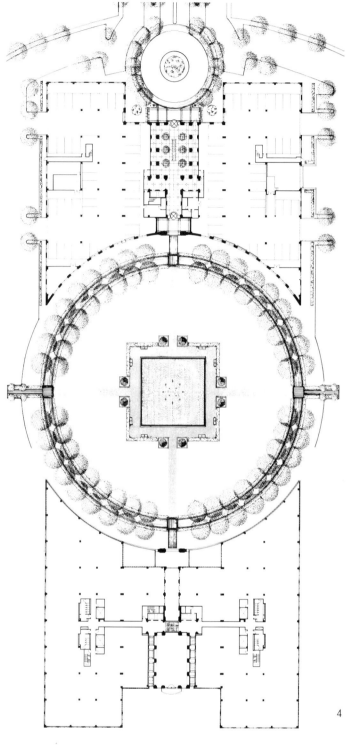

4

2. Atrium
3. Atrium
4. First (top) and second
   (bottom) floor plans

NATIONAL BANK OF COMMERCE

San Antonio, Texas
1984

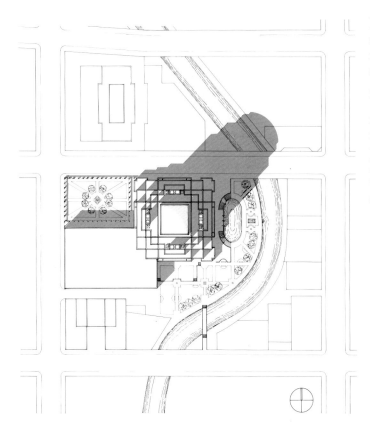

Located on the edge of downtown San Antonio, the 31-story headquarters building reaches out beyond the realm of the surrounding urban area for its contextual cues. This proposal for a 2.2-acre site fronting the San Antonio River Walk creates a high-rise mission-style building, embodying the stylistic characteristics of the mission churches typical of the Southwest. The strong formal organization of domes, arches, broken scroll pediments, and screen walls is enhanced by the use of limestone and precast concrete, materials which evoke the warmth and light-colored qualities of a regional architecture.

1.Site plan
2.Oblique view of model

2

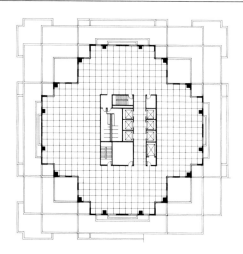

1

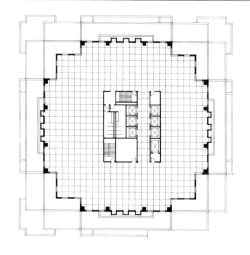

2

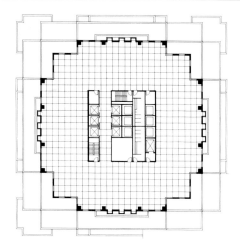

3

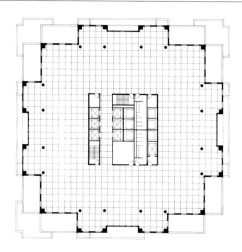

4

1.Typical highrise floor plan
2.Typical highrise floor plan
3.Typical lowrise floor plan
4.Typical lowrise floor plan
5.First floor plan
6.View of model from river
walk

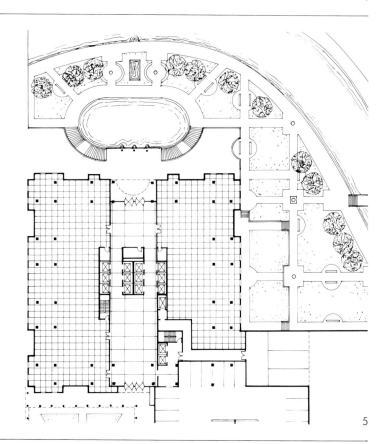

5

6

CNG TOWER

Pittsburgh, Pennsylvania
1984/1987

The Allegheny International Headquarters building derives its form from two considerations: the need to accommodate a large building program on the Z-shaped site; and a desire to establish a whole-block composition which incorporates the existing building into its total scheme. The complex asymmetrical massing expresses the interplay of contextual and architectural forces acting on the site.

At the crux of the complex a plaza is established, creating a focus to absorb the thrust of the diagonal Sixth Avenue, which terminates at this point. The plaza also allows for a dialogue between the new structure and its neighboring Midtown Tower building. The 60-foot width of this neighbor governs the dimensional module for the CNG building. Thus the building is divided into three 60-foot bays, each defined as an autonomous piece.

piece. These pieces are organized in a classical tripartite division and defined by the articulation of their centers and lateral edges to read as separate figures. The surfaces are sheathed in two different-colored granites, with their junctions expressed as quoining.

Overlayed onto the composition is the reference to three distinct urban scales. The traditional height of old Pittsburgh is articulated in the base and *piano nobile*. The intermediate 200-foot height of the Midtown Tower and the predominant streetwall is threaded through the fabric of the building skin at its midsection. At the top, the height of the more recent skyscrapers is met, and, in this case, the vaulted truss roof is symbolic of the importance and proximity of the converging waterways and the many bridges which transverse the Allegheny River.

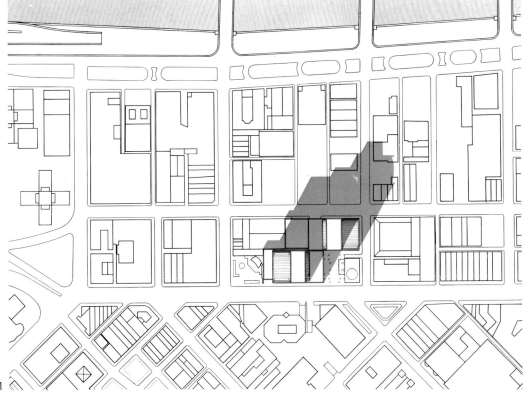

1

1.Site plan
2.Photomontage

2

1

1.Photomontage
2.Top of building, model
3.Base of building, model

4.Clay study model
5.Clay study model
6.Study model

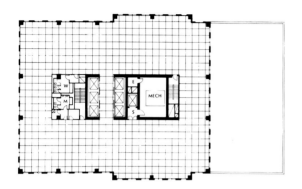

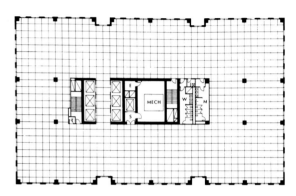

1

2

3

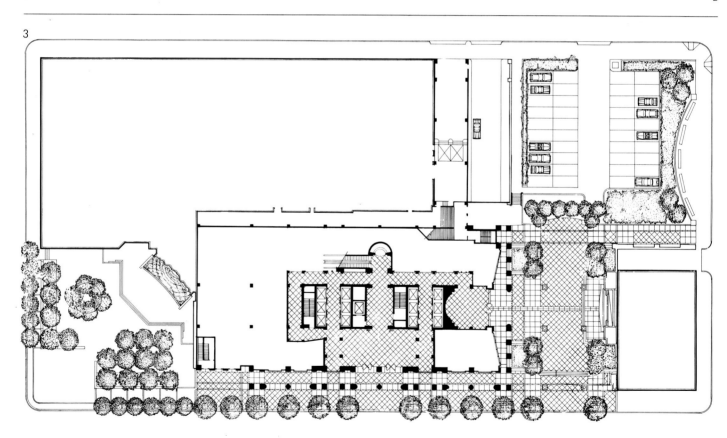

1. Typical highrise floor
2. Typical lowrise floor
3. First floor plan

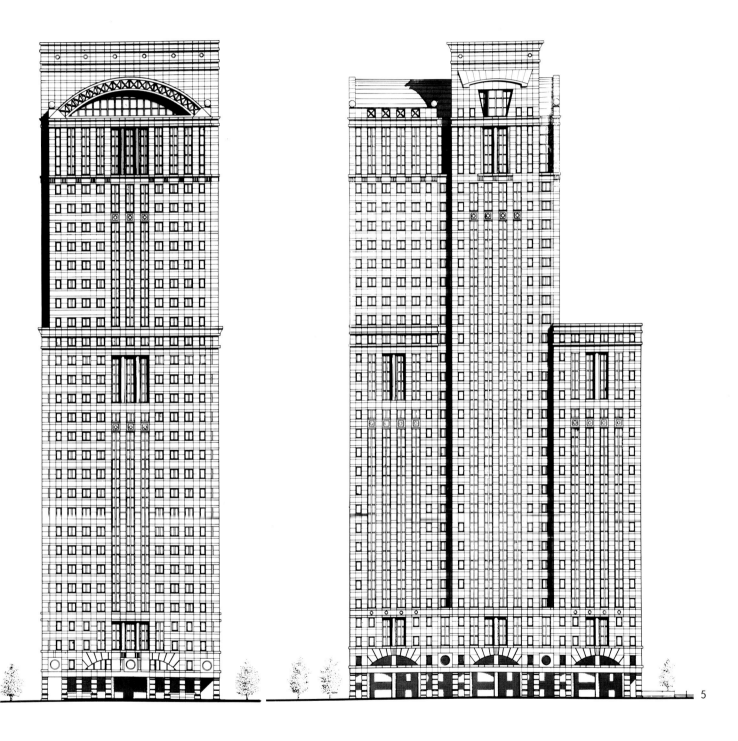

4. East elevation
5. South elevation

5

ONE O'HARE CENTER

Chicago, Illinois
1984/1986

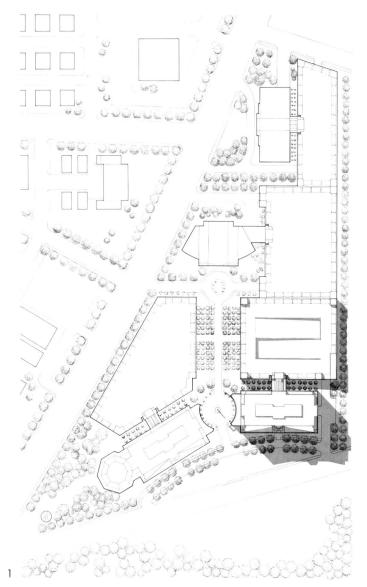

1

Located in the heart of Chicago's O'Hare business corridor, One O'Hare Center is the first development of a 17.5-acre Cook County Forest Preserve on one side, and by uninspired suburban office parks set in fields of parking on its other three sides.

The master plan is intended to structure growth in such a manner that the otherwise residual space typically created between suburban buildings becomes an asset. Through the particular massing of the buildings a collective sense of community is created within the total master plan. The residual spaces are thus well defined landscaped gardens. A sense of place is experienced immediately in the sequence of arrival through these gardens. This notion of place, and sense of belonging, is reinforced within the building through a series of public spaces and common amenities. An atrium, which unites the garage structure and office building, becomes the forecourt to the building. This transition space is focused by a waterfall feature. The arrival sequence culminates in a three-story lobby space, detailed in the same materials as the exterior of the building, and further embellished with ornamental metal work.

The twelve-story building's front facade is composed of a two-story granite base upon which sits an inflected curtain wall of blue-green glass, addressing the Forest Preserve and the city beyond. The other facades are clad in alternating vertical gray masonry piers and green glass windows, responding to the increasing urbanism of the business corridor immediately adjacent to the site. The building's imagery recalls some of Chicago's renowned buildings, such as the facade articulation on Louis Sullivan's Auditorium Building and the vertical expression of Raymond Hood's Tribune Tower.

2

1.Site plan
2.Aerial view

1.Oblique view from forest
  preserve
2.Oblique view from business
  corridor

3.Atrium
4.Elevator lobby
5.Typical floor plan
6.First floor plan
7.Forest elevation

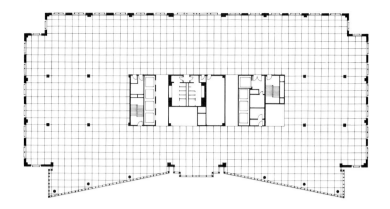

5

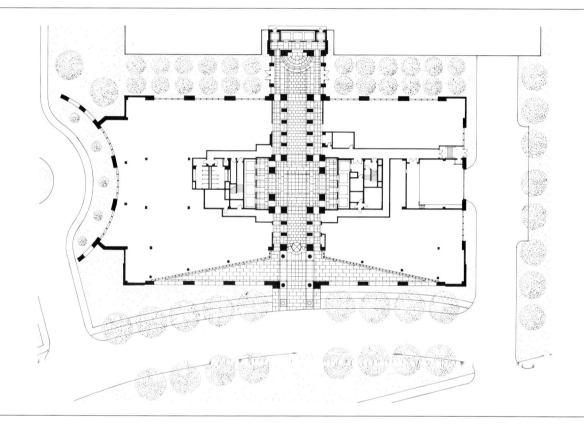

6

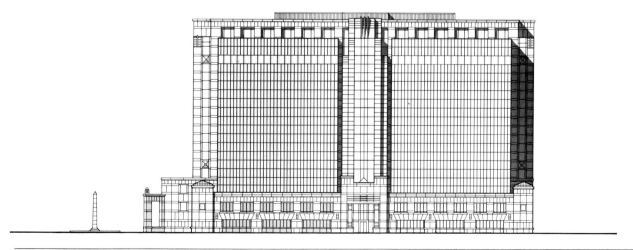

7

ABC PHASE II

New York, New York
1984/1986

In 1978, Kohn Pedersen Fox designed a building as part of the first phase of ABC's ongoing redevelopment of its broadcasting facilities on Manhattan's Upper West Side. Housing offices, technical facilities, and a newscasting studio, the 14-story Phase II building links into the existing first-phase structure.

The cascading profile of Phase II in its "as of right" setback profile reduces its impact and bulk as perceived from street level. Overscaled elements and a 25-foot window module introduce a rhythm which foreshortens the 225-foot-long streetwall and establishes a dialogue with the double-height fenestration of the many studio apartment buildings in the area. The undulating qualities of the surface and its interlocking fragments are intricately woven out of granite, brick, and glass. Marking the building's entrance is a bulging sphere, below which a loggia filters employees into the lobby. The lobby, in contrast, is a high-tech environment, sheathed in gridded-aluminum panels which house television monitors at intermittent points. An axis is established through the lobby space, up the escalators, to the core of the combined buildings.

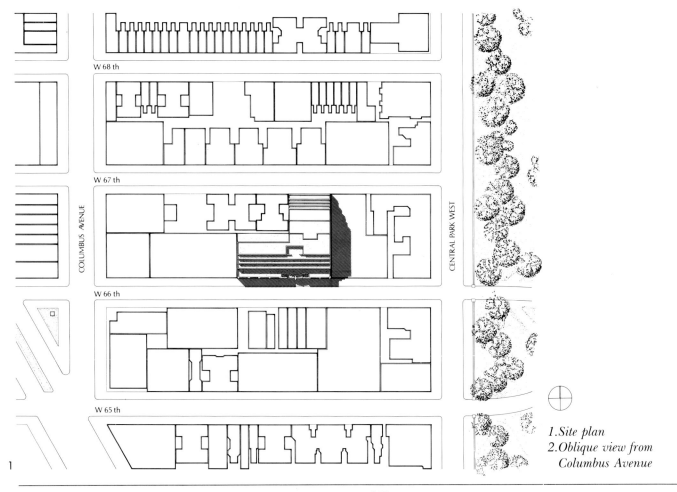

1. Site plan
2. Oblique view from
   Columbus Avenue

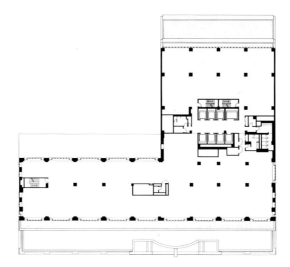

1

2

3

1.Eleventh floor plan
2.Second floor plan
3.First floor plan

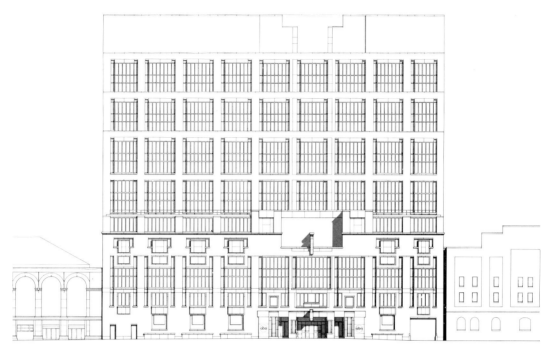

4

5

4.66th street elevation
5.Transverse section

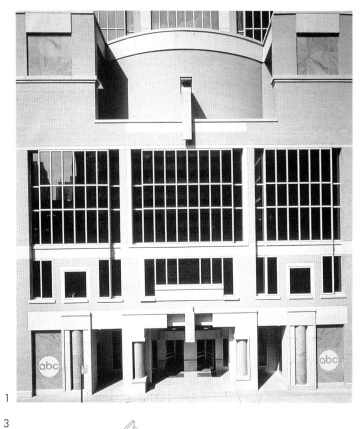

1

2

3

4

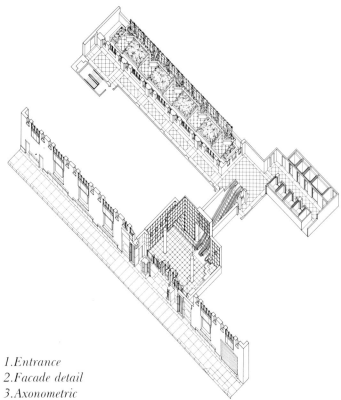

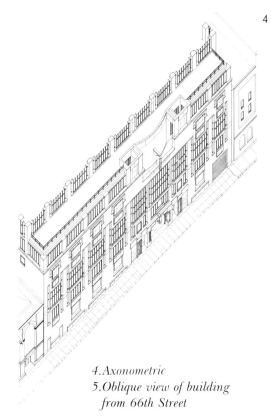

1.Entrance
2.Facade detail
3.Axonometric

4.Axonometric
5.Oblique view of building
from 66th Street

1000 WILSHIRE BOULEVARD

Los Angeles, California
1984/1987

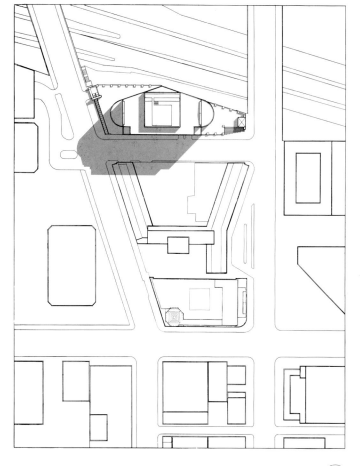

The ubiquitous array of tall modern office towers in downtown Los Angeles presents a bland backdrop to this uniquely shaped building set in the foreground at 1000 Wilshire Boulevard. The site is a sliver located between the truncated urban matrix and the Harbor Freeway, at the edge of downtown. The resulting building mass is a direct response to the contextual forces acting upon it. The facade, which rises to form a rectangular roof element crowned with three pediments, respects the rigidity of the city grid behind it. In contrast, the curved front bursts away from the central business district; alluding to the flowing form of the freeway and foretelling the river of cars to the west.

The resulting form is wrapped with a decorative skin developed in two shades of granite and two shades of glass, composing a pattern that serves to reduce the building's perceived scale. Every third floor is banded by a horizontal strip of gray glass, intersected by honed black granite pieces that demark the solid vertical framework. The overall effect is that of a woven fabric interlaced with varying textures of granite and glass.

In order to resolve the change in grade between the adjacent streets and to accommodate the required six levels of underground parking, the building sits on a podium elevated at Seventh Street, but at grade adjoining Wilshire Boulevard. The podium forms a pedestrian plaza, integrating a series of gateways which direct one towards the round loggia entrances located on the narrow ends of the building. The vaulted main lobby, detailed in black, green, and gray marble, is subdivided by a series of square-column bays, which open up onto the elevator lobbies on one side and a restaurant on the other.

1.Site plan
2.View from north

1

2

3

1. Base of building at Wilshire
   Boulevard, model
2. Base of building at Seventh
   Street, model

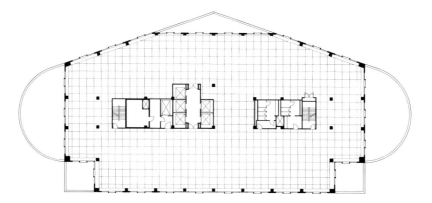

1

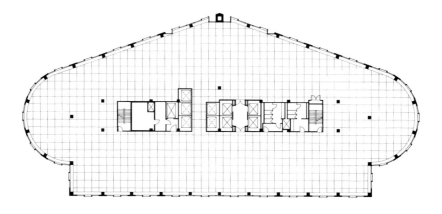

2

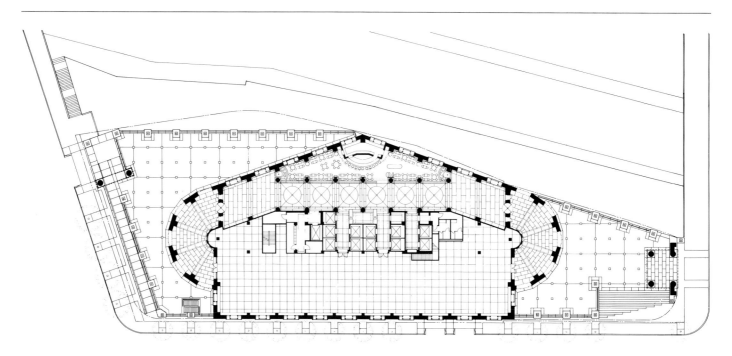

3

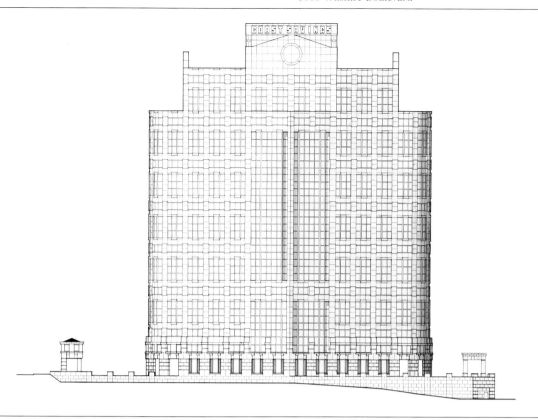

4

5

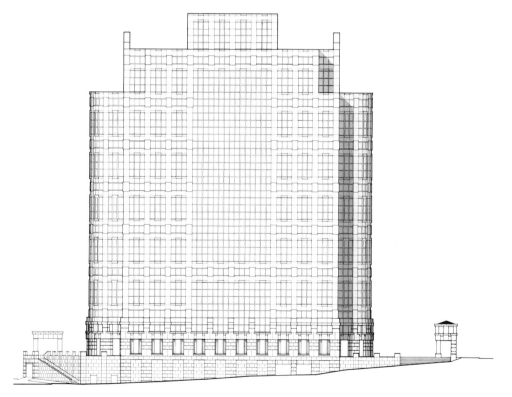

1. *Typical setback floor*
2. *Typical lowrise floor*   4. *Harbor Freeway elevation*
3. *First floor plan*   5. *Francisco Street elevation*

180 EAST 70th STREET

New York, New York
1984/1986

A great number of turn-of-the-century residential buildings located on Manhattan's Upper East Side have derived their inspiration directly from classical precedents. On Park and Fifth Avenues, residential towers, rising as symbols of power and wealth, are derived from classical urban forms. This 31-story building at Third Avenue and 70th Street is informed by these precedents.

The building's underlying classical theme and tripartite organization respond to the lower-scaled townhouses on 70th Street and to the larger-scaled buildings on Third Avenue. Its L-shaped mass establishes a frontal presence on 70th Street, with its side and back facades rising lyrically to address the vistas from Third Avenue. The tri-pedimented top which crowns the building is derived from William Kent's Holkham Hall. It rests on a punched-window brick tower, which fits into a decorative limestone base. On the *piano nobile* level, community facilities open onto a skylit garden atrium. In the lobby, pairs of mahogany Tuscan columns are set on a black-and-white checkerboard marble floor. A vaulted *trompe l'oeil* blue clouded ceiling caps the space.

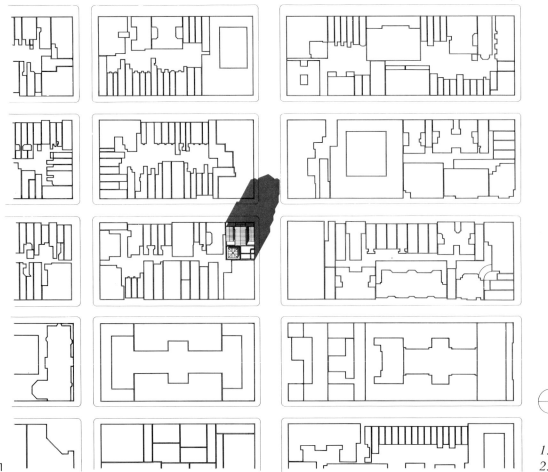

1. Site plan
2. View from 70th Street

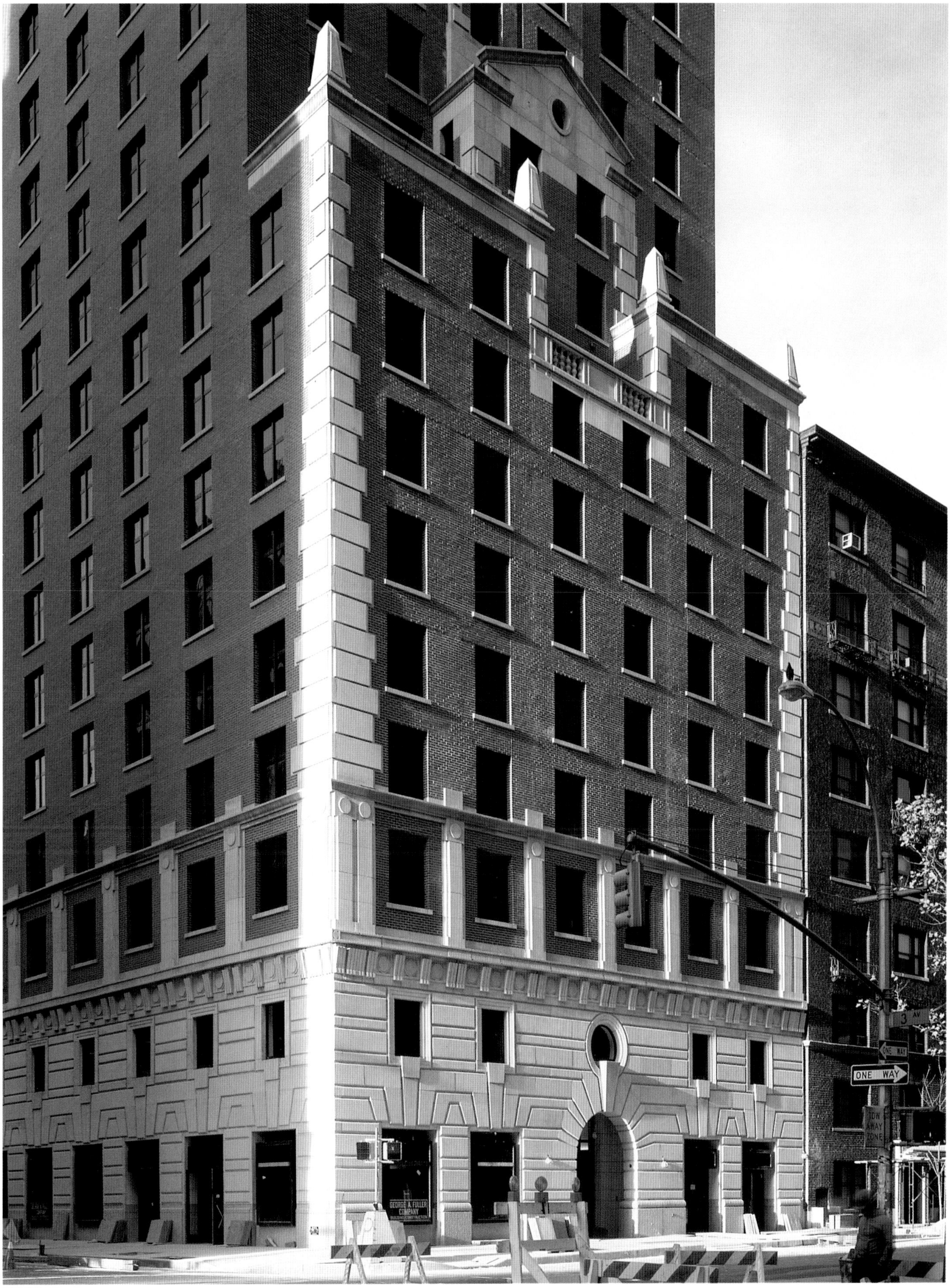

2

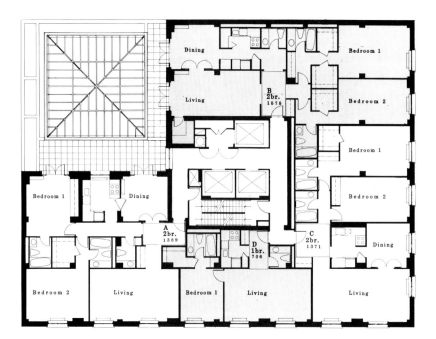

1

2

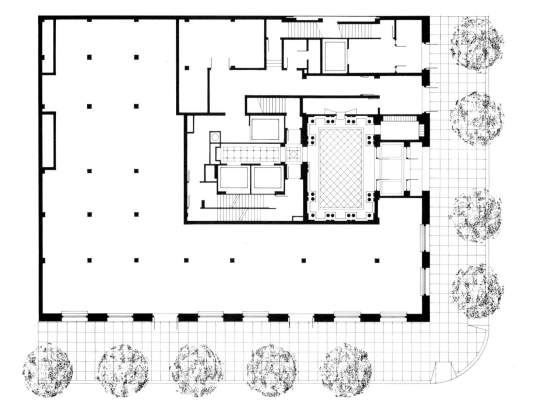

1. Third floor plan   3. 70th Street elevation
2. First floor plan   4. Third Avenue elevation

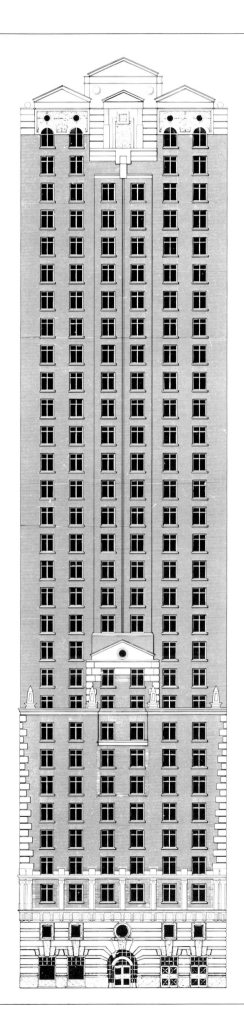

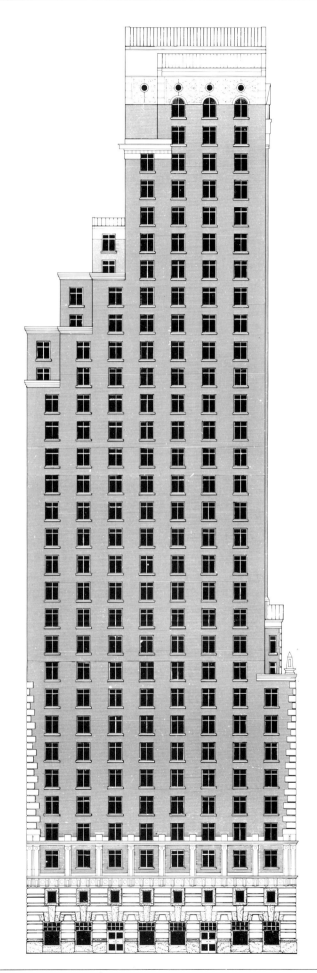

3

4

1. *View from Third Avenue,*
   model
2. *Top of building*
3. *Shaft of building*
4. *Base of building*

5. *Base*
6. *View looking north*

HYATT REGENCY

Greenwich, Connecticut
1984/1986

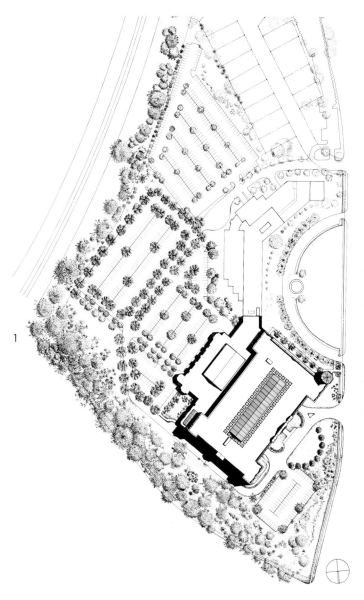

One of the primary concerns in the siting of this hotel was the establishment of a harmonious relationship between the existing structures on the site and the new building. The hotel building, which links to the existing L-shaped office structure to reestablish the old crescent, is anchored on its newly acquired end by the refinished vestigial tower. The 400-room, four-story hotel is internally organized around a 250-foot-long atrium space, which is subdivided into three parts and defined on its perimeter by a colonnade of monumental, paired precast columns splitting from the massive base piers, continuing upward to support the skylights above. Pilasters and arches carved out of the atrium's lining form the background, echoing and establishing a multifarious rhythm of planes. The atrium is developed in a subtle, airy palette, combining a variety of precast-concrete members, metal, and glass. Beyond the elevator lobby is a grand staircase, terminating the longitudinal axis.

On the exterior, a series of undulating planes reduce the perceived length of the building and morphologically tie it into the scale of its suburban neighbors. The buff-colored concrete base is surmounted by a brick-veneer shaft, which is capped by a copper roof, further integrating the project with its context.

1.Site plan
2.View of entrance

2

1

2

3

1. *View of north facade*
2. *Southeast corner, with pool pavilion*
3. *Long view of atrium*
4. *North entry, loggia*

4

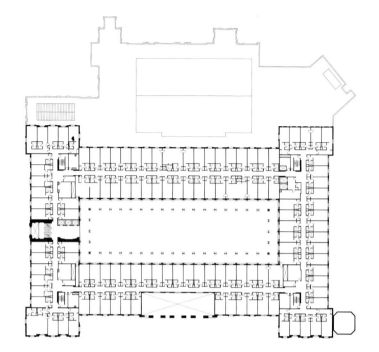

1

2

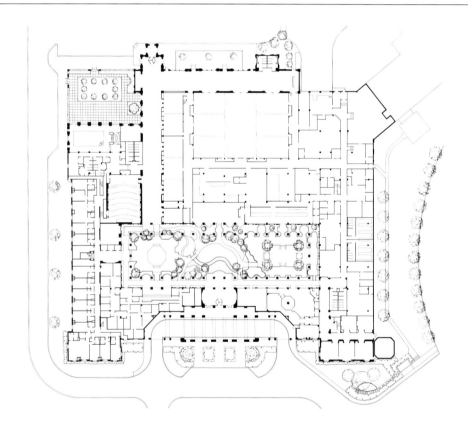

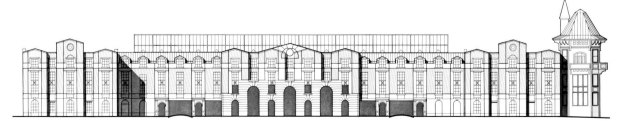

3

4

1. Typical floor plan
2. First floor plan
3. Entrance elevation
4. Atrium, north wall

1111 BRICKELL AVENUE

Miami, Florida
1984/1988

Set between the shores of Biscayne Bay and Brickell Avenue are twin 25-story office buildings at 1111 Brickell Avenue. As bookends, the towers address both urban context and seascape through the subtle differentiation of their respective massings. The design's iconography acknowledges the stylistic legacy of Miami's Art Deco architecture and derives much of its meaning and visual inspiration from this strong, regional tradition.

The pair of identical but mirror-imaged office towers atop a retail podium work in concert to address the two significant orientations which govern the site. One tower, its principal facade accentuated by canted glass planes, faces west and inland to address Brickell Avenue, a prominent tree-lined boulevard, and the city beyond. The other tower, its principal facade composed of an expansive, curved glass plane, looks east to the waters of Biscayne Bay. Each tower's orientation is further emphasized by the supporting stepped form of its glass

wrapper which straitjackets and directs it. The buildings' facades are composed of a hierarchical division of glass and metal, with an exaggerated and dense mullion quoining at the corners. At the skyline, the towers are crowned by twin, illuminated monumental lanterns of stainless steel and sandblasted glass.

Within the podium the tower lobbies are connected by a retail galleria which extends the length of the site— linking Brickell Avenue to Biscayne Bay. At eigher end, the galleria terminates in an entry atrium which features a grand stair that in plan echoes the profile of the principal tower facade directly above. Midpoint along the galleria and set between the towers is a skylit palm court, the centerpiece of the design. Throughout the interior the indigenous coquina stone used on the exterior reappears, highlighted by accent marbles and decorative stainless steel details.

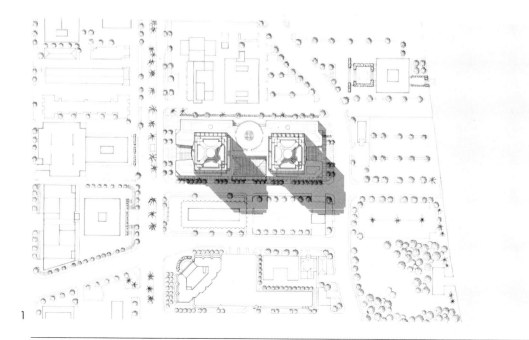

1.Site plan
2.Photomontage

2

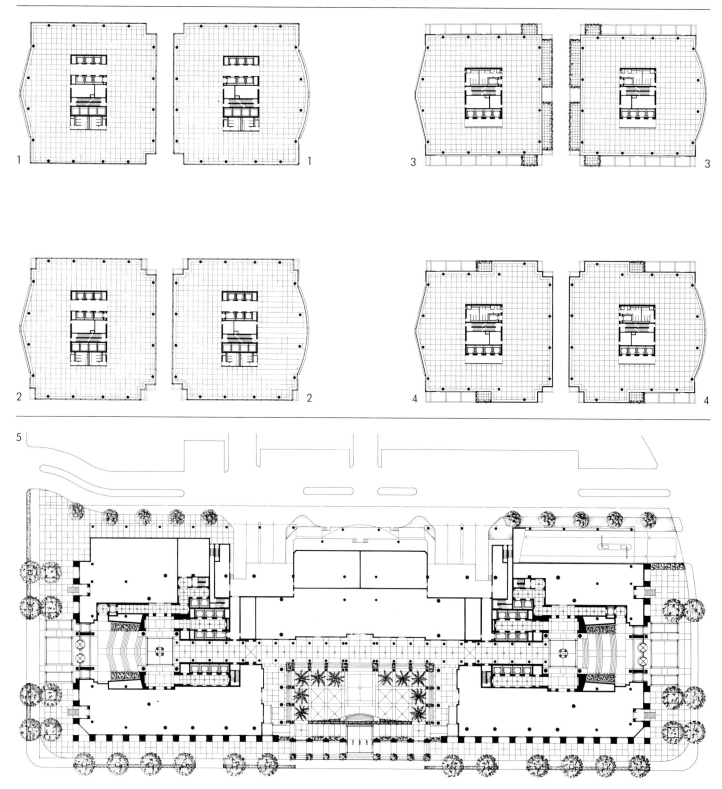

1.*Typical floor plan, 2
  through 4*
2.*Typical floor plan, 5
  through 14*

3.*18th floor plan*
4.*Typical floor plan, 21
  through 24*
5.*First floor plan*

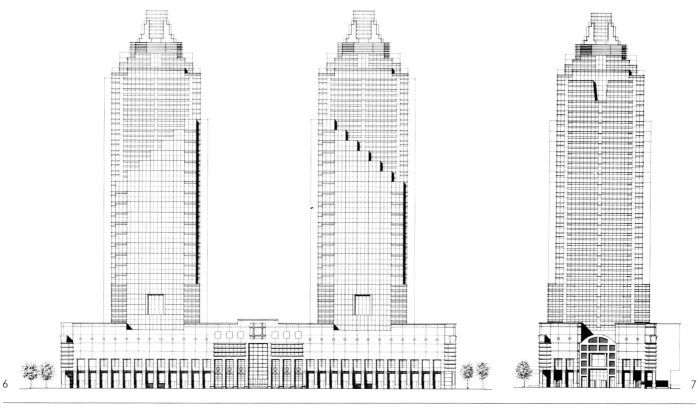

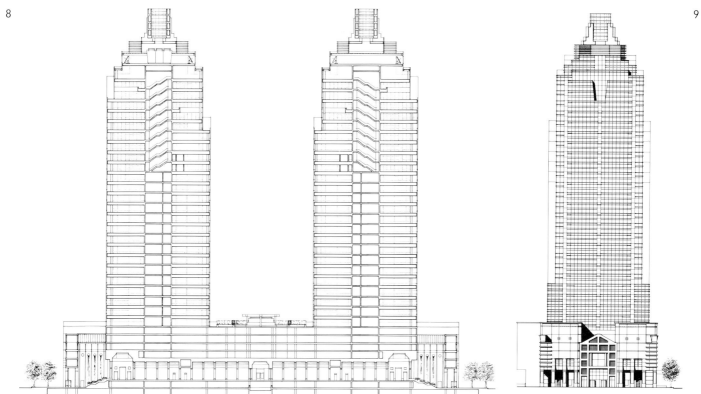

6.Southeast 12th Street
  elevation
7.South Bay Shore Drive   8.Longitudinal section
  elevation   9.Brickell Avenue elevation

1.Lobby
2.Palm court
3.Photomontage/Night view

500 E STREET S.W.

Washington, D.C.
1984/1987

Sited near the nation's Capitol Building, in an area composed of both residential and office buildings, this nine-story speculative office building completes a wall of modern office blocks along the northern edge of Washington's Southwest Expressway.

The building's form is derived from the 45-degree chamfered site boundary to the west. On the eastern side, the building is similarly chamfered to create a symmetrical composition. Marking the intersection of E Street and Sixth Street is an engaged polygonal tower. Its placement establishes a dialogue with the 200-foot-high spire of the nineteenth-century church across the street.

The building's precast-concrete facade is a neutral wrapper, modulated by four-story bays, transformed as localized conditions require. The repetition of these discrete units produces a rich fabric, enabling the scale of both vehicular and pedestrian movement to be addressed. The wall is composed of a combination of masonry elements which express the structural frame of the building, and glass/metal elements which express its utilitarian office functions. The reflective glass panels contained in the aluminum metal grid are placed flush with the precast base, denoting their constrained modern

character: a one-foot-deep recess at either side of the bay piece emphasizes the plastic nature of the material and allows the central panel to be expressed as a figural element in the gridded masonry field. Thus each bay describes multiple functional elements: the structural frame, the five-foot office planning module, the perimeter mechanical system, and the ten-foot width of the typical office.

The vertical bay windows penetrate the two-story attic zone, visually uniting the shaft of the building to its top. At the uppermost floor, a band of glazing introduces a horizontal reading which terminates the vertically striated facade of the shaft.

The stripped-down nature of the cylindrical tower's vertical glass elements produces the maximum visual tension at the building's primary viewing point. An airy roof pavilion, constructed of concrete piers with aluminum fins and an open web of painted steel members, caps the towers. While providing a gateway effect when paired with the similarly scaled church steeple, the tower contrasts with the spire in its lightness, openness, and sense of compression.

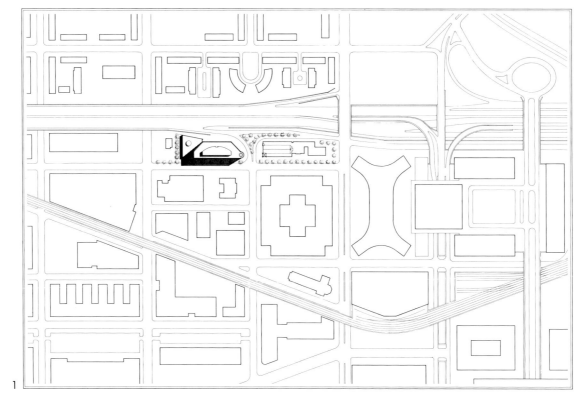

1

1. Site plan
2. View of model from
   intersection of E Street and
   Sixth Street

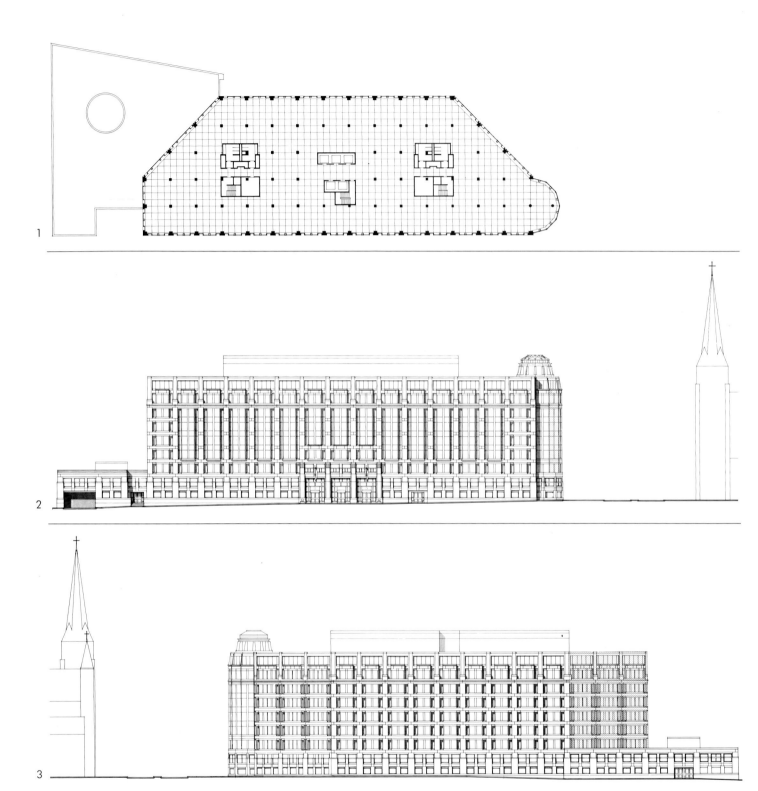

1. Typical floor plan
2. North elevation
3. South elevation

4

6

5

4. Model view of north
  elevation

5. Entry view of model
6. Elevation

383 MADISON AVENUE

New York, New York
1984/1989

The legendary Manhattan skyline will have a prominent new member added to it with the completion of the proposed 383 Madison Avenue building. This building, the third highest in Manhattan, will heighten the silhouette of what is already the tallest skyline in the world, evoking a sense of mystery and marvel and creating a dialogue with its neighboring Chrysler and Empire State buildings.

The dichotomy between the skyscraper as facade and object is dealt with differently here than in the Block 265 project. In Block 265, the facade is organized into a collage of contextual imagery which alludes to the city around it. In 383 Madison, the building retains its facadelike character throughout its entire height, a product of its cruciform shape whose lateral faces respond to the cardinal points of the grid of Manhattan in a frontal fashion.

The site, located in the heart of midtown Manhattan, is an atypical square block. The massing of the building is a direct response to the requirements of the previously untested Tier One provisions of the New York City Midtown Zoning Law. Simultaneously, it conforms uniquely to the structural characteristics of buildings that must respond well to lateral loads produced by winds. It has a profile that allows it to maintain the streetwall at the base, thereby tying into its context, and rise as an object in the sky.

The base itself is composed of layers of gray granite, which create an illusion of depth. Above, a taut, cagelike metal surface emerges, framing the glass panels which rise through a series of transitions, becoming lighter and airier visually, terminating with an almost lacelike effervescent crown. Although the entire shaft of the building is perceived as a monolithic piece, an integrated and sequential manipulation of scaled-down elements allows for a tertiary reading. This permits the expression of the separate parts as autonomous pieces which are in turn further broken down into base, shaft, and capital. In a classical manner, the individual pieces are completely striated and linked vertically. The surface is, therefore, held together vertically from base to top.

Fronting on Madison Avenue, a colonnade forms a large urban room with grand curved staircases at either end imposing on the space, leading commuters to the neighboring Grand Central Terminal. Within the base and directly above the lobby are four duplex levels designed as trading floors, above which are retail and dining facilities open to the public.

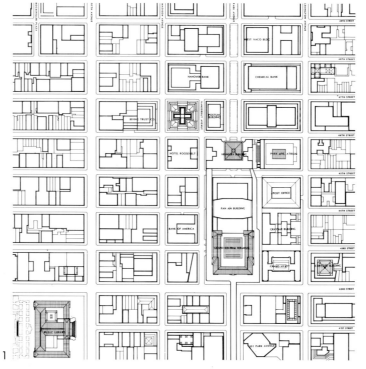

1. Site plan
2. Oblique view of model
3. Model view of Madison
   Avenue elevation

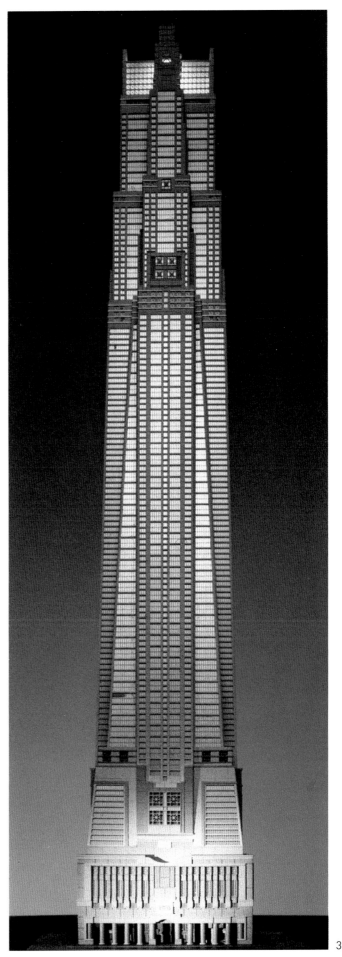

2

3

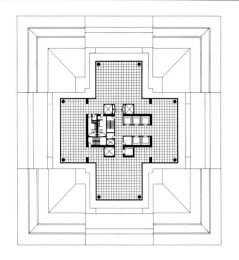

1

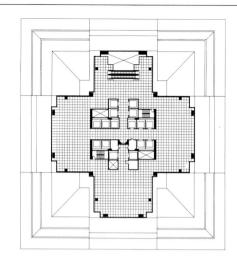

2

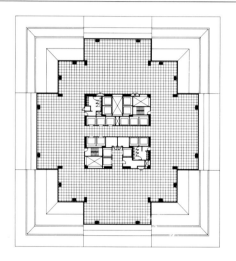

3

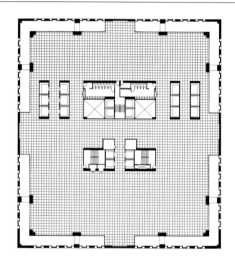

4

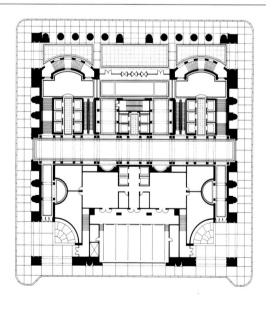

5

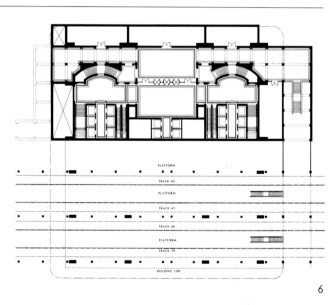

6

1. Typical highrise floor plan
2. Second skylobby floor plan
3. Typical lowrise floor plan

4. Trading floor mezzanine plan
5. First floor plan
6. Concourse floor plan

7

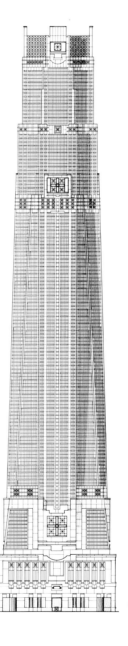

9

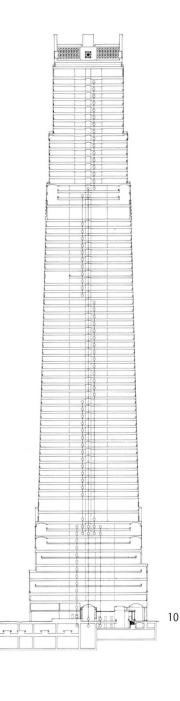

10

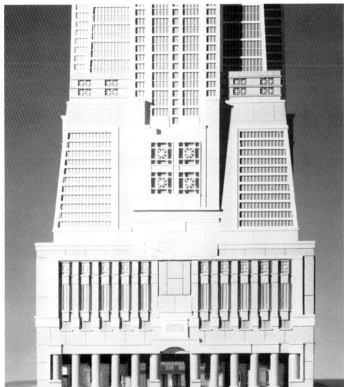

8

7. Top of building, model
8. Base of building, model
9. 47th Street elevation
10. Section

1

2

3

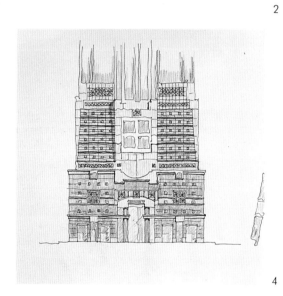

4

5

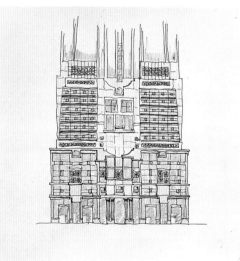

6

1-6.Facade studies

7

8

7.*Photomontage*
8.*Photomontage*

MELLON BANK CENTER

Philadelphia, Pennsylvania
1984/1989

Located on the axis of Philadelphia's historic City Hall tower, Mellon Bank Center establishes a clear iconographic link with the city's architectural centerpiece. The building is situated in a newly created special height district whose new zoning and height regulations supersede the city's traditional datum previously set at the height of the William Penn Statue, located atop the City Hall building.

The resultant compression of the Philadelphia skyline forced buildings to fill in the available green spaces at street level. The sudden release of this pressure allows Mellon Bank Center to assume a more natural architectural order.

At its base, a six-story granite podium anchors the westerly boundaries of the site and provides street-level lobbies on JFK Boulevard and Market Street. An open green space in the form of a topiary garden is set between the existing Six Penn Center building and the new podium. Set back from the street walls, the 53-story metal and glass tower rises above the podium in the form of a slender obelisk terminating in a pyramidal roof, thereby completing the traditional tripartite ordering of tall towers. The tower's metal and glass cladding is articulated to mimic the internal structure of the tower. The frame format of the exterior facade accents the corners with horizontal lacing and the centers with vertical columns recalling a vocabulary common to the Art Deco period. The tower's shaft opens in a series of large cornices, revealing the lattice-framed pyramid on top.

While Mellon Bank Center rises above its predecessors to mark the coming of a new generation of buildings to the Penn Center area, it remains mindful of its contextural responsibility to improve the liveability of the city, particularly at the pedestrian scale.

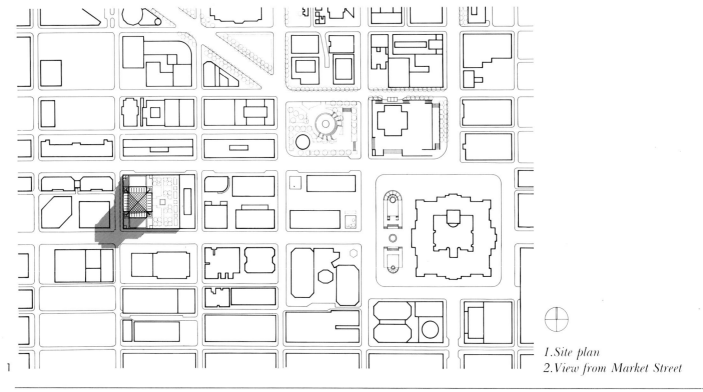

1. *Site plan*
2. *View from Market Street*

2

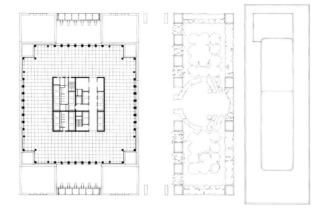

1

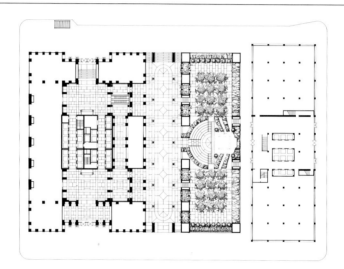

2

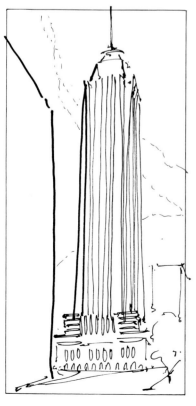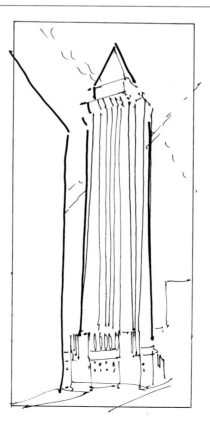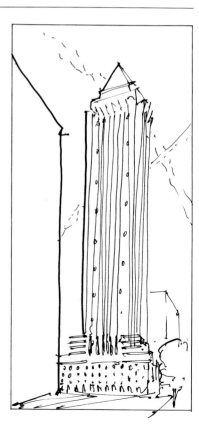

3

5

7

1.Typical highrise floor plan
2.First floor plan
3.Design studies

4.Market Street Elevation
5.Typical curtain wall study
6.Context model
7.Context model

70 EAST 55th STREET

New York, New York
1984/1986

This 25-story office building is located in midtown Manhattan, on a midblock site, between Park and Madison Avenues. The solution addresses the problem of reinforcing the streetwall while still allowing the building to maintain an independent identity. To achieve this, a classical tripartite division of base, shaft, and top is employed. The base respects the cornice line established by its Park Avenue neighbors and relates in scale to the plaza across the street. The large pilasters which rise above the entry support oversized lighting spheres, whose quality serves to emphasize and focus the visual center of the base while simultaneously gesturing up towards the shaft of the building. The square shaft sets back from the base and rises to the twenty-first story. Above this level, the corners are indented to form a cruciform shape which, in turn, gives way to twin towers.

The front, side, and back facades are differentiated from one another by a subtle variation in the use of materials. The front is a combination of light gray and green granite, detailed to give the facade a play of light, shadow, texture, and color. The edges are accentuated with large granite quoins which tie into the horizontal bands of punched windows. In contrast, the center is marked by a continuous vertical window panel that punctuates the otherwise solid mass of the building. The side and back facades, sheathed in brick, are flat and more restrained.

In the lobby, a procession of rooms is visually extended by a forced perspective garden which is inspired by the garden in the Palazzo Spada in Rome.

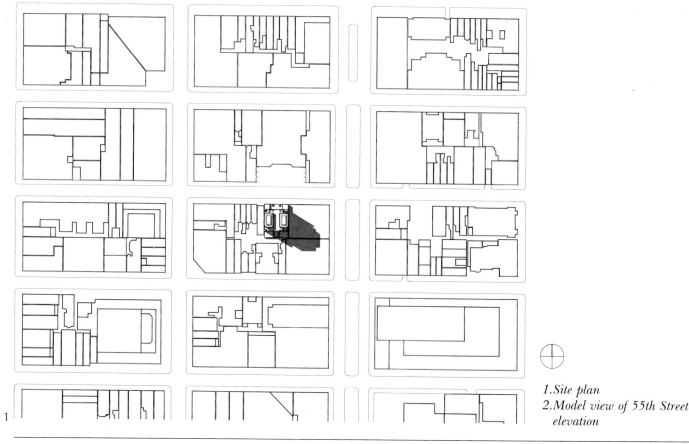

1.Site plan
2.Model view of 55th Street elevation

1

1. *View of model from*
   Madison Avenue
2. *Overhead view of model*

2

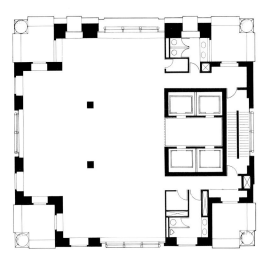

1

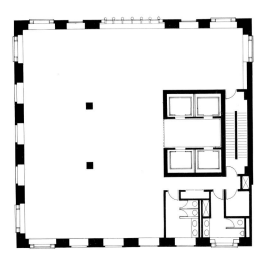

2

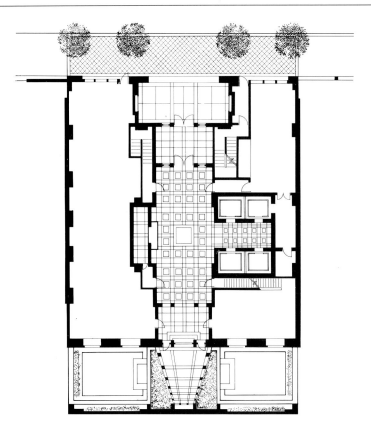

3

4

5

1. Typical floor plan, 22
   through 25
2. Typical floor plan, 7
   through 19

3. First floor plan
4. View of base, model
5. Lobby, model

101 FEDERAL STREET

Boston, Massachusetts
1984/1987

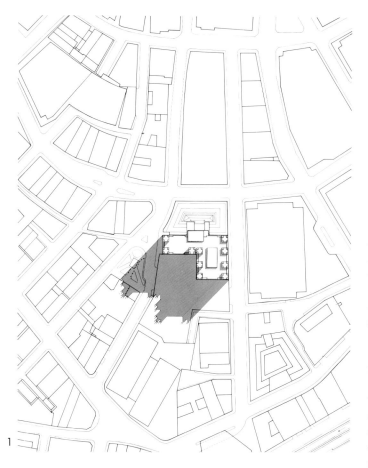

1

When part of the site for the initially proposed 75 Federal Street development could not be assembled, an alternative project adding to the existing 75 Federal Street building was designed. The 101 Federal Street site borders the city's financial district, an area dominated primarily by structures of a classical tradition, and abounding with examples of buildings with strong profiles and polychromatic dispositions. The adjacent 75 Federal Street building is a rare example of the Art Deco style within the district. 101 Federal specifically addresses the basic textural considerations of the predominant urban fabric and the compositional characteristics of its 21-story pyramidal neighbor. The 35-story building mass is designed as a neutral backdrop, against which the cascading northern profile of 75 Federal can be appreciated. The awkward configuration of the site and a dense program results in a bulky mass rising the full height of the building. Three semidiscrete entities subdivide the mass and allow for a series of local symmetries to resolve the complex massing condition.

101 Federal introduces into the basic substructure of its facade the vertical striations present in 75 Federal. Horizontal elements are allowed to weave through these vertical planes, tying the fabric together. The lower third of the building maintains the same floor-to-floor height of its neighbor, above which a new floor-to-floor height is employed. In order to compensate compositionally for this difference, decorative pieces are inserted above the standard windows. At the 10-story level, the building begins to subdivide, first into two and then into four masses. The decorative system developed further reinforces this constantly subdividing form. The building's warm gray limestone field is highlighted by a series of black and white marble and granite elements and an intricate metal gridding. This decorative metal grid used to articulate the surfaces evolved from the decorative theme explored in the interiors of the Procter & Gamble General Offices complex.

Internally, a two-story pedestrian galleria lined with shops ties into 75 Federal Street's lobby and links the existing business district on the east to the commercial district on the west. The new lobby's mood and palette complements the existing lobby of 75 Federal Street and reinforces the external system employed on 101 Federal Street.

1.Site plan
2.Northeast view of model

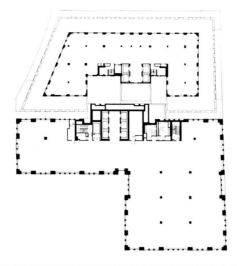

1

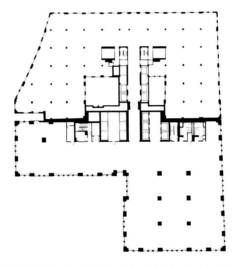

2

3

1.Typical highrise floor plan   3.First floor plan
2.Typical lowrise floor plan   4.East elevation

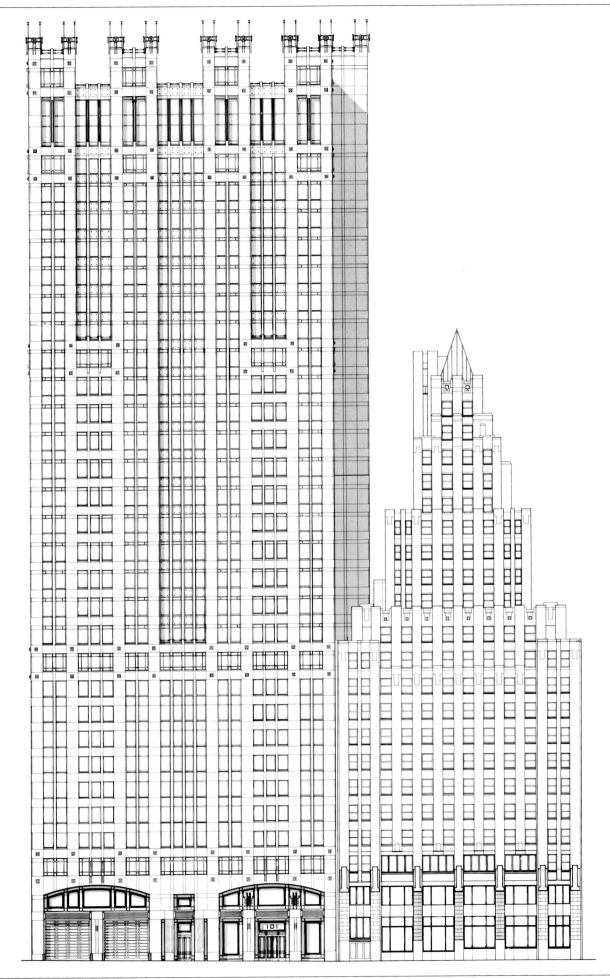

4

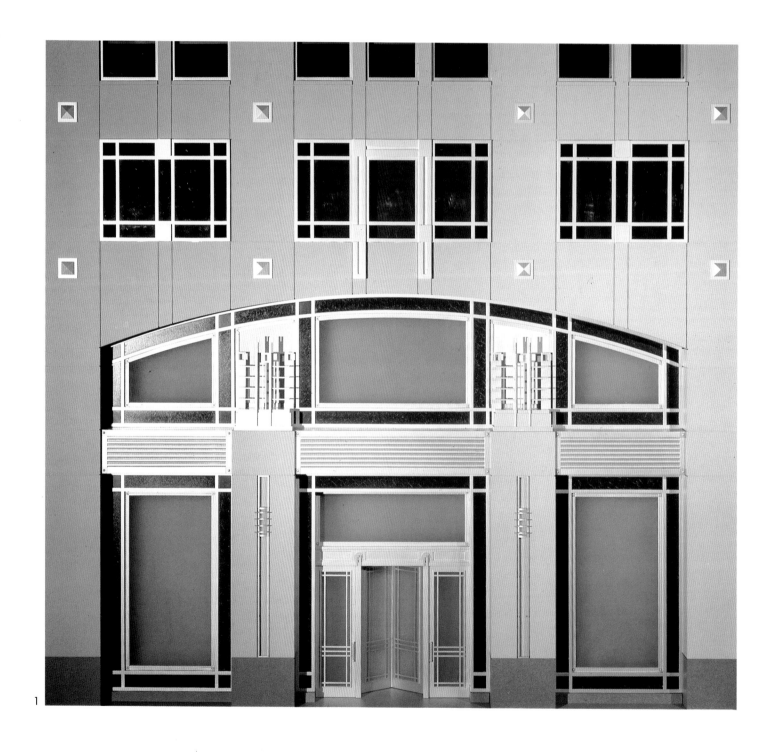

1

1.*Entrance detail, model*
2.*Southwest view of model*

2

PRUDENTIAL–HILTON TOWER

New York, New York
1984/1988

This 34-story midblock office tower, situated in midtown Manhattan, faces onto two narrow crosstown streets and is sandwiched between a residential building and the thin-slabbed Hilton Hotel. The building sets back from its podium, rising to establish a frontal stance onto the flanking streets. The highly articulated aluminum and glass facades of the tower are capped by domed lanterns to mark the building's presence in the skyline and to reinforce the visual connection with the avenues. The solidity of the side elevations, sheathed in granite with punched windows, absorb the thrust of the Hilton Hotel slab and relate to the adjoining masonry residential building.

At its base, the building holds the streetline and is scaled to pedestrian activity. A city-mandated through-block connection is provided. This four-story vaulted glass galleria, lined with shops and cafes, acts as an interstitial zone between the Hilton Hotel and the office building. Centered on the tower's mass and independent of the galleria is the main lobby entrance. Dual hexagonal lobbies assembled in an array of marbles with stainless-steel and brass trim lead to the central elevator banks through circular rotundas.

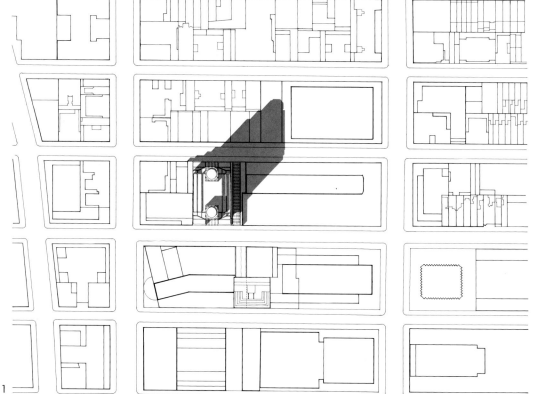

1. Site plan
2. Midblock view of model

2

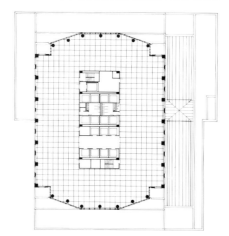

1

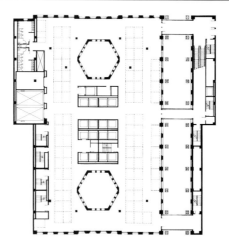

2

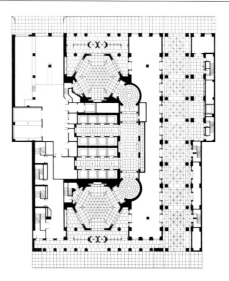

3

1.Typical floor plan
2.Exhibition floor
3.First floor plan

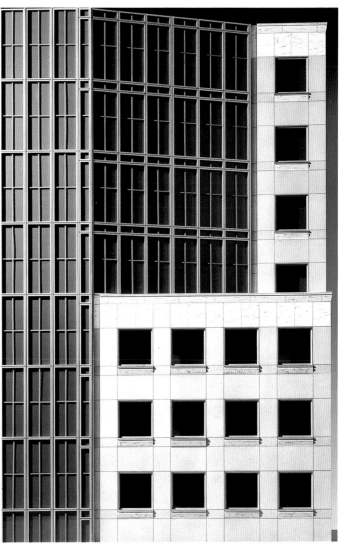

4

5

4.Galleria model
5.Facade study

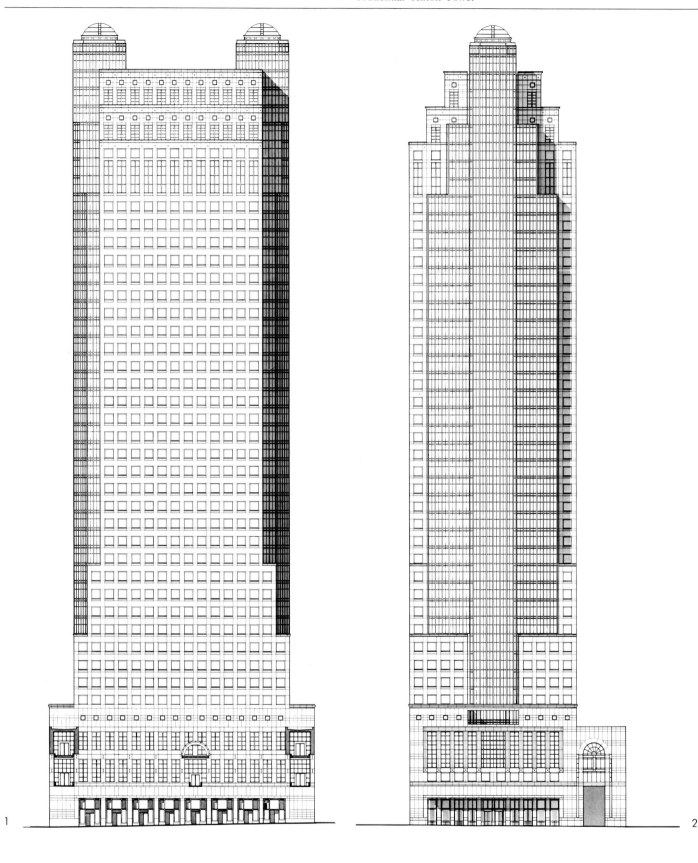

1

2

1.East elevation
2.South elevation

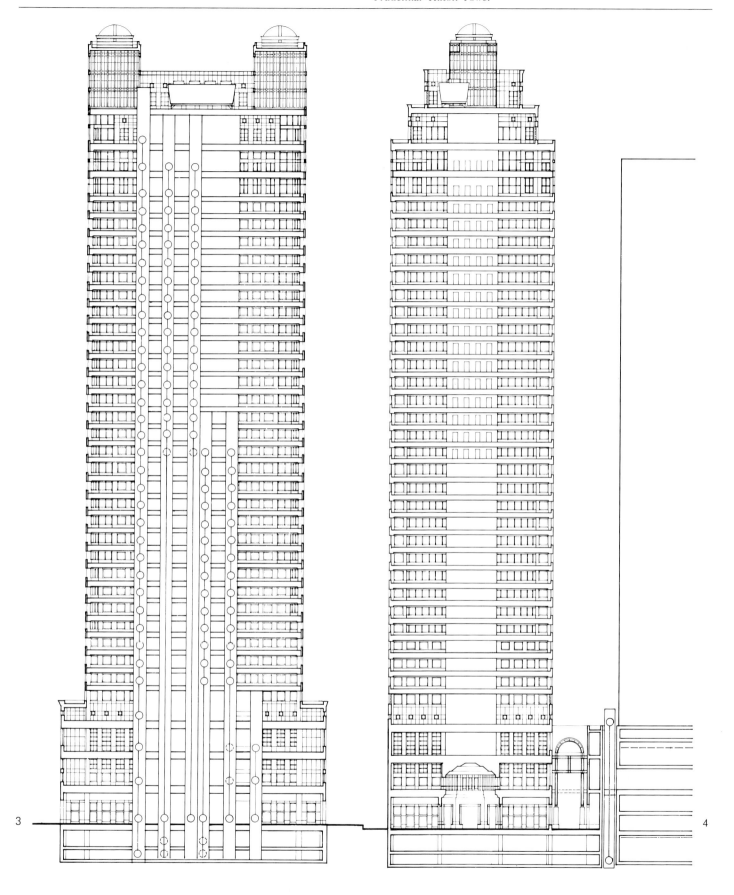

3. *Longitudinal section*
4. *Transverse section*

LINCOLN CENTER MINNEAPOLIS

Minneapolis, Minnesota
1984/1987

Twin towers, built in two phases, rise 35 stories on a 300-foot by 300-foot site. The pair of buildings preserves the integrity of the city's north-south axis, established by the neighboring courthouse building's twin slabs. The diagonal planes of these facades absorb the thrust of the axis, while the undulating east and west facades reinforce the streetwall. The configuration of the paired structures establishes a figure-ground relationship which complements the urban realm and provides adequate independent view corridors for each tower on this narrow site. Each phase is resolved as a single tower piece, flanked by contextually responsive accoutrements, resulting in complex building masses. The buildings, therefore, oscillate between a modernist objectlike structure in a landscape in the first phase, to a more traditional set of buildings upon completion of the second phase.

The buildings are delineated by a polychromatic development of their granite and marble surfaces and the vertical and horizontal striation of their decorative elements and motifs. The tripartite organization and its compositional field of punched windows interrupted by centered vertical fenestration groups are similar to those designed for the CNG Tower.

The entry progression commences on the main axis at the gardenlike pavilion, through a double-vaulted space, up a pair of escalators to a central lobby core. This space is composed of two squares, divided by a five-foot zone, with a series of marble columns which rise to meet the shallow vaults. Many of the exterior materials reappear in the lobby space.

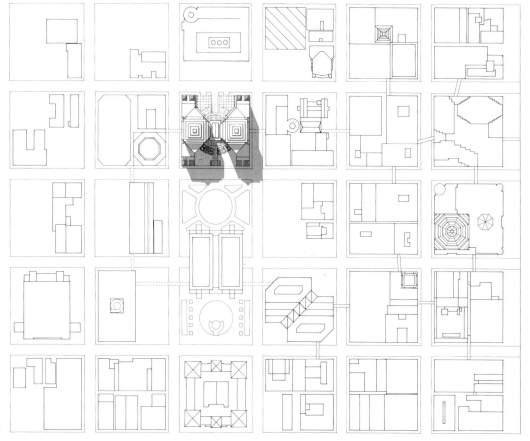

1
1.Site plan
2.Southeast view of model,
 Phase I

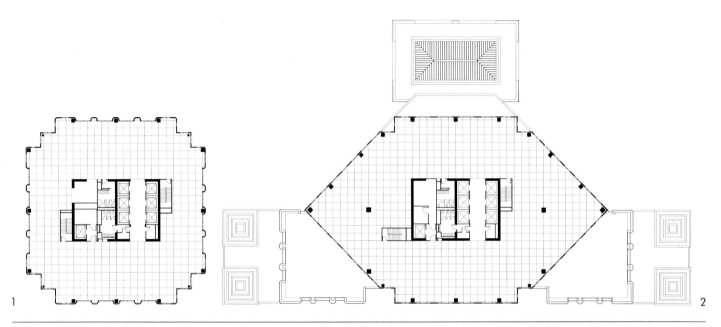

1

2

3

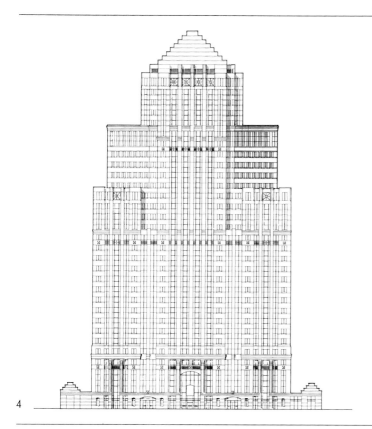

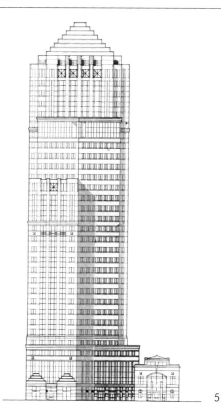

4

5

6

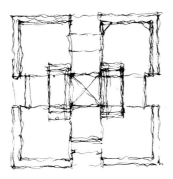

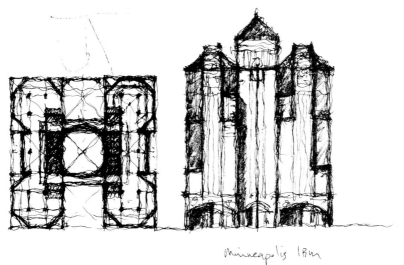

Minneapolis IBM
9-24-84

1.Typical highrise floor plan   4.East elevation
2.Typical lowrise floor plan   5.North elevation
3.First floor plan   6.Design sketches

1

2

3

1.Northeast view of model
2.Photomontage
3.View of entrance pavilion,
  model

712 FIFTH AVENUE

New York, New York
1985/1987

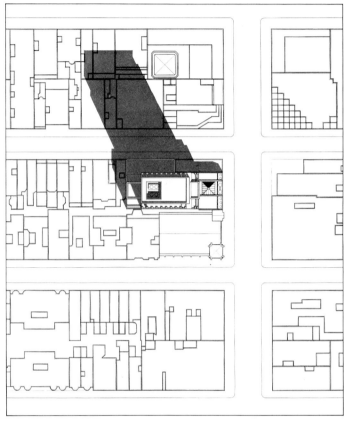

This mixed-use tower rises 50 stories above the street on one of Fifth Avenue's best preserved blockfronts. Its facades date back to the turn of the century. Two of these, both recently landmarked structures on the site, will be incorporated into the project. A third, new facade will be built adjacent to these two, which is compatible with the historic character of the blockfront while filling a gap which interrupts the streetwall today.

This street wall fronts a new retail entity whose central focus will be the Lalique glass panels within the central Coty building's facade.

The tower's shaft is clad with a series of white Vermont marble piers within a field of punched windows. The corners are turned with black granite quoins.

The tower's midrise is marked at an elevation which recognizes the datum line established by the surrounding development from the 1920's.

The crown of the building is setback in the tradition of New York skyscrapers as it emerges from the piers which mark the tower's four facades.

1. *Site plan*
2. *View of model from Fifth Avenue*

2

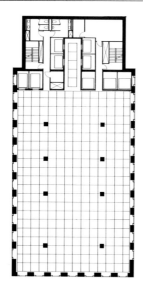

1

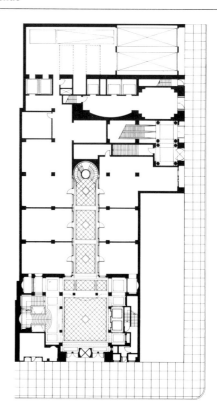

2

3

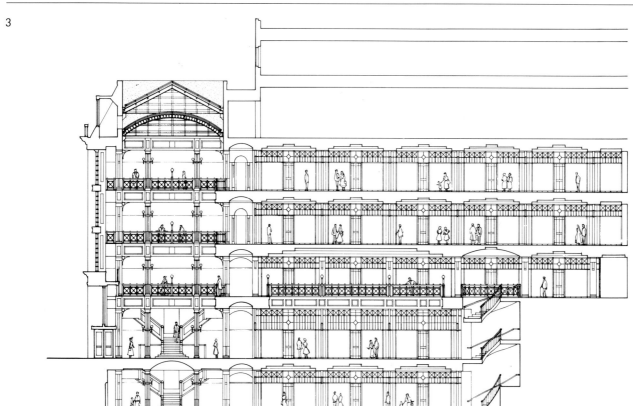

1. Typical office floor plan
2. First floor plan
3. Longitudinal section
   through atrium

4. 56th Street elevation
5. Fifth Avenue elevation

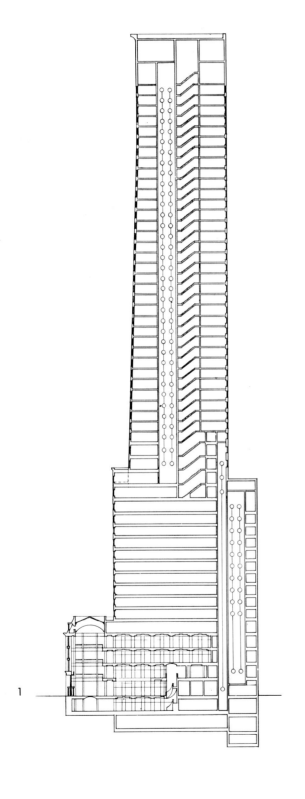

1. Longitudinal section
2. View of model from Fifth
   Avenue
3. Context model

3

BLOCK FIVE–SEATTLE OFFICE TOWER

Seattle, Washington
1985/1987

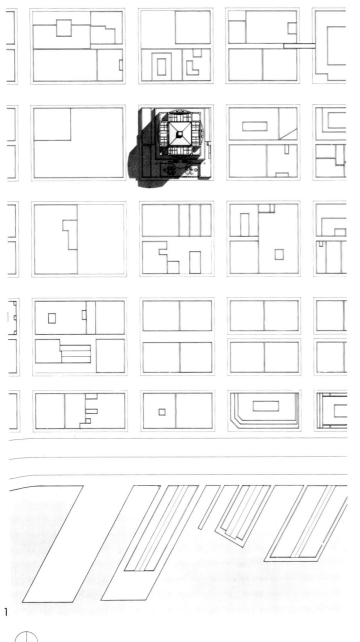

Unlike many of the firm's earlier works, where the response to external forces molded the shape of the building, Block Five office tower is an ideal form selected for its adaptability to the specific context. In geometrical terms, a circle resides within the square. The interaction of these two primary figures is reminiscent of the Renaissance fascination with platonic relationships. Through minimal distortions, particularly at its base, the building responds to the surrounding conditions and scale. Taking advantage of the steeply sloping site and the western orientation towards the ocean, movement through the base is directed in a sequence that starts with the formal Third Avenue lobby, followed by a series of transitions which open up into an outdoor plaza facing Second Avenue. This plaza is flanked by two low buildings, one of which is the historic Brooklyn Building.

In the base, four 30-foot-square corners define the zone which becomes the internal core. These solid corners are discrete entities, acting as points of both focus and transition. On the exterior, they are expressed as piers rising through the entire structure, containing the bulge of the vertical glass cylindrical bays in the shaft of the building. Above the blue-green glass tube, the square erodes into a cruciform plan that rises to the fifty-third floor and culminates as a pyramidal cap. Block Five emulates many older buildings in Seattle's downtown core; elements like the top of the Smith Tower, the vertical lines of the Seattle Tower, and the Skinner Building's limestone elegance strongly influenced the design.

1. *Site plan*
2. *Oblique view from Second Avenue, model*

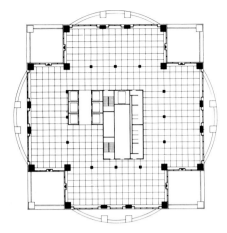

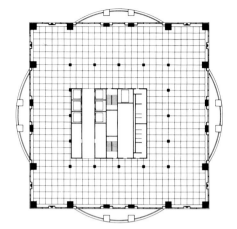

1

2

3

4

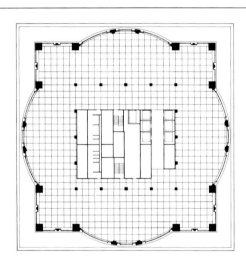

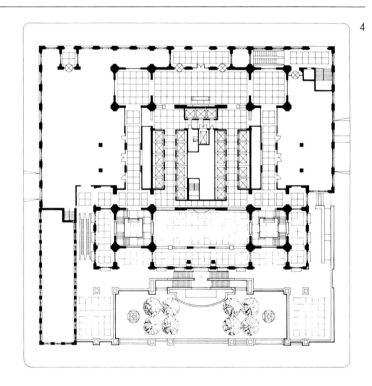

1. Levels 48–55
2. Levels 45–47
3. Levels 6–44

4. Level 3
5. East elevation
6. South elevation

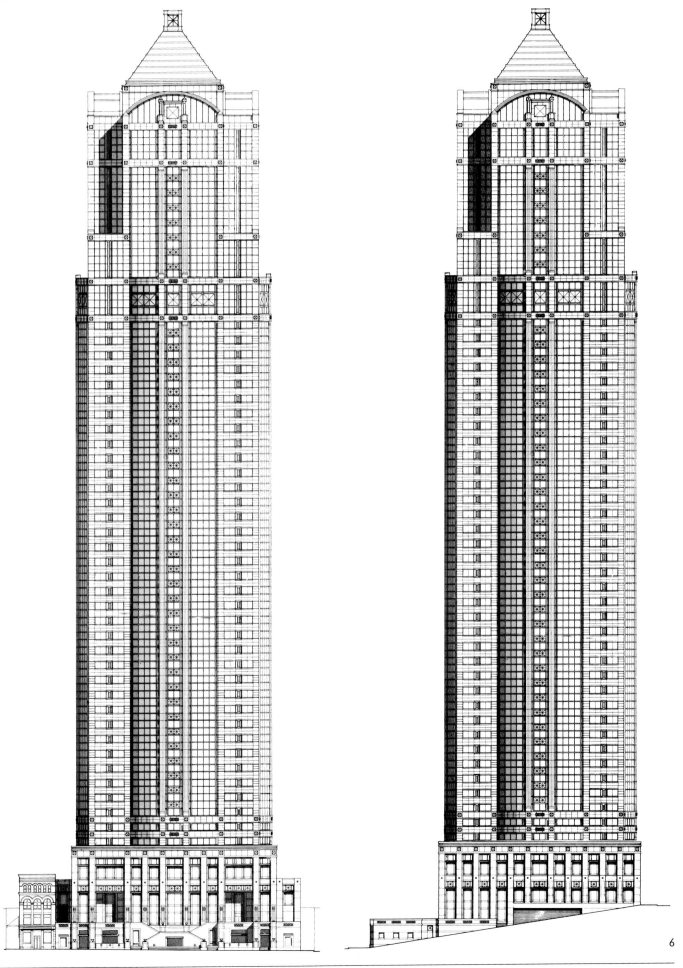

5

6

1. *Base of building, model*
2. *View from Third Avenue*
3. *Top of building, model*

2

3

SUFFOLK COUNTY COURTHOUSE, COMPETITION

Islip, New York
1985

The proposed courthouse is located on a flat 100-acre site at the outer fringe of a suburban New York development. The major exterior elements of the complex, the garden and the parking, are conceived of as a formal, highly ordered landscape that defines a micro-context for the building. In the center of the site, an open pear-shaped field with the courthouse as its focus is carved into the surrounding forested parking areas. Manicured lawns to the west afford grand vistas of the building from the main entrance. To the east, a series of gardens offer a more intimate scale. As in a French classical garden, an accord exists between the natural element and the architectural—in the interplay of open and closed spaces, transitions and contrasts, geometry and irregularity.

The building plan is determined primarily by its program. The separation of the program into three basic components (courts, offices, and judicial spaces) and the provision for the construction of the building in three phases were key issues in the generation of the design concept. The resulting building is an assemblage of the basic components, each of which is developed as an independent architectural and structural entity, then woven together into a coherent whole.

The office component is accommodated in the central cruciform building with its central core and radial atria. The courtrooms are organized vertically on five levels in four wings. Public access to the courtrooms is through the atria. These serve both to connect and separate the courtrooms from the office space, providing a sense of orientation and natural light. The courtrooms connect at their rear to the judges' corridor and are served by a prisoners' secured area from between each two. Judges' chambers are located in the slender outer towers, adjacent to the courtroom wings.

In keeping with the character of Long Island and the nature of the design, a traditional palette of brick and limestone with a granite base and copper roof elements is proposed.

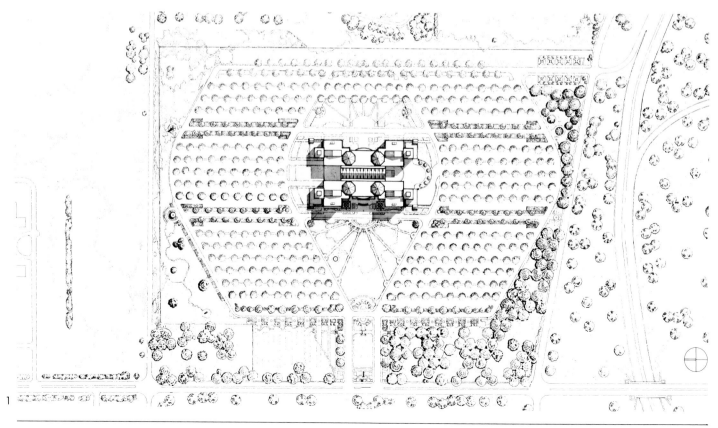

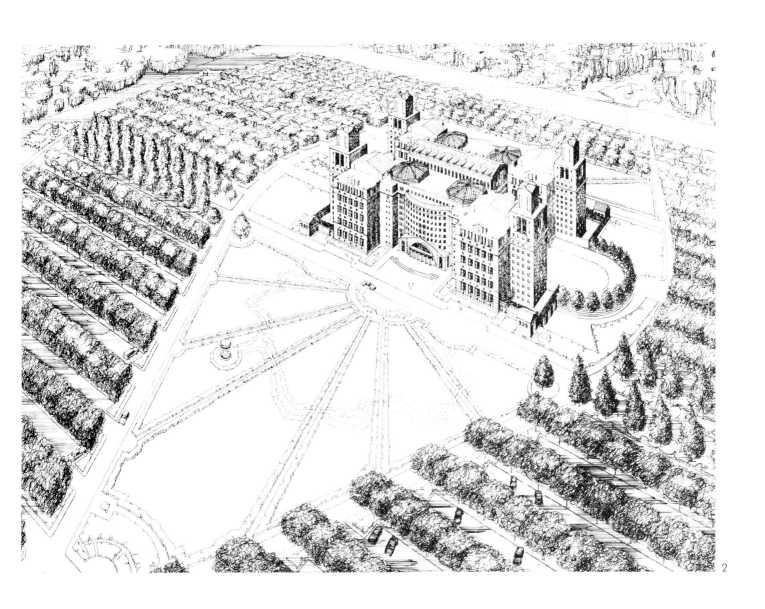

2

1. *Site plan*
2. *Aerial view*

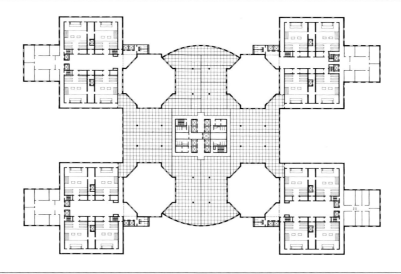

1

2

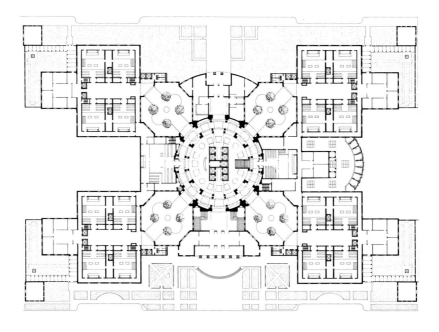

3

1. Typical courtroom floor plan
2. Typical juryroom floor plan
3. First floor plan
4. View from entrance

1

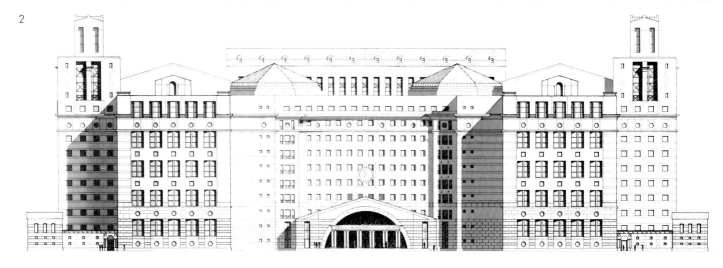

2

1.*South elevation*
2.*East elevation*

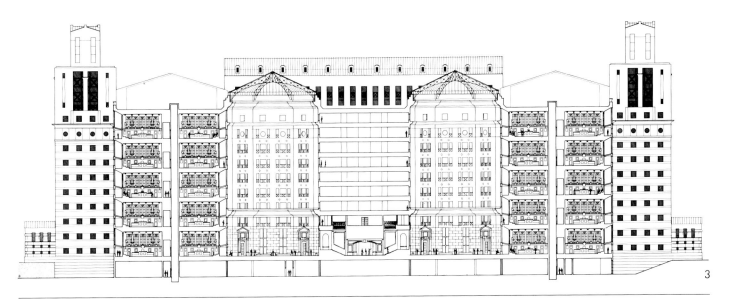

3

4

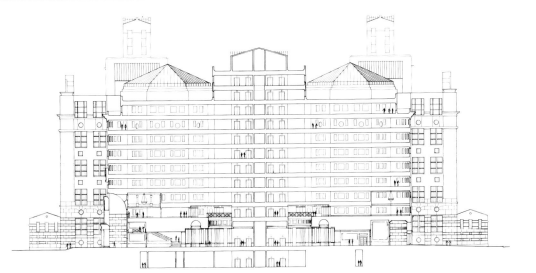

3.Longitudinal section
4.Transverse section

SHEARSON LEHMAN BROTHERS PLAZA

New York, New York
1985/1988

The Shearson Lehman Brothers Plaza building is located on the edge of the Hudson River, on the northern perimeter of downtown New York in an area which marks the infiltration of tall office buildings into the established medium-scale loft residential neighborhood. To interpolate this contextual juxtaposition, the architects have manipulated the mass of the building, within the limits of a prescribed master plan, to create two separate readings: that of a tower addressing the water and that of a building stepping down to the lower residential scale. To reinforce the dual reading, a subtle equipoise is established between the curved, taut waterside facade and the slender, more transparent city-side facade. The mass is capped by a gabled copper roof with battered buttresses, reminiscent of older waterfront structures that were once located in the area.

To accommodate a single major tenant in the lower seventeen floors and multiple tenants above, a staggered-core system with a skylobby at the eighteenth floor is employed. The lower-level core is situated on the party wall with the adjoining computer center, allowing large open floor plates with maximum natural lighting. At the upper levels, where the exterior is exposed on all four sides, the core shifts to the center, facilitating a more conventional office rental floor plan.

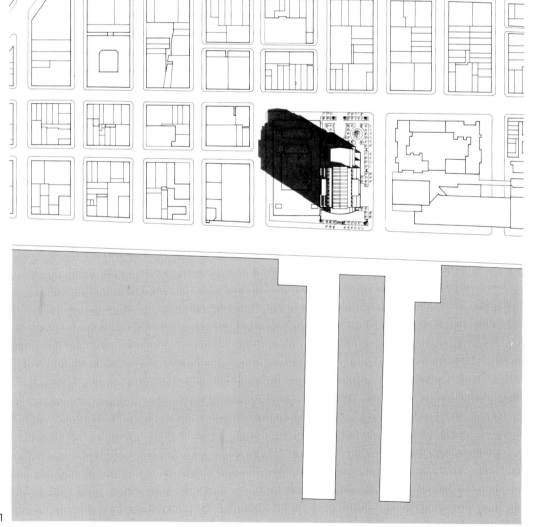

1

1. Site plan
2. Southeast view of model

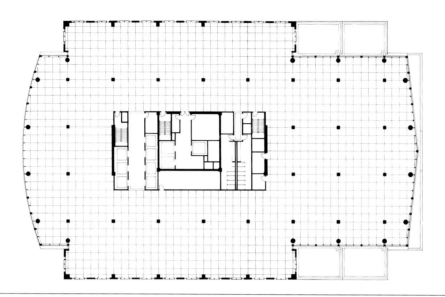

1

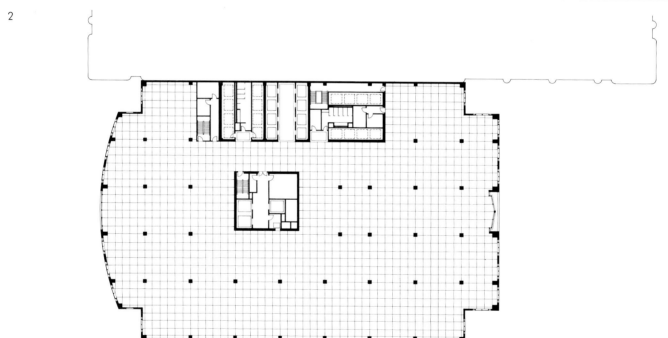

2

1.Typical highrise floor plan
2.Typical lowrise floor plan

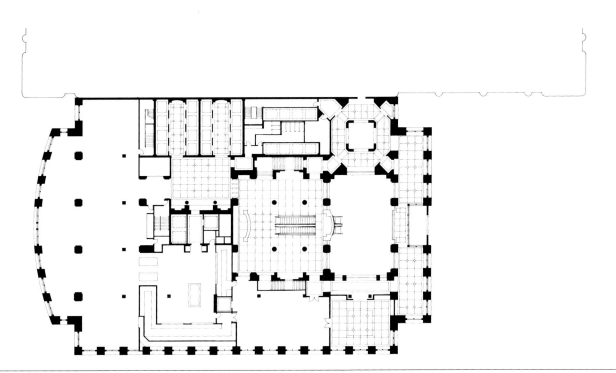

3

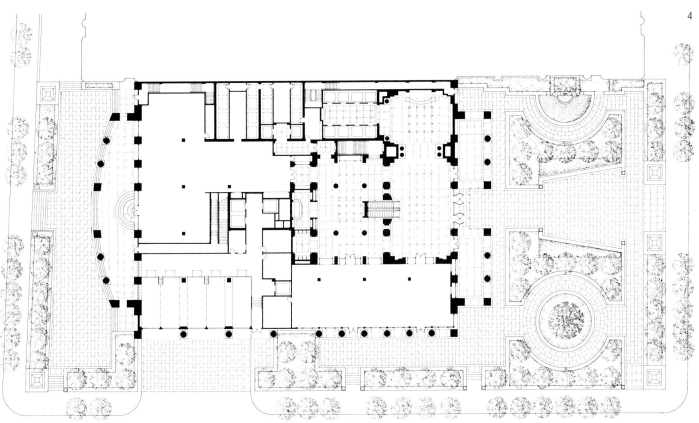

4

3.*Second floor plan*
4.*First floor plan*

1

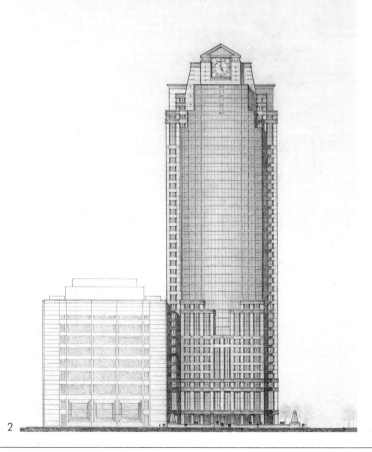

2

1.Photomontage
2.Elevation study

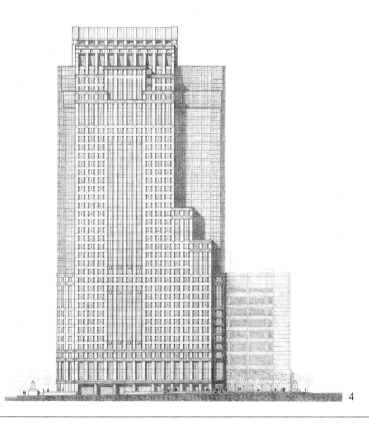

3.Photomontage
4.Elevation study

125 SUMMER STREET

Boston, Massachusetts
1985/1988

Located on a commanding triangular site, onto which six streets converge, this building functions as both an isolated object and as a part of the existing urban fabric. The 45-story hexagonal tower anchors this nodal site, forming a visual focus for the neighborhood.

At its base, this city-block complex incorporates four existing nineteenth-century town houses, interweaving the new structure into an old urban fabric. Straddling the northern edge of the block is a winter-garden galleria, lined with retail and dining facilities, and flanked by cylindrical entry pavilions on either end. In plan, two ideal forms are nestled within the irregular city block. The linear winter garden and the semicircular office lobby coexist, asserting an internal order on the triangular configuration of the site. In a sympathetic gesture to the delicate scale of the lower existing town houses, the tower is set back in layers from the streetline. The tower, sheathed in stone with punched windows, rises to two pronounced cornice lines at the thirty-fifth and forty-second levels, and is capped by a decorative Hawksmoorian top. With its allusions to earlier, memorable buildings, its respectful, formal relationships to surrounding buildings, its sculpted facades and ornamental top, this building has an accessible, colorful character at pedestrian level and an individual identity on Boston's skyline.

1

1. Site plan
2. Contextual model

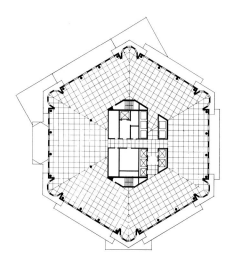

1

2

3

4

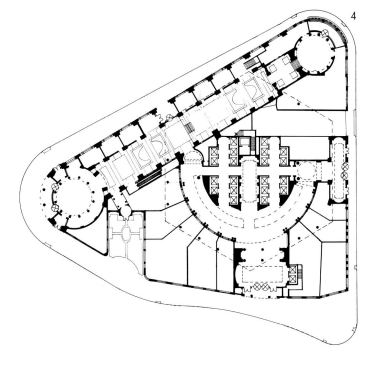

1. *Typical highrise floor plan*
2. *Typical lowrise floor plan*

3. *Second floor plan*
4. *First floor plan*
5. *Elevation*

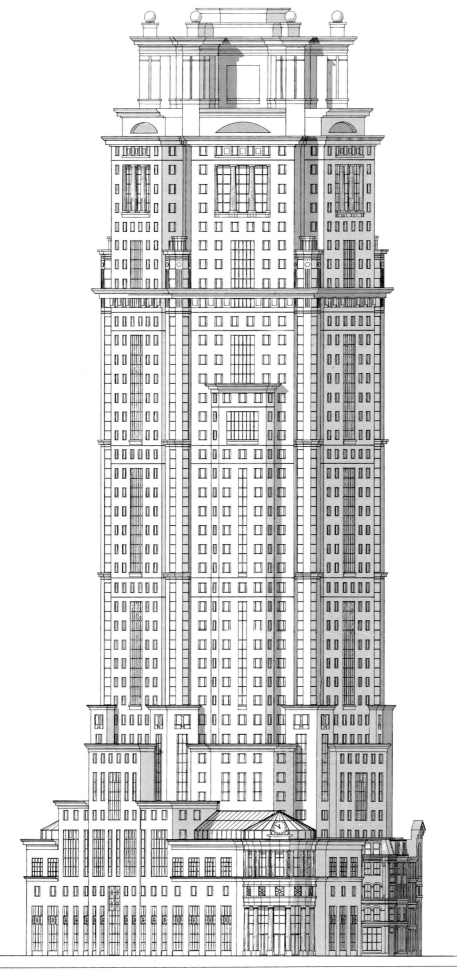

SOUTH FERRY PLAZA, COMPETITION

New York, New York
1985

This competition entry is a festive medley of forms lining Manhattan's southernmost waterfront. Flanked by two existing terminal buildings on the site, the 51-story office tower proposal serves to visually anchor Whitehall Street, dramatically underlining its position as terminus and gateway. The striking monumentality of this complex structure presents a language of allusion and metaphor which capitalizes on the utilitarian character of the program.

On the northern side of the building, a cylindrical shaft above a base terminates the main axis of Whitehall Street. This form allows light to model its surface, implying space beyond. The striated southern side of the building with its vertical towers straddles the main ferry slip. The isolation of the vertical forms creates a tension between the figurations of the skin and the symmetrical masses, resulting in an assemblage of pure geometrical responses to both internal and external demands.

Facing Whitehall Street, the colossal loggia of the base demarks the building's entry. Beyond this heroic colonnade is the main entrance, sheathed in glass. This transparent tissue becomes the terminus of the axis at the ground level, affording views of either a docked ferry ship or of the harbor beyond. The building's waterside base is lined with protruding slips and an arcuated facade that echoes the 1907 Whitehall Terminal building's sensuous ironwork and stone construction.

Internally, the existing terminal structures are integrated into the composition by converting them into a waiting room and retail hall. A series of escalators link the lower main processional route with these elements. Above that level, a separate elevator lobby provides access to the office tower and observation deck.

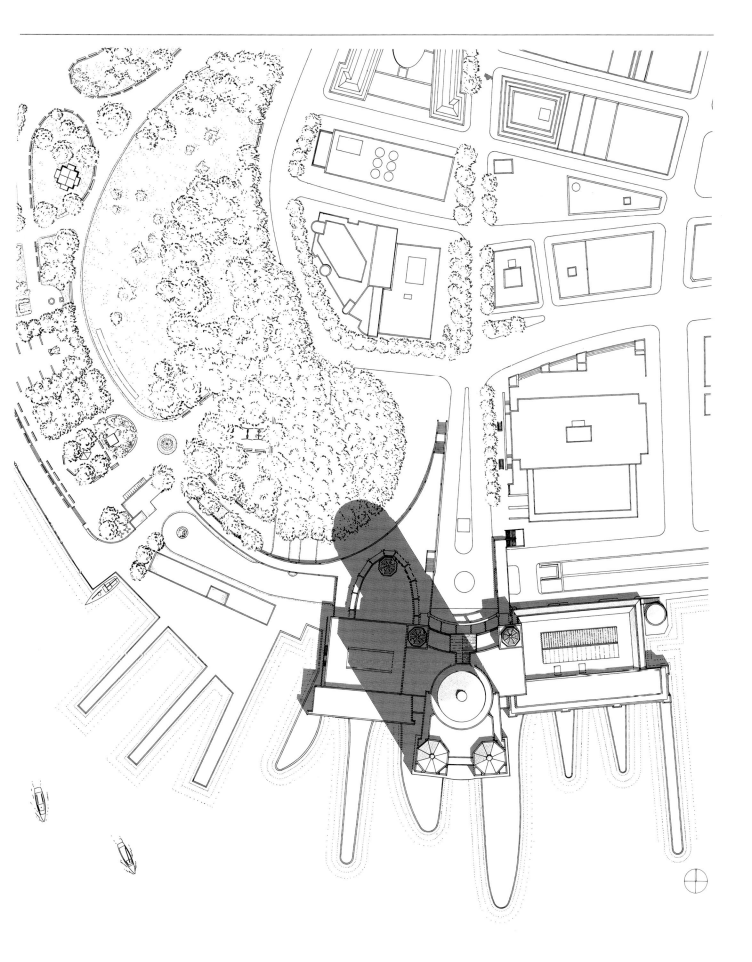

1. *View from harbor*
2. *Site plan*

2

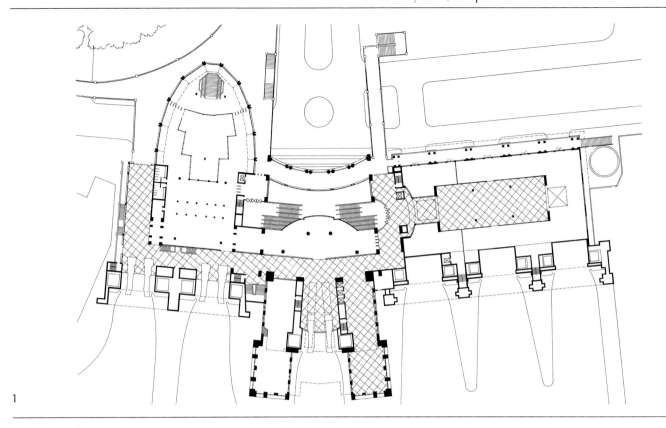

1

2

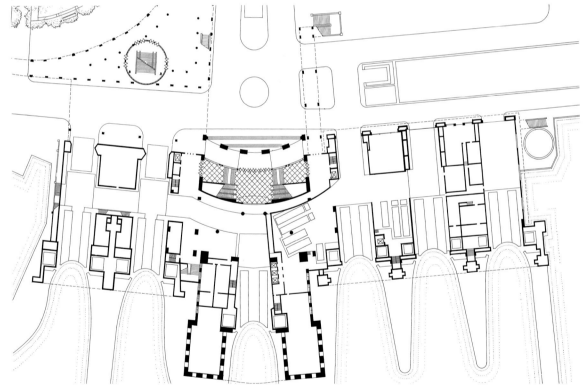

1.Loggia—second floor plan
2.First floor plan

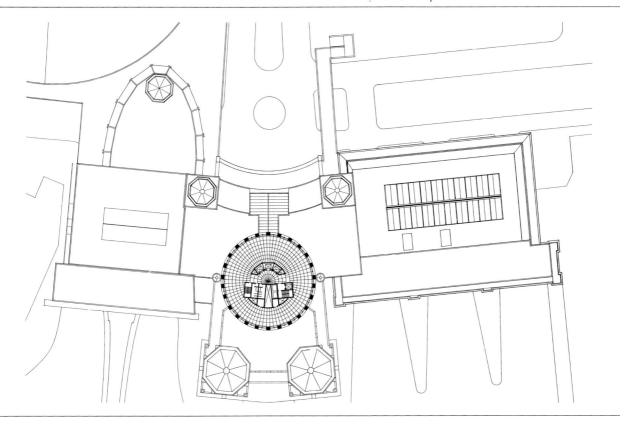

3

4

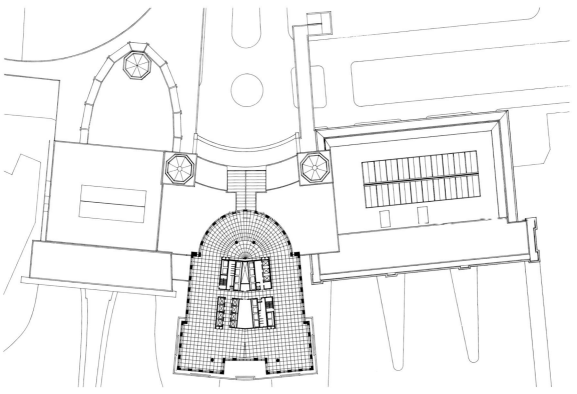

3. *Floor plan, 44 through 50*
4. *Typical floor plan*

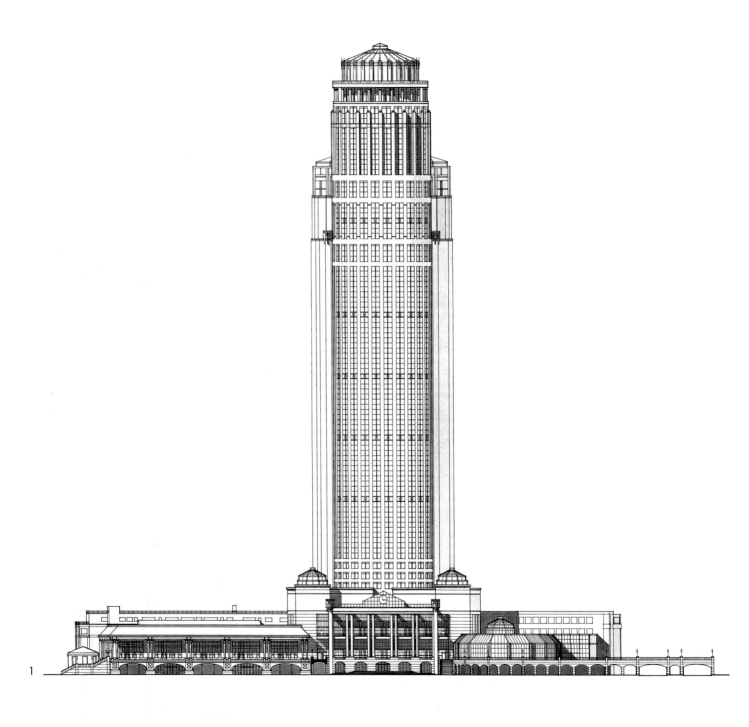

1

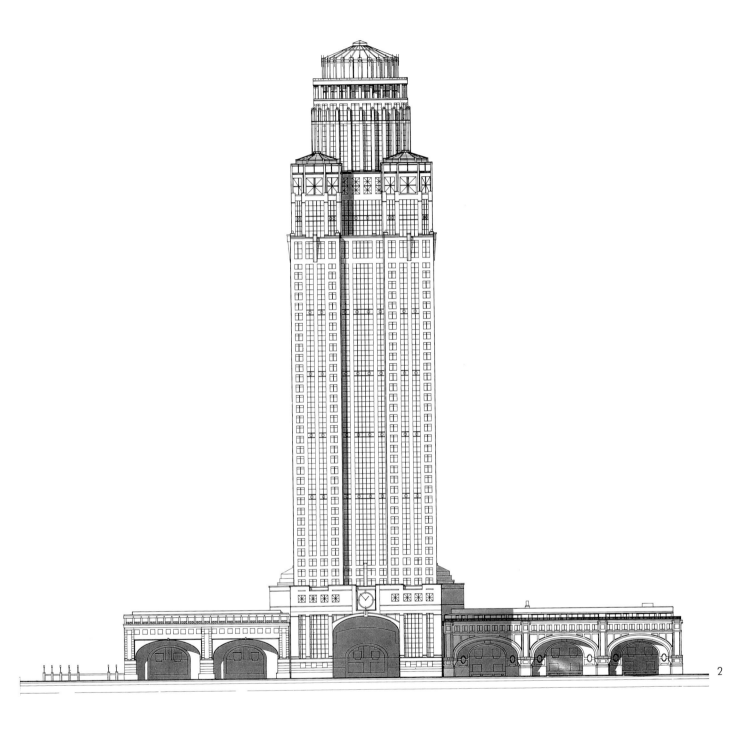

1.North elevation
2.South elevation

2

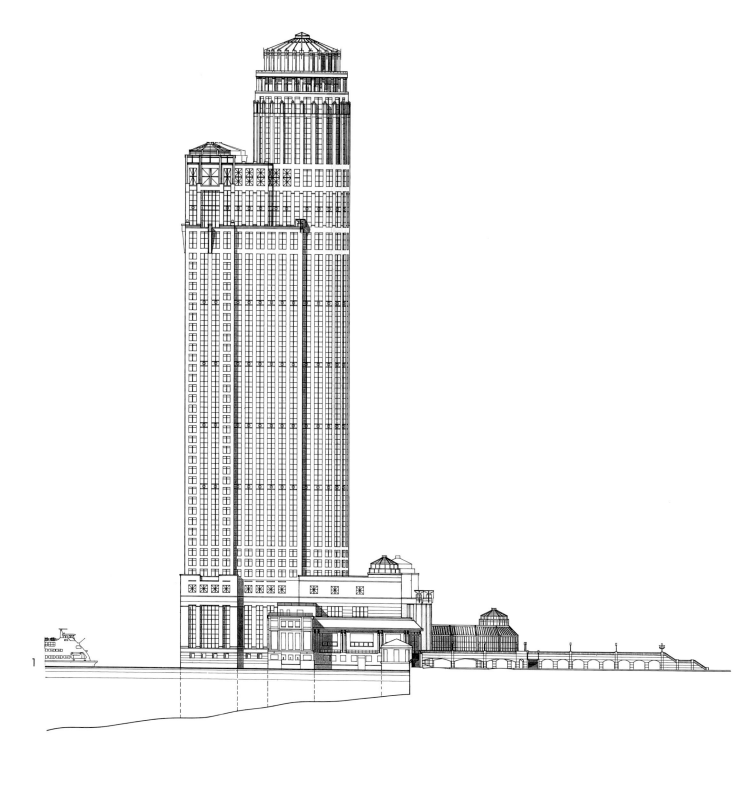

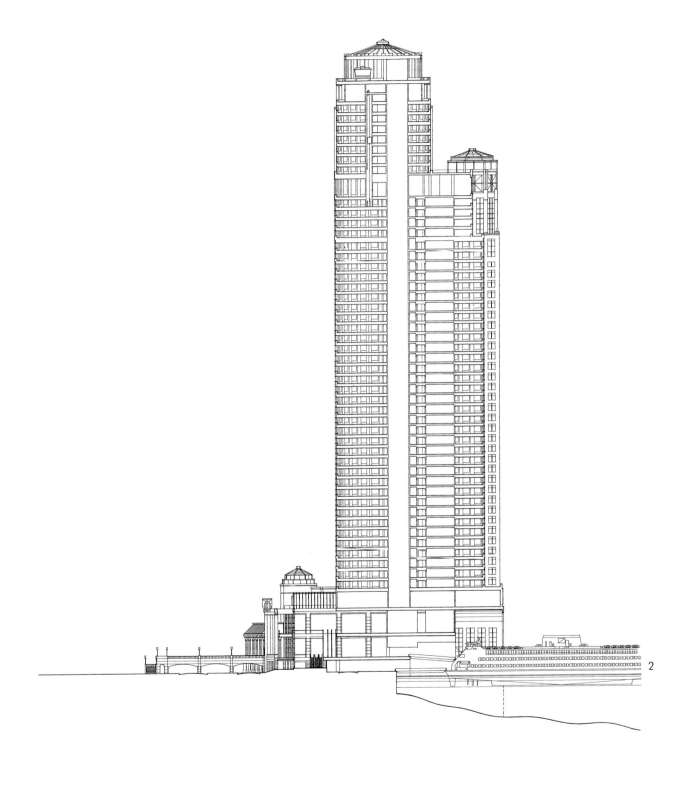

2

1.East elevation
2.Longitudinal section

STANFORD UNIVERSITY BUSINESS SCHOOL EXPANSION

Palo Alto, California
1984/1987

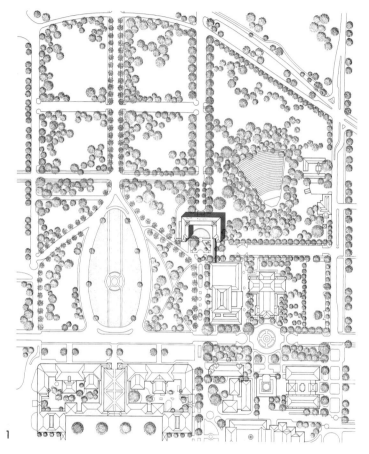

1

Like the Bucknell University Performing Arts Center, the addition to the Stanford University Business School creates a building form and vocabulary which melds into the architecturally rich context.

The nexus of Stanford's campus is a massively proportioned Romanesque quadrangle, designed by H. H. Richardson. Located diagonally across from the Business School and the new expansion site, this rusticated, sand-colored, stone building possesses an arcuated base and a series of internal courtyards which generate a high level of intricacy and a multiplicity of spatial readings.

The Business School expansion convincingly emulates the ideals of its predecessor's architectural expression, as well as its dense massing and selection of materials. It is a U-shaped, three-story, stone and stucco building, predominantly housing faculty offices on its upper two floors while devoting the ground floor to classrooms, lounge areas, and a trustee boardroom. Programmatically, one of the primary concerns of this building design was to create a variety of public spaces which would establish a sense of community. An open arcade, located on the inner perimeter of the U-shaped form, threads the semipublic areas together and serves to activate the courtyard. A traditional collegiate passageway bisects the U form, allowing for the visual and physical extension of the space, with key programmatic insertions placed at the points of intersection. Above, primary circulation elements formally and psychologically unite the faculty office areas.

The building envelope discreetly expresses the subdivisions of the building's functions and users by sculpting the mass and astutely unifying architectural elements to reflect the building's hierarchy.

2

1.Site plan
2.Overhead view of model

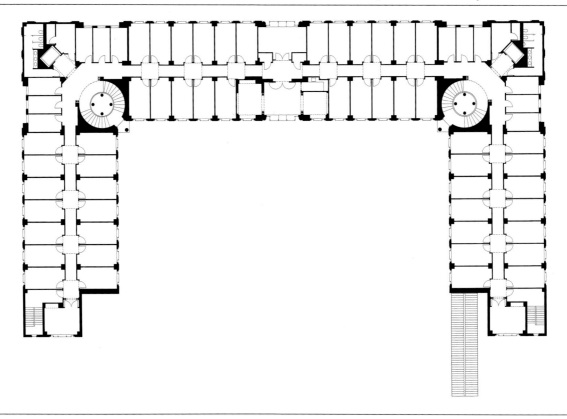

1

2

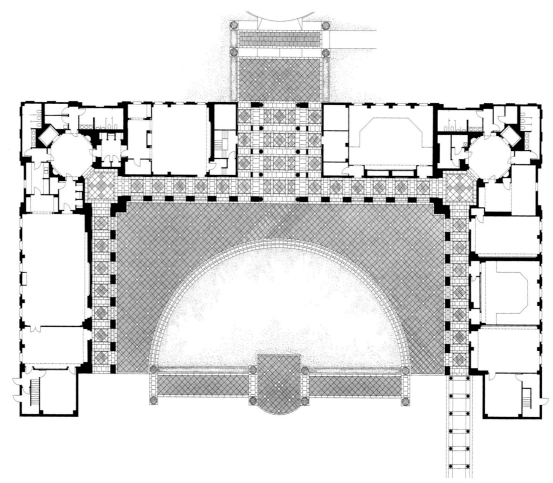

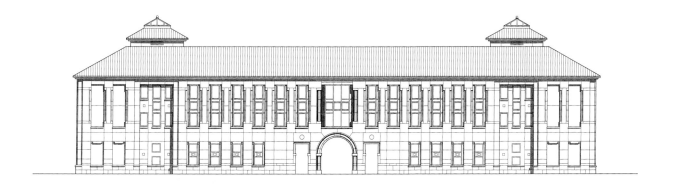

3

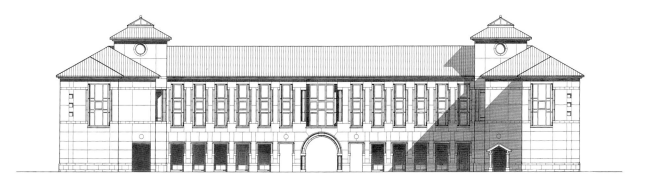

4

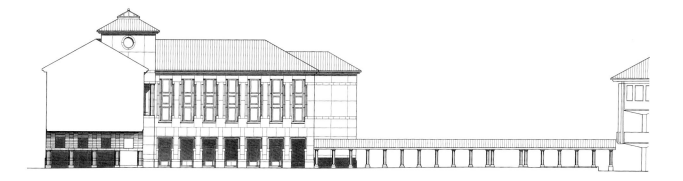

5

1.First floor plan
2.Second floor plan

3.South elevation
4.North elevation
5.Transverse section

UNITED STATES EMBASSY

Nicosia, Cyprus
1986/1988

The site for the American Embassy in Cyprus is located in a residential suburb of Nicosia, the capital city, in an area which is gradually evolving into a diplomatic sector.

The design *parti* for this embassy compound reestablishes the typological ideal organization of an embassy as Chancery and Ambassador's Residence, expressing both these functions as independent elements within an overall framework. The resulting composition is deformed by the circumstantial conditions imposed by the site's own geometry, the scale and character of the context, and the restrictions set by the adjacent monastery (which owns the site), the city of Nicosia, and the United States State Department.

The compound's perimeter membrane varies, acting as a building (motor pool and security command posts), wall, column, or pergola, as required, with the Chancery and Residence at a prescribed distance from it. The zone between this outer layer and the buildable area is developed as a series of exterior rooms, each delineating the processional route; transforming from architectural and formal to landscaped and informal, thereby reflecting the hierarchy of spaces from public to private.

The Chancery's protracted rectilinear mass addresses the main boulevard, presenting a stately front which mediates between its modern and its traditional context. It is a protective shell, containing a pool of offices and idiosyncratic support facilities.

The Residence is safely nestled behind it, orienting itself towards the adjacent olive grove and monastery. This building's pure configuration, which is based on a vernacular type, is sliced open, physically uniting its courtyard and garden. A cylindrical element housing the residential entry hall and library resolves the collision of the Chancery and the Ambassador's Residence by hinging the opposing grids in plan and by serving as a volumetric mediator. The eroding masses of both the Chancery and the Residence acknowledge the tension created at this point.

In the compound, the various buildings and the perimeter wall are united by a one-story sandstone base. This local sandstone is the primary cladding material on the Chancery, but the upper portions of the remaining structures are stucco, subtly differentiating them from the more symbolic Chancery. A singly sloping terra cotta roof serves to connect the separate buildings visually and to consolidate the compound's architectural character.

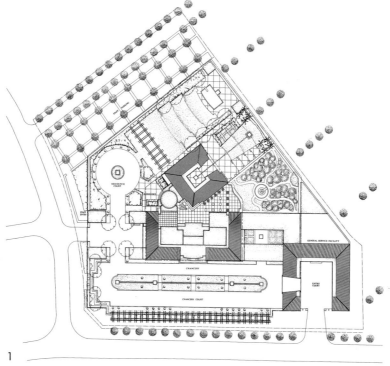

1

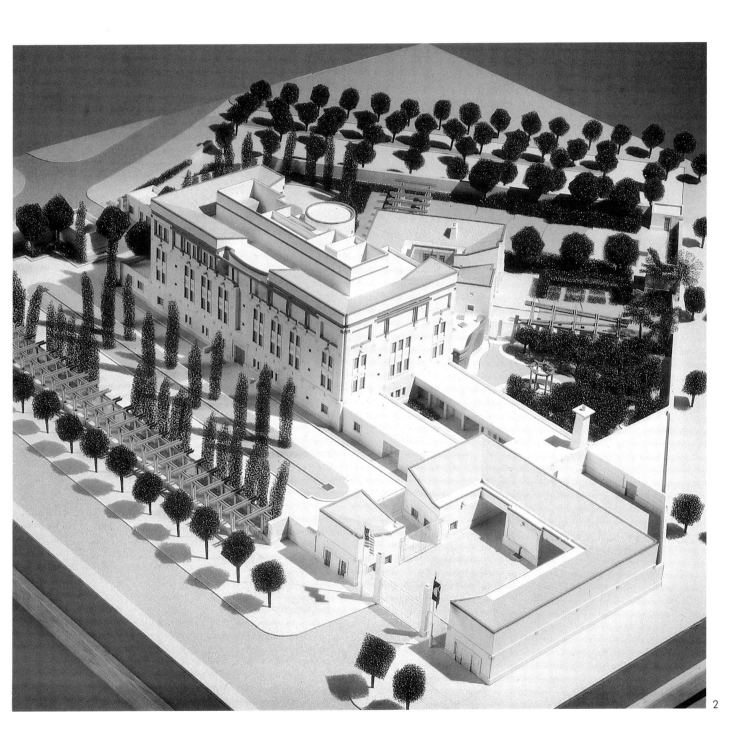

2

1.Site plan
2.Model

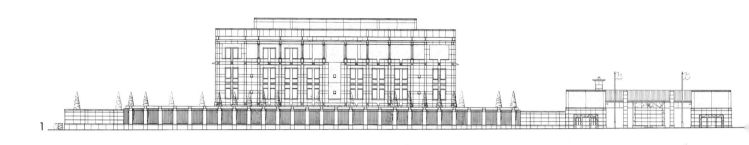

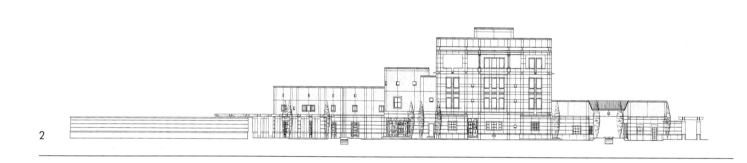

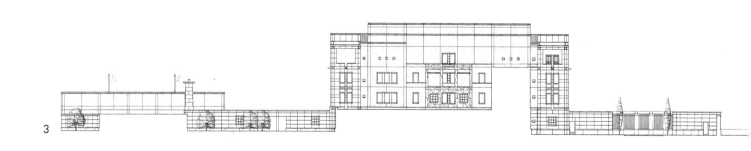

1.*Street elevation*
2.*East elevation–chancery*
3.*South elevation–chancery*

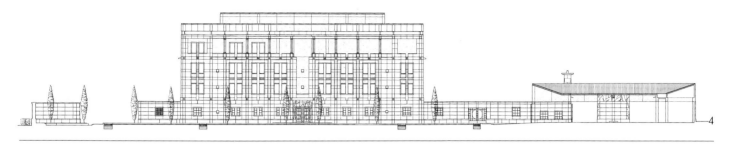

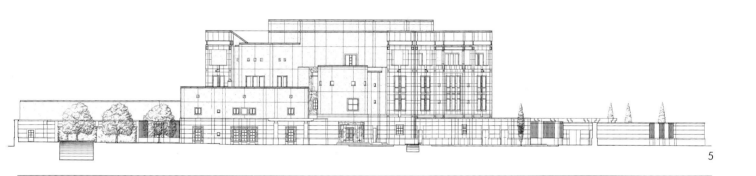

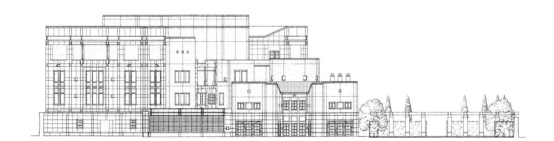

4.*North elevation—chancery*
5.*East elevation—residence*
6.*South elevation—residence*

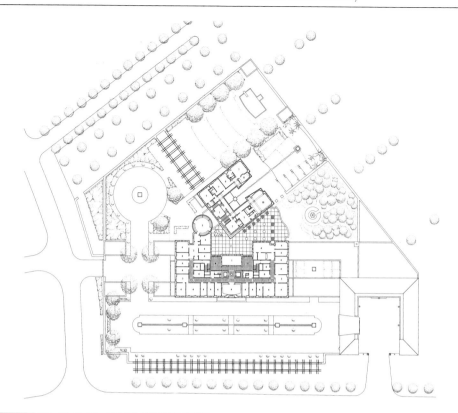

1

2

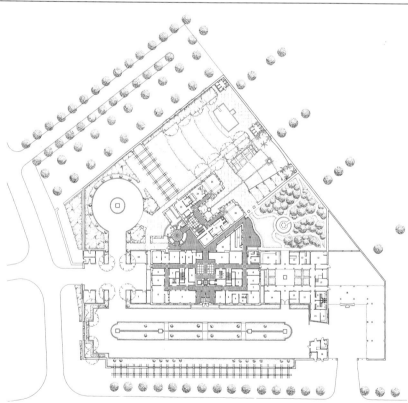

1.*Second floor plan*
2.*First floor plan*
3.*Chancery lobby axonometric*
4.*Residence axonometric*

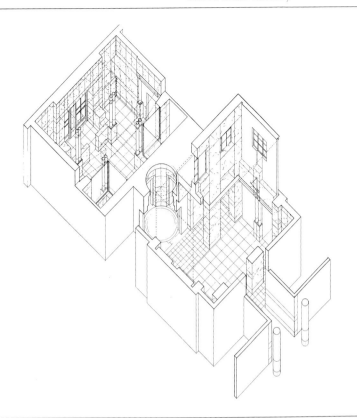

3

4

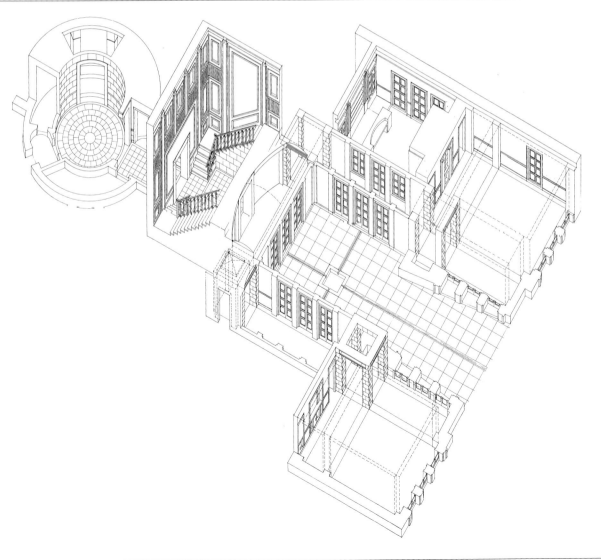

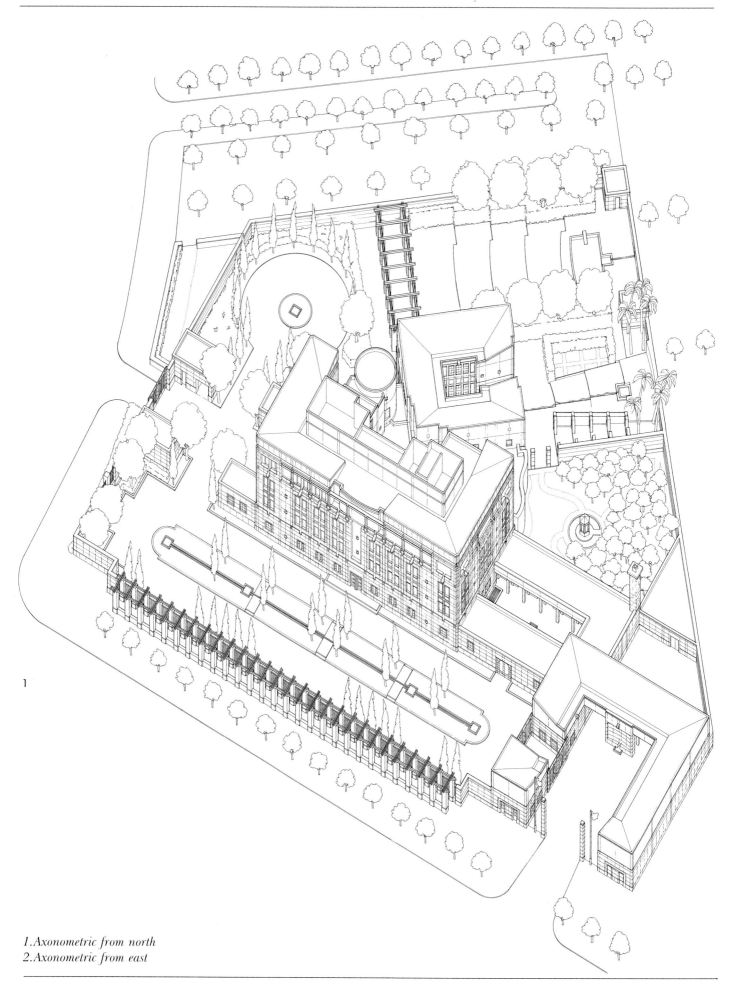

1
1. *Axonometric from north*
2. *Axonometric from east*

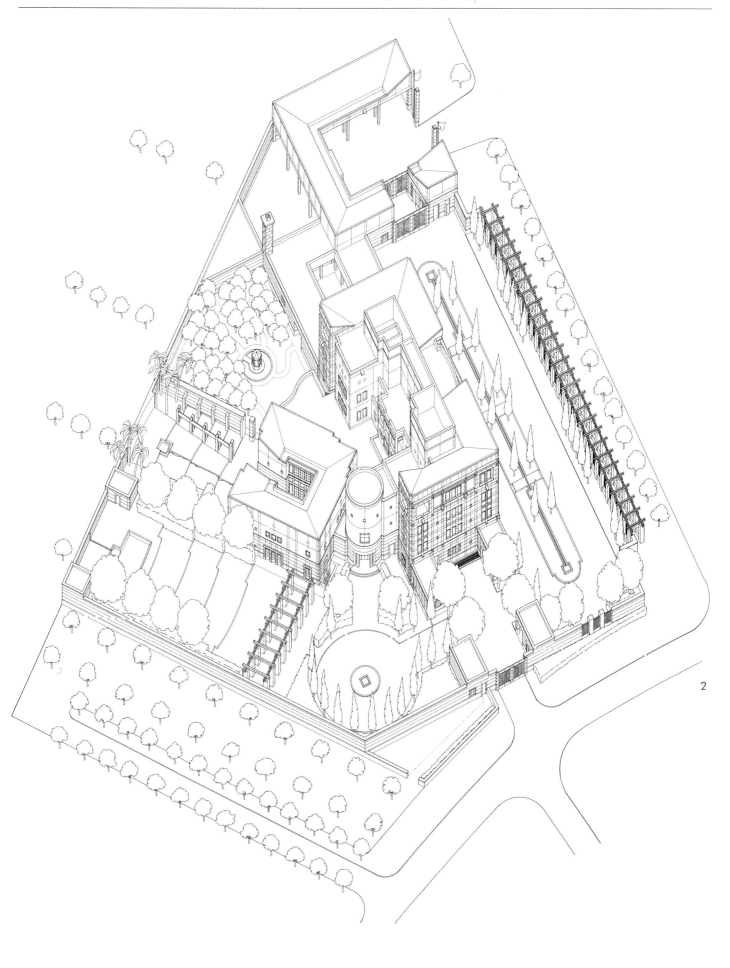

2

CANARY WHARF TOWER

London, England
1986/93

Canary Wharf Tower is designed as the first building group within a master plan whose guidelines were established by the project's clients and their planners prior to the project's inception. The complex occupies three sites on a redeveloped wharf adjacent to the River Thames, located to the east of London's City Center. The design solution evolved as a response to the master plan, to the building's larger context, and to its program.

The character and tradition of London's river architecture is a source of inspiration for the Canary Wharf Tower's architectural development. Reference is made to the clustered spires of the Houses of Parliament and the nineteenth- and twentieth-century bridges spanning the Thames. Industrial waterfront forms, particularly derricks and riggings, are also considered. The project's design reflects the perpendicularity and delicacy common to all these forms, and establishes an architectural vocabulary which speaks of its proximity to the river both texturally and chromatically.

Programmatic requirements dictated unusually large trading floor facilities and office floors throughout the project. These large areas are arranged in C- or H-shaped wings around shared atria which rise up through the building. Large trading and mechanical floors are placed beneath and between these atria to define the

program's five user groups. The fifth, consisting of a hotel, is placed atop the central tower. Here, the voids of the atria below become solid in the form of a rooftop dining facility whose form participates in the articulation of the tower crown.

The structural grid, also an outgrowth of programmatic exigencies, combines with each floor slab's edge and the building's curtainwall system to further define Canary Wharf Tower's architecture. Fifteen-meter spans provide extremely large column-free bays of interior space, while at the corners, these columns are expressed on the facade and engage in a dialogue with the series of cantilevered slabs supported by them. The project's curtainwall system is composed of a basic grid of stainless-steel mullions infilled with tinted vision and spandrel glass, ribbed stainless steel, and white marble. The wall is developed as a thin, exoskeletal surface whose rhythmic hierarchies are derived from contrasting patterns and textures as opposed to any reliance on readings of depth for comprehension. It is in this that the building skin adopts an attitude of using a modern vocabulary combined with local compositional techniques. Its larger compositional goals, however, may be likened more clearly to traditional ones in their use of devices such as symmetry and triangulation.

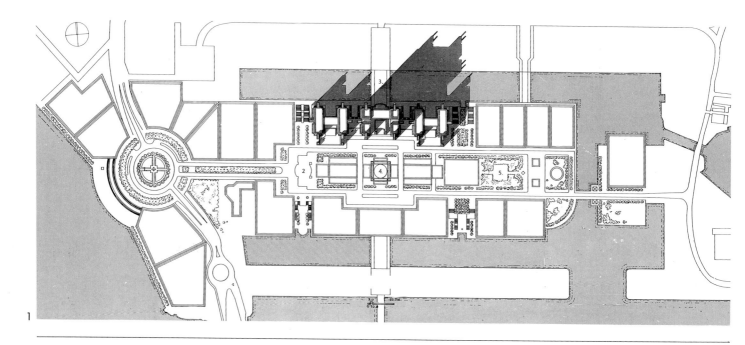

1

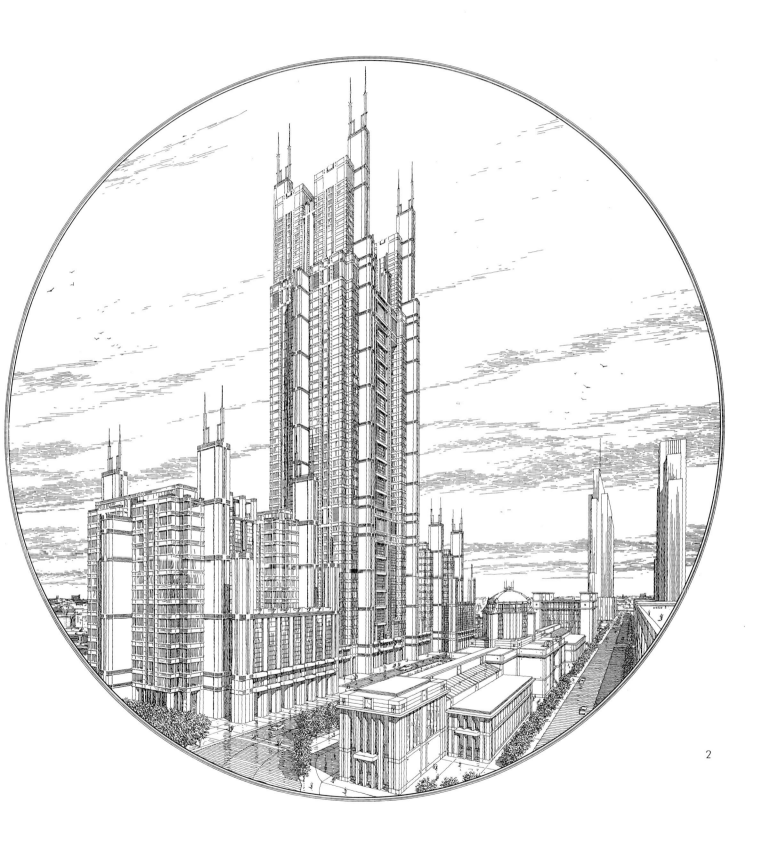

2

1. Site plan
2. View to northeast (perspective)

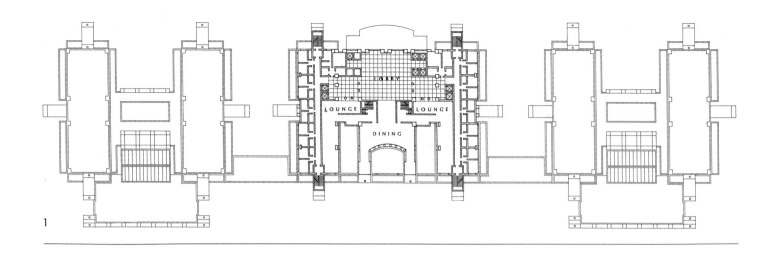

1

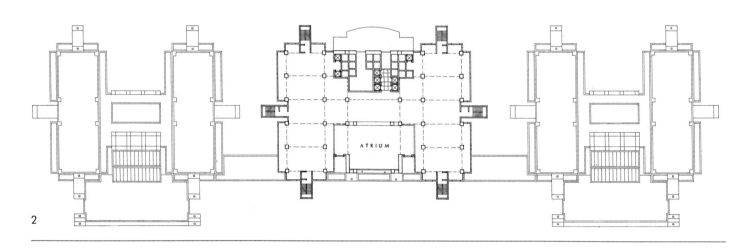

2

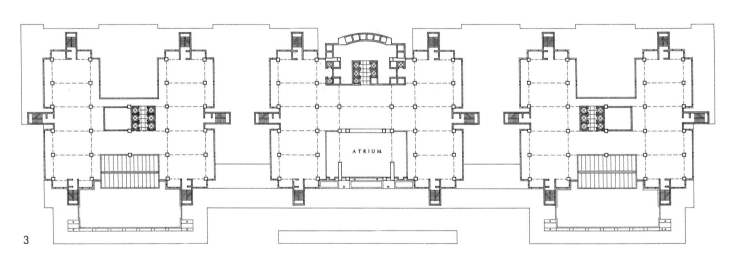

3

1.Hotel lobby (levels 41 and 42)
2.Levels 23–28
3.Levels 7–12

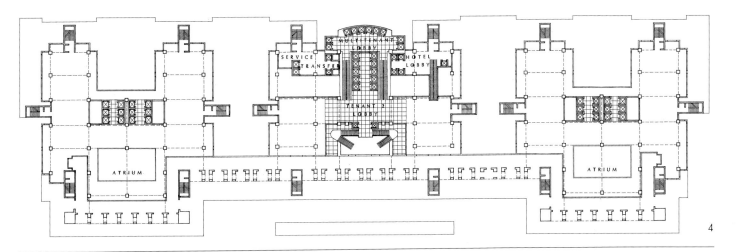

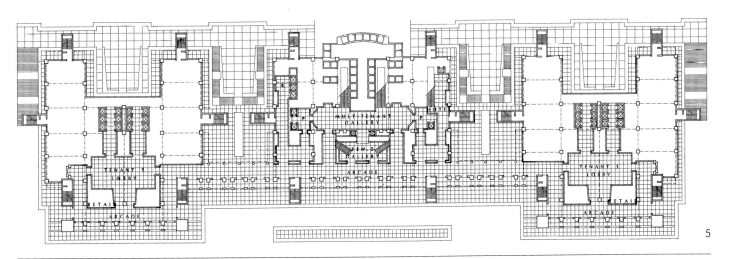

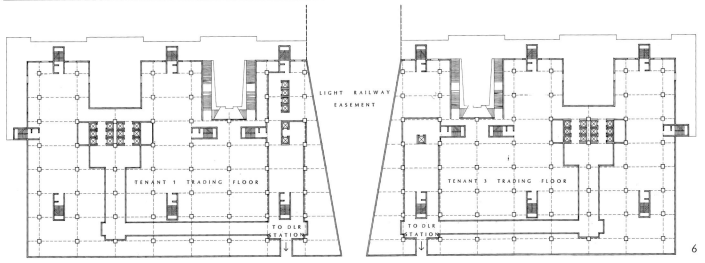

4. Upper lobby (level 2)
5. Grade lobby level
6. First level below grade

1

1. South elevation
2. North elevation

2

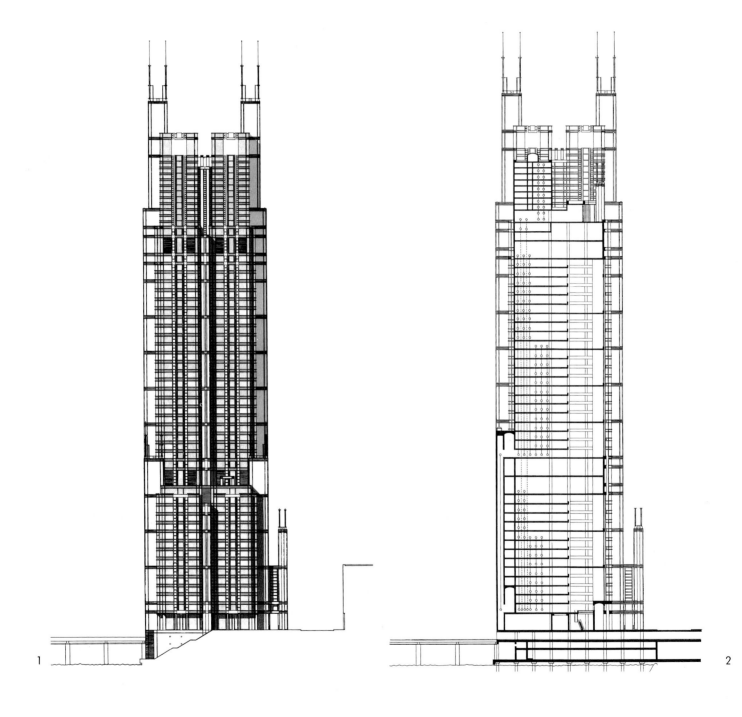

1 2

1.West elevation
2.Transverse section
3.View to northwest

3

WORK ON THE BOARDS

GARRISON CHANNEL PLACE

Tampa, Florida
1984/1988

1

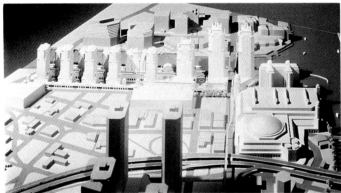

2

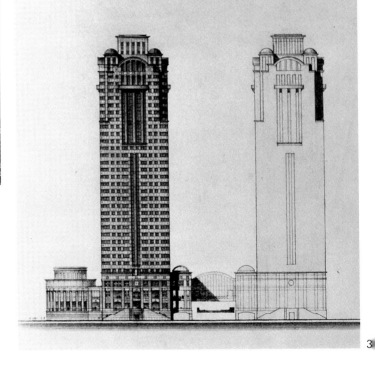

3

1.Aerial view of model
2.Aerial view of model
3.Elevation study

NEW YORK TRADE MART

New York, New York
1984/1989

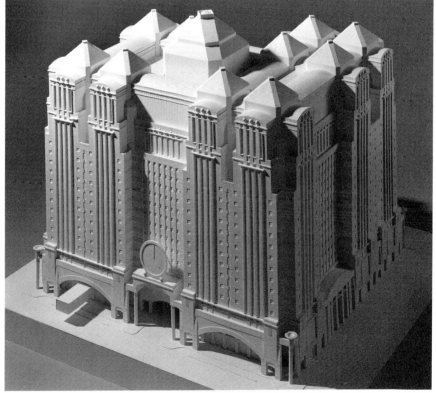

1.Site elevation
2.Oblique view of model

LINCOLN PROPERTIES
CULTURAL DISTRICT

Dallas, Texas
1984/1987

"Lincoln"

Oblique view of model

GATEWAY CENTER

Boston, Massachusetts
1985

*1. Aerial view of model,
   scheme 1*
*2. Aerial view of model,
   scheme 2*

300 EAST 64TH STREET

New York, New York
1985/1987

View of model from 64th Street

FIDELITY BUILDING

Boston, Massachusetts
1985

1.Elevation study
2.Aerial view of model

Chicago, Illinois
1985

Oblique view of model

TAYLOR-WOODROW PROJECT

San Francisco, California
1985

Oblique view of model

AT&T CORPORATE CENTER, COMPETITION

Atlanta, Georgia
1986

1.Photomontage
2.Aerial view

ONE FOUNTAIN PLACE

Cincinnati, Ohio
1986/1990

Oblique view of model

INTENTIONS, PROCESS, AND EXECUTION

An Interview by
Sonia R. Cháo and Trevor D. Abramson
with Kohn Pedersen Fox

November 1985

INTENTIONS

Question: Is there an underlying philosophy which unifies all the work of KPF?

Mr. Fox: I don't think we're 100 percent unified, and I don't think it's necessary. We have three senior design partners and they each approach our design philosophy in their own way. I think the strength of the firm comes from the interplay of these people one against the other and one with the other.

Mr. Kohn: We have a unity of purpose to design, to detail, to execute our work to the highest level of quality possible. We are not easily satisfied. While our senior design partners share a common overall philosophy, there are differences in certain areas of their design approach. Those differences tend to influence each partner along with the contribution of fresh ideas presented by the younger design talent. A real synergism—a positive competitive environment of ideas and execution—exists and inspires greater achievement.

Mr. Pedersen: Our partnership is an assemblage of diverse personalities and it has always been our intention to allow for the full expression of this diversity in the design of our buildings. But past that personal, stylistic level, it is our shared view of the individual urban building and its role within the city, as a whole, that unites our work.

Mr. Louie: There is a fairly broad stylistic range of expression in our work but, over time, there has been a certain amount of cross-pollination which has begun to give our work some identifying traits. On one level, for example, the KPF windows have somewhat identified our work.

Mr. May: We're very competitive with each other around the set of problems that we've loosely defined for ourselves, in concert, I'm sure, with other members of the architectural community. In a way, I sometimes think of our efforts here as being analogous to the work that Picasso and Braque produced at the beginning of the century, which came out of one studio, and was indistinguishable—early cubist work; yet maybe that's presumptuous.

Question: Please categorize the different phases of the firm's design philosophy. Which buildings best represent each stage of development?

Mr. Pedersen: The great majority of our buildings have been high-rise commercial structures built within the urban fabric. To trace the evolution of our work is to trace the path of a series of strategies aimed at bringing the primitive characteristics of this building type, which by nature make it insular, autonomous, and discrete, into a more social state of existence so that it can once again

assist in shaping the public realm within our cities.

For me, our work began in an almost visceral sense with the interaction between two sets of forces: those forces that are internal, coming from the building itself and those that are external, arising from the building's context. During that period, the shape of the building was the central issue. Since these forces were thought to exert almost physical pressure, from within and without, it was inevitable that as the pressures were altered, the mass was altered as well. Our buildings took on distinct fronts and backs as hierarchical pressures acted upon internal form. Eight Penn Center, with its glass front and concrete back, curving on the diagonal corners, and 333 Wacker Drive, with its great curved surface on the river cornered by an altered geometry on the city side, are the more obvious examples of this period.

Thinking of a building as a product of pressures was useful up to a point. However, it didn't help us much with issues of scale and place. We reasoned that since most of the contexts we were building in gave off confusing and contradictory signals, wasn't it possible for the building itself to be composed of diverse pieces, each drawn in reference to different conditions within the context? We intended to "gather" the meaning of our buildings into, hopefully, an artistic unity, often combining retrospective gestures with those that were intended to be prophetic in nature. Certainly, we agreed, a large building could be more sensitively scaled to the city if it was made up of distinct pieces. In a way, we intended to introduce the complexity of the modern city into the individual building itself. Buildings such as Hercules, the Goldome Bank for Savings, and Houston

265 and 142 are representative of these intentions. The buildings of this period—and it still continues in our work—were very highly charged. They had substantial visual energy directed at the "difficult unity" of which Bob Venturi has written. However, the attempt to achieve unity through this strategy may not have been realistic.

The individual building could go only so far in representing the complexity of the city. Consequently, our buildings became less complex. They started to achieve a greater sense of homogeneity. The issue of the tall building, addressing the public realm, presenting a facade to the street which would join with other buildings to make a continuous and cohesive unity out of the street became a dominant preoccupation in our work. We started to introduce classical compositional techniques, primarily those that were aimed at encouraging the textural environment and unification of surface. This less active, perhaps more conservative point of view is obvious in Logan Square and certainly in Procter and Gamble.

Since these buildings, our work has largely focused on surface, not that form or shape is less an issue. While there have been substantial stylistic oscillations during this period, some work being more overtly historic, such as East 70th Street, while others are almost collaged, like 383 Madison Avenue, we like to think that these stylistic swings are taking place within the boundaries of more focused intentions.

Mr. May: I think that in the collage work one of the elements we were collaging was a component of history. We became interested in that per se, which I think led to a more thorough understanding of the meaning of history, and the use to which it could or should be put. The latest phase of our work is one that's much more strongly tied to the history of architecture. There's a feeling of continuity between our current work and the past.

Question: What is the new direction the firm is taking in the designs of its office buildings?
Mr. Kohn: The firm's work will continue to be sensitive to the context, to the spirit of the place within which the building is to be built. Certain sites will call for a more literal response to historical precedents, that is, classical architecture. But I believe that, in general, our designs will tend to be less literal; they will be simple and strong in form, more homogeneous in external appearance but still appropriately embellished with decorative elements and with a rich sense of detail to give visual interest and a sense of human scale. Also, the state of the economy and the marketplace will influence the high-rise office building to become more simple in its form and detail.

The Seattle office building in many ways symbolizes the direction that our firm's design is heading in. The building is a strong, easily perceived form, classical in the arrangement of its parts and proportions. It is a modern office building that pays respect to the past as well as to the present and future, and it is enriched through its detail and decoration.

Question: Your architecture exhibits a constant shift towards a classical predilection. What led you to this and why did you feel that a shift from modernism was necessary?

Mr. Louie: A failing of modernism is that it ignored the lessons of 4,000 years of history. It divorced itself from art and historical development and based its aesthetics solely on the expression of utility. To quote Bruno Taut, "Serviceability becomes the actual content of aesthetics." Their tenet denied the humanist qualities of classicism, reducing its architecture to a technical exercise. Our shift toward classicism is clearly to counter the negative effects of the past sixty years. As a result of this misguided period, architects have suffered a tremendous loss of stature and credibility.

Mr. May: I think we've come to understand the limits of modernism, and—from my own perspective, perhaps because I am as interested in painting as I am in architecture—I've come to see modernism as being a little bit too subservient to the world of art, and a little too derivative of art movements per se, which is meaningless in a work of architecture, architecture having its own set of problems to solve. Problems such as scale really don't exist in painting. Paintings were almost always relatively small. The orders of architecture were really designed and evolved in response to the problem of scale. It is how to break down the very large wall that architecture is automatically involved in. You can apply the orders of architecture: columns, moldings, string courses, cornices; these become natural, logical ways to deal with scale. Kahn used to say that when the wall evaporated, the column emerged, and that shows an understanding of the nature of walls and columns.

The problem of contextualism doesn't exist in art at all (with the possible exception of site art). Most art is made to be looked at in an isolated instance, hung on a wall with space to the right and left so you look at it, and appreciate it all by itself. Most painting and sculpture isn't meant to be juxtaposed with other painting and sculpture. But buildings are always meant to be seen in the context of other buildings or nature, so they have to have a language and establish a dialogue, feel comfortable, talk to one another in framing spaces that say something coherent. If they're all talking a different language, you have chaos, as in many cities where the modern sits cheek by jowl with the classical, each shouting its own language. The problem with modernism is that it tried to invent a new language, and a little bit like Esperanto, it doesn't work. Not because it was a bad language, but because there was a language there to start with, which everyone used and understood.

The permanence of architecture—the need to have a building last and stand up and be detailed against the elements—isn't really paralleled in art. That's not a problem of art. And then the sense of permanence; the sense that you can't, if you don't like it, take it off the wall and put it in the closet.

We have come to realize that the architecture of the past fifty or sixty years had clay feet, was founded on false premises. The modernist movement was too respectful of the art currents of the time, without ever admitting it. Why indeed should a building look like a cubist painting or minimalist sculpture, which many of the products of the last fifty years closely paralleled.

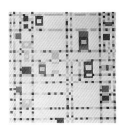

Mr. Pedersen: The history of modern architecture is almost exclusively written through the freestanding building. Our intentions, for reasons which I have already discussed, have made it necessary that we design buildings that encourage visual linkage. Classicism is an architectural language devoted to edge and boundary. It allows for the simultaneous autonomy and joining of pieces. Classical compositional strategies are uniquely suitable to an architecture of urbanism, where not only pieces but in fact buildings must link to form coherent walls and surfaces. The traditional city is adequate evidence of its success.

In the traditional city, the public realm, meaning the streets and squares, has to be dominant over the private realm, as represented generally by the buildings themselves. The idea that a building stands as an object in space has been prevalent for the last fifty years. While this concept was valid at the outset, it has decimated almost all our American cities. Presently, urban buildings, as representative of the private realm, are visually dominant over the spaces that represent the public realm. I consider that condition to be antiurban. The tall building must begin at its lower levels by acting as a facade that can join with other facades to create the urban walls that define a street. Once it meets that need, the tall building can rise as a freestanding object to fulfill the demands of its own program. We do this by treating the tall building initially as facade and then as object. The composition of the surfaces then assumes a primary role.

My work focuses on the compositional strategies of the classical language without adopting the specific motifs of that language. I can employ symmetry, centering, gridding, layering, and so on, without being the least bit interested in the Tuscan order.

Question: Can architects today legitimately copy motifs of the past? Is it necessary to alter motifs and forms to demonstrate the contemporaneity of the usage? Is it acceptable, for instance, to do a Georgian facade without the kind of distortion that would show it to be obviously of today?
Mr. Louie: Historically, architecture has always borrowed from its past in some fashion. Motifs were copied, translated, altered and synthesized to represent their particular cultures in time and place. Romanesque architecture, for instance, cannibalized and reused ancient Roman columns. This represents some 600 years of time difference. Georgian architecture, on the other hand, is only 260 years old. Seriously, though, I think

this is a very sensitive issue. Architects are still on precarious ground, having lost their stature as master builders in our fling with modernism. I do feel that in the hands of a master, both literal and interpretive use of motifs is possible. What I fear most is that the same mindless attitude that proliferated glass boxes will destroy the renewed interest in classicism.
Mr. Pedersen: We are now doing a tower in Boston atop an existing Greek Revival structure, much as the Customs House tower was built upon an earlier building. In this case, I feel, it is necessary and legitimate to use motifs, if you will, from the existing into the new. The context demands it, and my sense of architectural morality will accept it. It is, however, the question of how these motifs are to be drawn from old to new that is of interest to me.

The specific motifs of the classical language evolved over centuries in response to the realities of construction. The issue for me is authenticity. If we choose to build as the Greeks did, then it is legitimate to decorate as did the Greeks. However, if we build with the steel frame, we must decorate the surface upon it so that the surface represents, with a degree of fidelity, the structure behind. This does not mean that the surfaces become a literal representation of structure. Surface has one set of responsibilities and structure another. It means that as the horizontal load upon the vertical support was the genesis of the classical language, so too may the structural frame be the motivating force behind the expression and extension of that same language. I am completely convinced that classicism is sufficiently flexible and elastic to accommodate this seemingly modernist point of view.
Mr. May: I think the issue of the copying of motifs of the past is really irrelevant. The central premise of modernism was to start with a clean slate, and reinvent everything; that was a primary error of the modernist point of view. They demonstrated a total lack of willingness to look to precedent, to models in history. The word *copy* is a pejorative, you know. But I think a willingness to be informed by precedent—the thousands of years of dealing with all the problems of making buildings: the problem of entering a building, framing a door, a set of steps, making a portico, an entry vestibule, et cetera—that is the issue.

Question: But you're talking about elements there. What about the language?

Mr. May: Well, that's what I'm saying; the elements are more important than the language. The language is sort of a grammar, a vocabulary, and a discipline which I, for one, would be perfectly willing to use. Another legacy of the modern movement is that building has become a very cheap and rudimentary activity. The builders expect to get bulk square footage very cheaply. There was a time when they were willing to spend a lot more, so it's hard to get the details that were once lavished on a building.

Mr. Pedersen: If one were to think of a system of architecture which every architect ought to adopt in producing work that would find itself within an urban context, and with my lack of confidence in a great percentage of the architectural profession, I would immediately say that it ought to be decreed that classicism should be used verbatim for the remainder of time. Only architects of tremendous ability can achieve good results in the modern language, whereas architects of very mediocre ability achieved acceptable results in classicism. So, while I may not feel personally comfortable with using the classical language, I nevertheless think that the literal use of classicism is as legitimate today as it was two hundred years ago.

Question: Do you initially approach a design problem with analysis of historical precedents?

Mr. Pedersen: There are certain historical precedents that dominate all of our work. When one looks to history, however, one must look very specifically to discover solutions to problems that are again relevant to our age. Let me give you an example. I have said that much of our work is focused on the surface representation of the facades. Because developers want to get every inch out of an available volume, deep recesses are difficult to achieve. We must achieve, almost like the painter has always had to achieve, the illusion of the third dimension within the reality of two. Through Colin Rowe and Judy Di Maio we were led to the analysis of the late-sixteenth-century Italian Mannerist architecture of Vasari, Vignola, and Michelangelo. During this period, they were purposefully trying to flatten their surfaces and stretch them laterally. Painting during this time was attempting to accomplish similar objectives. To achieve this illusion, they introduced vertical and horizontal gridding upon their surfaces. Centered, figural material was then placed within the gridded boundaries. Surfaces were built up as a series of layers, almost like the layers in a piece of plywood. The implications of these compositional techniques have

tremendous meaning for a faithful representation of steel-frame construction which is, by its very nature, a grid. ABC Phase II, 383 Madison Avenue, and 500 E Street S.W. are buildings of ours which directly employ this historical precedent.

Question: Define postmodernism. Are you postmodernists?

Mr. May: I don't think we invented it, so maybe perhaps we don't have to define it, but the three key ingredients are: an interest in decoration, contextualism, and history. All three of those were noticeably missing in the modernist era. Postmodernism also seems to include a more ironic use of history, rather than a direct use of history, or a willingness to use it for what it has to offer. Perhaps our work is different than some postmodernists' work, because it doesn't have that humorous or ironic component. I don't think our work is fully classical either, although the apartment house on 70th Street tends toward that direction in a more complete way.

Mr. Pedersen: The term *postmodernism* was invented by an architect-journalist for whom I have low regard. Wright was very much interested in decoration. Aalto was very much interested in context and Kahn in history. The term only has meaning when placed in juxtaposition to the distilled, sterile concept of modernism that is unfortunately the product of too many second-rate architects. Modernism is and can be as flexible and elastic as classicism. Hasn't Le Corbusier been called a great classicist for his brilliant inversions of the classical language? Modernism will be expanded to include classicism and classicism expanded to include modernism. When that happens, we will need another quick-witted journalist to coin a new phrase. It will probably be the same one; he works fast.

Ms. Conway: We use ornament as an integral and logical expression of the building's parts to relate them to surrounding buildings and to give them a human, pedestrian scale. I suppose we are postmodern in the sense that often we draw from the language of classical or Art Deco architecture in developing our decorative systems, but the primary references are to the buildings themselves, not to history per se. Our planning, too, could be called postmodern to the extent that it strives for symmetry, for classical progressions of movement, for rooms as opposed to spaces. But I don't think we're at all interested in grab-bag historicism, irony, humor, or some of the trendier aspects of postmodernism.

Question: Can you evaluate the determining role of architecture as culture in relation to urban design? When one starts looking back at historical precedents, where does one draw the line between responsible architectural reinterpretation, literal interpretation, and kitsch?

Ms. Conway: Well, first one has to define *kitsch*. I believe what we mean by kitsch is an imitation or simulation of something that, by pretending to be real, programs a sentimental response. The role of architecture as culture is never pretense, though there are always, in any time, examples—usually bad ones—of architecture that pretends. If by literal interpretation one means reproduction, that, in my opinion, is merely a specialty craft. It may be a valid solution to a particular problem, but it has nothing to do with the mainstream of architecture as a creative process. What you call responsible architectural reinterpretation, on the other hand, is what serious architecture has always been about: continually refining and adapting 4,000 years of architectural language to solve the problem at hand. The modern movement broke with that tradition, abandoned that language and invented its own vocabulary. But even within the modern movement there is a process of responsible architectural reinterpretation, of adapting that particular vocabulary; seldom does new architecture spring full-blown without reinterpretation of the past.

Mr. Louie: Architecture has always been a reflection of its culture, marking its values at a certain time in history. It should be representative of all that has come before and be prophetic as well. Whether we can evolve a language that marks our time and place clearly as a result of our understanding and synthesis of our past remains to be seen. I don't think that the application of a particular type of ornament drawn from history is wrong as long as its purpose and syntax are correct. As children display characteristics of their parents, so should buildings.

Question: Yes, but what about the responsibility that one takes on, in terms of defining an urban realm today, with the vocabulary of another time and place.

Ms. Conway: Well, there has been a serious problem in modern architecture related to popular culture and readability. One way in which some designers are now responding to that problem could be called kitsch: mindless re-creation of easily recognizable images of premodern buildings or, in some cases, deliberate tongue-in-cheek mimicry of low art. But the problem of popular culture is not solved simply by pandering to an uneducated preference for nostalgia. One can make a very good case that the Bauhaus, the International Style, and modernism in general were also pandering to popular culture. They did it by romanticizing the machine, which their proponents believed was the salvation of the masses. For example, the planning of Le Corbusier was a glorification of the automobile and, indeed the automobile today is a dominant force in popular culture. If one spends one's life in an automobile, one needs only points on a map: objects to drive to and from and park under or around. The building as sculptured-object-in-the-park makes perfect sense. String this plan along the highway and there's no more need for detail or human scale. There's no more city at all. That's the absurdly logical conclusion of Le Corbusier's planning. And when the reductive forms of modernism are extruded to the highrise and economized to the developer's bottom line, there's no more sculpture either. There's no more need to identify place because there is no more place. Unfortunately, while popular culture has embraced the automobile, it has not found the consequences of planning around it to be very satisfying. People now sense that the machine has taken away at least as much as it has given us, and that not all machines are friendly. The popular reaction is Disneyland. It's the only place that people can go to and feel comfortable with, that they can identify, in their imaginations, with ideas of town and city—ideas that still have very real meaning to them. And, yes, people do embrace kitsch as an alternative to anonymity. But just because these popular yearnings are not intellectualized does not mean they're not valid. These yearnings are terribly important, and I think that serious architecture must respond to them. But that does not mean that architects have to resort to kitsch to satisfy people. I think the architect's responsibility is not necessarily to put traditional design back into the city, but to put traditional values back into the city, which may or may not mean using the vocabulary of another time or another place. I think there's also a responsibility to try to create traditional values in the suburban environment, to try to focus these anonymous agglomerations we've created, to knit them together in some way and to give them, too, a sense of place.

Mr. May: Kitsch is just bad art, false art. Sentiment before content. I don't think kitsch is part of the problem. Kitsch really refers to a kind of sloppy sentimentality in place of substance.

Mr. Pedersen: When there is no relationship between the appearance of things and the reality of things, the opportunities for kitsch arise. Scenographic intentions lead to sentimentality. Architecture loses its stability.

Question: Has modernism produced any worthwhile contributions to the traditional city?
Mr. May: To the traditional city? (long silence) Better it weren't there, better it never happened. A blight on the landscape.
Mr. Louie: Modernism was a self-conscious break with the past. Its principles and expressions are so diametrically opposed to the humanist principles that created the traditional city that any contribution would be purely coincidental. On the other hand, an obtuse contribution may be that it has made us more aware of the liveability of the traditional city, which has led us to where we are today.
Mr. Pedersen: Within the fabric of the traditional city, buildings of great public significance were isolated as set pieces. The buildings of modern architecture which contribute to the traditional city function as similar figural pieces. The Guggenheim Museum in New York is such a building. The dynamic of the juxtaposition between object and wall is only successful if both are represented. Unfortunately, the modern city presents less and less wall against which figural object reading is meaningful.

Question: Now, Bill [Pedersen], you've been quoted as saying that if a building looks good out of its context, it is not a good building. Can you elaborate on this authenticity to place by comparing your 333 Wacker Drive building in Chicago and the Block Five tower in Seattle?
Mr. Pedersen: Oh, you're really pinning me down there. The implication of that statement demands that a building's character and composition be drawn from its context. 333 Wacker Drive is primarily focused on shape to join it to its context. Its shape was created by the external pressures of context acting upon the relatively neutral medium of internal space. If one looks at the building's plan, this can be easily seen. The surface that clads this shape is not drawn from the immediate context or from the larger context of Chicago itself. It acts, rather, in juxtaposition to it. Our Seattle building takes a different tack towards context. The shape of the building was selected, almost from a series of platonic absolutes, for its compatibility to its centralized site. (Remember that 333 was on an edge site.) The surface of the building was abstracted from the character of many Seattle buildings, the Smith Tower being the most

influential. If you wish to more accurately compare my position at the time of 333 Wacker Drive with my present position, we should substitute South Ferry in New York for the Seattle tower. Then we can compare two responses to edge sites which are rather similar. South Ferry, indeed, responds to external pressures as literally as did 333. It truly has a city side and a water side. Yet it created this response to context by joining platonic pieces into a unified composition without distorting the integrity of the pieces. Quite a different approach to achieving a similar objective. Additionally, the character of the building's surface comes directly from an interpretation of lower Manhattan. So, as you can see, my basic intentions towards a building's relationship to its context have not changed. I have chosen to accomplish the same task with different artistic responses.

Question: What architects, specifically, do you admire, and/ or do you consider your mentors?
Mr. Louie: There was an article printed once in the *Harvard Business Review* called "Everyone Who Makes It Has a Mentor." I think it's more true in the business world than in architecture. It's reversed in architecture to some extent where we tend to select our mentors, those whose body of work we entrust as tutors. I've always admired and found inspiration in Louis Kahn's work as well as Wright's and some of Aalto's. Not only for their aesthetic content but for the fact that they were master builders who were humanists as well. There are no sentimental references in their work, but single-minded genius pushing the envelope of expression. Exploring their work is like listening to Beethoven's Ninth; it inspires confidence. There are others whose consistent pursuit of quality such as Pei and Cossutta I find admirable. Similarly, I have found the inventive genius of Wagner and some of Hoffmann's work sources of decorative inspiration. I would be remiss in not mentioning Bill Pedersen as a constant source of influence.
Mr. May: I was always very enamored of the work of Alvar Aalto and Frank Lloyd Wright. I've come to really love Frank Lloyd Wright's very early work, the work around 1906: the Larkin Building, the Robie House, Unity Temple. Now, currently, I'm more interested in neoclassical, and, I guess, the American classicists such as McKim, Mead and White, the English Palladians, and Palladio. Roman architecture has always had a special interest for me. I was introduced to that by Kahn and his fascination with Roman architecture. Kahn had a profound influence on everyone, I think, who came into

contact with him, in that he elevated the pursuit of architecture to such a high level. He was so serious about the effort. He imbued the effort with almost a religious and poetic content. Yet he had a very firm grip on the nature of the profession and its realities, and the history of architecture.

Mr. Pedersen: "Admiring" and "considering one's mentor" are two entirely different things. I feel that Colin Rowe has been a spiritual mentor in my career. My architectural pantheon is reserved for those architects who produced a body of work that rose out of a profound worldview. Throughout history, I suppose, there are many who qualify. However, the modern movement made the association between personal philosophy and artistic accomplishment more intensely focused. Frank Lloyd Wright, Le Corbusier, Mies van der Rohe, and Louis Kahn stand out, for me, in the highest relief. Architecture without the stabilizing influence of personal philosophy becomes hollow and without meaning. Architecture was, for them, a religion as well as an art.

Question: There exists in academic circles a certain stigma attached to commercial architecture, and in most cases, justly so. What, if anything, sets KPF apart from other commercial architects? Can you break away from this stigma?
Mr. Kohn: There's no question there has been a stigma attached to commercial architecture. I think those architects not doing commercial work tend to support and reinforce this notion and also may be jealous of those who are achieving outstanding results with large-scale projects. There is no question that a great number of architectural firms doing commercial work do it very poorly; not really architecture, just bad buildings. But it's kind of ludicrous to say commercial architecture in itself is not worth our best efforts, because what, in fact, influences the life of the average person in our urban areas more than commercial architecture? Cities are made up of commercial buildings. We have aggressively engaged commercial architecture with a design philosophy that calls for improving our cities, providing a vitality, a sense of place, an environment for pedestrians. Designing quality architecture for commercial buildings is the contribution we intend to make.
Mr. Fox: Even though we design speculative office buildings, we provide a high level of design and detail in those buildings which other architects do not. Many architects will take a commission and turn out a formula-type building. We approach each project as an individual challenge, with its own very special program, requirements, and design. Although many of our projects are for commercial clients, we achieve very unique buildings for that clientèle. So I do not think we are deserving of that charge.
Mr. Pedersen: We have tremendous sympathy with the intellectual issues that have been put forth during the last ten years. We owe a great deal to people like Colin Rowe, whose ground-breaking ideas and points of view in regard to the evolution of architecture during this period are absolutely fundamental to the architecture that we produce. So in a sense, our architecture has come from academia; we'd like to feel that we have taken it a step further, in that we've built it and we detail it.

Question: Your link with academia is obviously strengthened by the number of young people in the office. What is the role of the young blood in the office, and how do the partners interact?
Mr. Pedersen: Young people of tremendous promise, academic promise at least, were attracted to this office initially because they understood that there was a sympathy between what was taught in school and what in fact they would be experiencing after they left school.

Having come to us and found this to be the case, I think that their energies and their points of view, which were well conditioned and well established in an academic situation, have strengthened the debate that takes place within the office, and have fed it, and allowed it to build.

Mr. May: I don't think talent, insight, and inventive genius necessarily come late in life. What comes late is an understanding of the process, and the methodology of building these buildings. I think a lot of our young people supply very important input. Some of them are very creative, very inventive and very resourceful people. There is a kind of synergism in our firm between maturity and youth.

Mr. Cioppa: The role of the young person in the firm is really two-fold. We expect to get from them a certain level of work, and also a certain freshness of ideas, since they come directly from university environments where things are less pragmatic. On the other hand, their role in the office is really also for themselves, in terms of their own learning, and exposure to the process of building and designing buildings. The relationship of the partners to them has changed as we have grown. It was really more direct, a more universal relationship in the early stages than it is now; and, while granted, the design and administrative partners work directly with some of the younger people, the partners have become icons for the young staff.

Mr. Louie: The kind of architecture that we do takes a tremendous amount of energy both in terms of design and execution. They are a necessary evil to our process, and I mean that in a positive sense. The handcrafted quality of our work cannot be pulled out of a standard detail drawer. They are the means by which new expressions are explored. There's a dynamic tension between innocence and wisdom I find at times frustrating, at times invigorating. Without this constant challenge, however, we would ultimately stagnate in our own glory.

Question: In many architectural firms, all of the partners want to partake equally in every aspect of the work. The arrangement here deviates from that norm. Can you elaborate on the administrative structure of KPF?

Mr. Cioppa: I don't think there's any lack of desire in the partnership to participate in all aspects of the project. We just do not, quite frankly, because we realized very early on that people, be they partners, employees or associate partners, are really equipped to do certain things better than other things. Administratively, the partnership is set up to allow each of the functions of architecture to follow its course without all the claptrap

of running a hundred-and-fifty-person organization. That is to say, marketing doesn't have to worry about administration, and design doesn't have to worry about administration; so that the management of the project, the management of the office, and the management of the staff is really taken out of the equation on a daily level of marketing and design. This is, of course, a simplification of the process. It's really the interaction that's more important than the separation of the duties. In a general way, everybody is involved in administration, just as, really, administration is involved in design.

Question: KPF has generated a high level of quality and detail in these buildings which set them apart from the standard developer boxes. Many of your buildings are indeed speculative. How are they made feasible?

Mr. Cioppa: They're really made feasible by the desire of our clients to have a product somewhat better, in terms of its design quality and detail, than the normal developer building. They're also made feasible, quite frankly, by the willingness of all of us and our staff to put more into a building than perhaps one would normally expect from an architectural firm, or at least one as large as KPF. So what makes it possible is really two things: our willingness to do it, and our client's willingness really to go an extra percentage, if you will, in terms of the cost of the building.

Mr. May: It costs more to do a good job. It costs more for us to design it; it costs more to build. There has to be a willingness to spend more money; good buildings cost more money in construction and they cost more in fee—there's no magic formula. It takes more effort, which translates into dollars. We think we're clever, and spend money well, but I'm sure other architects are equally clever. The boxes you see dotting the landscape are done very cheaply, and very quickly. Our buildings are designed to do more than the boxes did. They do more environmentally, they do more contextually—they deal more with the problems of scale—and to do all those additional tasks takes more dollars.

Question: The development market has become far more competitive and, as a result, the clients have become more sophisticated. Whereas before their attitude was "Let's build this building for as little as we possibly can," developers now recognize the value of quality buildings.

Mr. Kohn: Americans have become increasingly conscious of the designer product—in jewelry, cars, clothing. The designer product seems to be more valuable in the eyes of the consumer. Real-estate developers have realized that they can market their product better, lease more space when the building's design is associated with a name architect. In addition, a quality building is more desired by the enlightened public. Developers of today are more professional than they were thirty or forty years ago. The majority are college graduates interested in the arts as well as in business, so, while they share a common goal with all developers for a strong bottom line, they are concerned today with taste, achieving an outstanding building, and leaving their mark on their cities and regions. Tax laws, particularly related to depreciation and market conditions, play a key role in the quality of our buildings. In the fifties, when depreciation was for seven years, the buildings were not built for long-term ownership. Thus, quality was minimized. When markets are overbuilt and rents become competitive, building costs must be reduced, thereby affecting quality. Developers play an increasingly important role in shaping our cities. We have been fortunate to attract developers who do care, who are creative, and who are doing quality buildings and want to use us to achieve something special—to make a positive contribution.

Question: To what extent are you involved with the developer in creating a project? And bringing it about?
Mr. Fox: We have not been involved in initiating projects. We have never, that I can recall, been instrumental in developing a project.

Question: Do developers come to you and say "This is the general area." Can you recommend a good site?
Mr. Fox: Sometimes that happens. In most cases, they have a site and they have a general idea of what they want to build. In some cases, we have been involved in site selection, but that hasn't happened too often. We have not sold ourselves as the instigator of the development; maybe we should.

Question: Getting back to planning. You're involved with some large projects which started off as planning projects. To what extent is KPF involved with the development of a project?
Ms. Conway: That depends on the individual project. Let me say that I'm the only person in the whole firm, top to bottom, who's not an architect or designer by training. I am a planner by training, and my initial inclusion as a partner in KPF was to handle zoning, master planning, EIS responses, and other predesign analyses related primarily to suburban office building commissions. Our early planning work was mostly technical in that it was

aimed at getting already funded projects built: solving traffic, access, and parking problems; managing drainage; avoiding adverse environmental impacts; relating building heights to surrounding development; and so on. Now that we're more involved in urban sites and large project feasibility studies, our planning is increasingly concerned with urban design, and my own work tends toward intensive programming with large corporate users to shape these projects to their needs.

Question: Do you involve clients in the design process?
Mr. Louie: Oh, they pay the bills. (laughter) At least most do. Seriously, though, they insist, and we insist that they become an integral part of the design process. Most clients come to us after they've done their homework. Usually they know our work. They understand their economic limits. We understand our architectural ones. The key in the process is to bring these two points of view as close together as possible. It is our role to translate their programmatic needs into an architecture that is more than economically inspired. Our best clients are those whose economic models are as flexible as our clay.

Mr. Kohn: I think it is crucial that clients be involved. The more they're involved, the more supportive they are of the design. Clients can be somewhat paranoid and suspicious of the architect; they do not understand what he or she does. It is a mystifying procedure, somewhat archaic, and, for some, it is hard to understand what the fee provides. They see a lot of sketches and drawings but are more accustomed to buying a tangible product: paying money for objects. It is a very difficult procedure for the average client to understand. The key to success is to involve clients in the decision-making process, so that the building becomes real to them very early. We do this by meeting with them at least once every two weeks or so in the early design stage. We keep them thoroughly informed and request that they make decisions on a regular basis. We provide them with enough material in a structured way to make those decisions. That's the key to management, in fact: to know what you need, and when; to get the decisions you need to keep the project going forward; and to continue to motivate the client. One of the reasons we have had some success is that we have been able to keep the client as a team member moving with us from the concept to the detail, to the completed building itself, in a timely way.

Mr. May: We're not a prima donna sort of a place, where we do one or two schemes and say "Take it or leave it." We do a variety of schemes, so that the developer can see the full scope of possibilities that the problem has to offer, and help choose the one that moves forward. This is sometimes risky, but it does involve them in the process, and we've found that when people are involved, they become excited about what we are doing, and in the long run are willing to support it. Whereas, if it's all yours, and they haven't made any significant input into the product, they're less willing to pay for it. We are looking for their support when the budgetary crunch comes, as it always does!

Mr. Pedersen: We always come to a client with a series of alternative possibilities in the initial meeting. These alternatives have been developed in clay massing studies. We work with small-scale models that generally have a large segment of the context surrounding the building, because the dialogue between the internal forces and external forces is so crucial to our work. Using clay models is quite helpful, particularly for office structures in an urban context, because they demonstrate the action of the external context upon the individual building quite clearly. By showing four or five alternative schemes within that context, it's easy for a client to understand which succeed and which fail. We don't have to sell very hard, because we understand which succeed and which

fail. Through a reasonably logical explanation of the process, they are quickly able to grasp it as well.

The bullnose detail is a crucial detail here, in that it allows for the horizontal strapping of that surface to be more evident. It gives it, I think, a rather remarkable play of light on the surface itself; the curvilinear shape allows the light to be received in a very special way. It highlights the lighting of the surface.
William Pedersen

The KPF window was first
developed on the Hercules
building and Logan Square
hotel at about the same time.
It serves to deal
simultaneously with a sense of
surface and depth in the
facades' treatment. The center
panel in its flush alignment
holds the surface of the wall
and the side panels move back,
revealing depth.
Arthur May

The punched window—as we see it used in 70th Street and 125 Summer Street creates, in a sense, a blank sheet of paper on which to draw longer-scale elements. We see this also in the establishment of the niches on the Logan Square hotel. The punched windows are used in a simple and repetitive pattern, flush with the surface. They establish a wall for the placement of the two- or three-story 'windows'.
Arthur May

The stone is not intended to imply a load-bearing characteristic. It was intended to only act as a surface cladding. This probably owes a debt to people like Otto Wagner, who at the time when he was working with stone cladding, late in his career, was very much interested in expressing it only as a surface-cladding material. He went to the extent of applying exterior fasteners to it, so that one would never get the sense that that stone was load-bearing; it was only held up.
William Pedersen

The metal detailing of the bridge that spans between the two towers is very dense. The metal offers another level of refinement, a level of detail, that says that the piece has been put together very carefully. It's on a two-foot module, and it has an ABA rhythm to it, so that it takes on another level of richness as well. The whole piece is centered with a vertical on it which then organizes it in a more figural fashion.
William Pedersen

They haven't found a way of
making precast any thinner
than six inches yet, so we still
have at least that advantage
over other materials. That's
one of the reasons we used it
in Buffalo. The 1901
building has a lot of depth
and articulation on its facade.
The precast was an ideal
material because it allowed us
to develop details which would
complement the pattern of the
existing building.
William Louie

Multi-layered frames give a glass curtain wall more depth. We are limited in the amount and the type of details we can use in a glass wall. By varying the colors of mullions and glass, and manipulating the depth and width of the mullions, we can generate a variety of readings that convey scale, vitality and structure so that it's more than just a taut, wallpaper-like surface.
William Louie

The stainless-steel grilles are
decorative opportunities.
When one has air intakes, one
can wish they weren't there, or
take advantage of them. But
rather than making a whole
architecture out of them, as
some have done, one simply
makes them secondary
architectural embellishment
which falls within the larger
framing system of the
construction itself.
William Pedersen

When we first set up the internal volumetrics of Procter & Gamble—the four-foot columns, which were pretty much part of the system—we needed an element of refinement to create a more comfortable scale relationship. The juxtaposition and the layering of the linear decorative system, derived from the work of Wright and the work of Wagner, established a very nice balance between the volumetric and the linear qualities. The manner in which that decorative system is put together is consistent with the exterior detailing.
William Pedersen

COMPREHENSIVE LIST OF WORKS

Project/Date		Project Team	Building Information
AID ASSOCIATION FOR LUTHERANS HEADQUARTERS Corporate Headquarters Appleton, Wisconsin 1974/77		*Architect:* John Carl Warnecke and Associates *Partner in charge:* A. Eugene Kohn *Partner in charge, design:* William Pedersen *Project planner:* John Smart, Patricia Conway, Mike Koenan *Project director:* Sheldon Fox *Client:* Aid Association for Lutherans	*Structure:* Steel *Exterior:* White aluminum plate, glass *Interior:* Drywall, fiberglass, fabric, red oak, plaster *G.S.F.:* 500,000 *No. of floors:* 2
ABC ARMORY RENOVATION Studio, Office Building New York, New York 1976/77		*Partner in charge:* Sheldon Fox *Partner in charge, design:* William Pedersen *Project planner:* Patricia Conway *Project director:* Robert Cioppa *Client:* ABC	*Interior:* Gypsum board, paint *G.S.F.:* 45,000 *No. of floors:* 3
KINCAID TOWERS Office Building Lexington, Kentucky 1977/79		*Partner in charge:* A. Eugene Kohn *Partner in charge, design:* William Pedersen *Partner in charge, planning:* Patricia Conway *Project director:* Laurence Goldberg *Associate Architect:* Johnson/ Romanowitz, Lexington, Kentucky *Client:* Kentucky Central Life Insurance Company; Huber, Hunt and Nichols	*Structure:* Steel frame *Exterior:* Precast concrete, aluminum, tinted glass *G.S.F.:* 430,000 *No. of floors:* 25
SEVEN LINCOLN SQUARE WABC-TV Studio/Office Building New York, New York 1977/79		*Partner in charge:* Sheldon Fox *Partner in charge, design:* William Pedersen *Senior designer:* Paul Rosen *Partner in charge, planning:* Patricia Conway *Job Captain:* Gary Stluka *Client:* ABC	*Structure:* Steel *Exterior:* Brick, glass *Interior:* Gypsum board, glass, metal partitions, quarry tile *G.S.F.:* 99,000 *No. of floors:* 6
30 WEST 67TH STREET Office Building New York, New York 1977/79		*Partner in charge:* Sheldon Fox *Partner in charge, design:* William Pedersen *Managing partner:* Robert Cioppa *Partner in charge, planning:* Patricia Conway *Senior designer:* Curtiss Fentress *Client:* ABC	*Structure:* Steel frame *Exterior:* Painted aluminum, glass *Interior:* Gypsum board and paint *G.S.F.:* 250,000 *No. of floors:* 14
AT&T LONG LINES EASTERN REGIONAL HEADQUARTERS Oakton, Virginia 1977/80		*Partner in charge:* A. Eugene Kohn *Partner in charge, design:* William Pedersen *Partner in charge, planning:* Patricia Conway *Senior designer:* Robert Evans *Project managers:* Charles A. Schmitt, Rick Schweber *Job Captain:* Arthur Korenstein *Client:* AT&T Long Lines	*Structure:* Steel *Exterior:* Brick, tinted glass, aluminum *Interior:* Brick, tinted glass, aluminum *G.S.F.:* 430,000 *No. of floors:* 3

Project/Date		Project Team	Building Information
BUNKER HILL Mixed-Use Complex Los Angeles, California 1977		*Partner in charge:* A. Eugene Kohn *Partner in charge, design:* Arthur May *Client:* The Maguire Partners	*Exterior:* Granite, glass *G.S.F.:* 2.0 million *No. of floors:* 40
AMOCO BUILDING AT COLUMBIA PLAZA Office Building Denver, Colorado 1977/80		*Partner in charge:* A. Eugene Kohn *Senior designer:* Curtiss Fentress *Project manager:* Laurence Goldberg *Job captain:* Bun-Wah Nip *Client:* Reliance Development Group	*Structure:* Steel frame, concrete core *Exterior:* Aluminum, glass *Interior:* Brick, glass *G.S.F.:* 750,000 *No. of floors:* 36
MANHATTANVILLE COLLEGE CONFERENCE CENTER Office, Learning Facility, Master Plan Purchase, New York 1977		*Partner in charge:* Sheldon Fox *Partner in charge, design:* William Pedersen *Partner in charge, planning:* Patricia Conway *Senior designer:* William Louie *Associate Architect:* Kohn Pedersen Fox Conway Associates, Inc. *Client:* New York Telephone Company	*Exterior:* Brick, limestone *G.S.F.:* 325,000 *No. of floors:* 2
ABC WASHINGTON NEWS BUREAU Studio Facilities Washington, D.C. 1978/81		*Partner in charge:* Sheldon Fox *Partner in charge, design:* William Pedersen *Partner in charge, mgt.:* Robert Cioppa *Senior designer:* Paul Rosen *Job Captain:* Gary Stluka/Dow Jarrett *Client:* ABC	*Structure:* Concrete *Exterior:* Granite, plate aluminum, tinted glass *Interior:* Granite, aluminum *G.S.F.:* 150,000 *No. of floors:* 7
EIGHT PENN CENTER Office Building Philadelphia, Pennsylvania 1979/1981		*Partner in charge:* A. Eugene Kohn *Partner in charge, design:* Arthur May *Partner in charge, mgt.:* Robert Cioppa *Senior designer:* Robert Evans *Job Captain:* Paul Pichardo *Client:* The Reliance Development Group	*Structure:* Reinforced concrete *Exterior:* Architectural concrete, reflective glass, aluminum frame *Interior:* Travertine, stainless-steel trim *G.S.F.:* 237,000 *No. of floors:* 23
ROCKY MOUNTAIN ENERGY COMPANY HEADQUARTERS Broomfield, Colorado 1979/80		*Partner in charge:* A. Eugene Kohn *Partner in charge, design:* William Pedersen *Project planner:* Mark Strauss *Project manager:* Charles Schmitt *Job Captain:* Bun-Wah Nip *Client:* Rocky Mountain Energy Company	*Structure:* Concrete *Exterior:* Brick, glass *Interior:* Brick *G.S.F.:* 265,000 *No. of floors:* 3

ONE LOGAN SQUARE
Hotel, Office Building Complex
Philadelphia, Pennsylvania
1979/83

Partner in charge: A. Eugene Kohn
Partner in charge, design: Arthur May
Partner in charge, planning: Patricia Conway
Partner in charge, mgt.: Robert Cioppa
Senior designer: Anthony Pellechia
Project manager: Myron Sigal
Job Captain: Timothy Hartley, James Outen
Client: One Logan Square Associates; Pic/Cigna; Four Seasons Hotels Limited; Urban Investment & Development Co.

Structure: Concrete
Exterior: Hotel: granite, clear glass
Office: granite, tinted glass
Interior: Granite
G.S.F.: Hotel: 400,000
Office: 600,000
No. of floors: Hotel: 8
Office: 31

---

333 WACKER DRIVE
Office Building
Chicago, Illinois
1979/83

Partner in charge: A. Eugene Kohn
Partner in charge, design: William Pedersen
Senior designer: Alexander Ward
Project manager: Gary Stluka
Associate Architect: Perkins & Will, Chicago, Illinois
Client: Urban Investment & Development Co.

Structure: Steel frame
Exterior: Marble, granite, glass, stainless steel
Interior: Granite, terrazzo, stainless steel
G.S.F.: 1.0 million
No. of floors: 36

FOUR SEASONS HOTEL
Feasibility Study
Beverly Hills, California
1980

Partner in charge: A. Euguene Kohn
Partner in charge, design: William Pedersen
Senior designer: Alexander Ward
Partner in charge, planning: Patricia Conway
Associate Architect: Daniel Dworsky, Los Angeles, California
Client: Four Seasons Hotel Limited

Structure: Concrete frame
Exterior: Architectural concrete, marble, exposed wood, brick
G.S.F.: 349,000
No. of floors: 18

PROJECT X
Office Tower; Feasibility Study
Houston, Texas
1980

Partner in charge: A. Eugene Kohn
Partner in charge, design: William Pedersen
Senior designer: Alexander Ward
Client: Century Development Co.

Structure: Steel frame
Exterior: Granite, low-reflective glass, high-energy-efficient glass
G.S.F.: 1.35 million
No. of floors: 63

PROJECT Y
Office Tower; Feasibility Study
Houston, Texas
1980

Partner in charge: A. Eugene Kohn
Partner in charge, design: William Pedersen
Senior designer: Alexander Ward
Client: Century Development Co.

Structure: Steel frame
Exterior: Reflective glass
G.S.F.: 1.9 million
No. of floors: 73

Project/Date		Project Team	Building Information
HERCULES INCORPORATED HEADQUARTERS Wilmington, Delaware 1980/83		*Partner in charge:* Sheldon Fox *Partner in charge, design:* Arthur May *Partner in charge, planning:* Patricia Conway *Senior designer:* Robert Evans *Project planner:* Mark Strauss *Project manager:* Demetrios Pantazis *Job Captain:* Ken Rose *Client:* Hercules Incorporated	*Structure:* Steel frame *Exterior:* Granite, reflective glass *Interior:* Brick, wood storefronts, clear glass, painted wood, painted steel *G.S.F.:* 680,000 *No. of floors:* 14
GOLDOME BANK FOR SAVINGS Office Building Buffalo, New York 1980/85		*Partner in charge:* A. Eugene Kohn *Partner in charge, design:* William Louie *Partner in charge, planning:* Patricia Conway *Project planner:* Laurence Goldberg *Job Captain:* Eileen Weingarten *Associate Architect:* Milstein Witteck Davis & Associates Buffalo, New York *Client:* Goldome Bank for Savings	*Structure:* Steel frame *Exterior:* Precast concrete, limestone, marble, reflective glass, aluminum mullions and bullnoses *Interior:* Brick, limestone, granite, precast concrete *G.S.F.:* 430,000 *No. of floors:* 12
TAMPA FINANCIAL CENTER Office Building Tampa, Florida 1980		*Partner in charge:* A. Eugene Kohn *Partner in charge, design:* Arthur May *Senior designer:* Megan Walker *Project manager:* Lawrence Goldberg *Associate Architect:* McElvy, Jennewein, Stefany & Howard Architects/Planners Inc. Tampa, Florida *Client:* Doran Jason Company	*Structure:* Parking: concrete Office: steel frame *Exterior:* Concrete, granite, glass *G.S.F.:* 517,000 *No. of floors:* 29
HOUSTON OFFICE TOWER– BLOCK 261 Houston, Texas 1981/82		*Partner in charge:* A. Eugene Kohn *Partner in charge, design:* Arthur May *Senior designer:* Megan Walker *Project manager:* Robert Landsman *Job Captain:* Alan Schwabenland *Client:* Wortham & Van Liew	*Structure:* Steel tube *Exterior:* Granite, glass *G.S.F.:* 1.0 million *No. of floors:* 40
HOUSTON OFFICE TOWER– BLOCK 265 Houston, Texas 1981		*Partner in charge:* A. Eugene Kohn *Partner in charge, design:* William Pedersen *Senior designer:* Sudhir Jambhekar *Project Manager:* Robert Landsman *Client:* Wortham & Van Liew	*Structure:* Composite tube *Exterior:* Granite, reflective glass, painted steel lattice *Interior:* Granite, marble, painted steel lattice *G.S.F.:* 2,500,000 *No. of floors:* 80
BATTERY PARK, COMPETITION New York, New York 1981	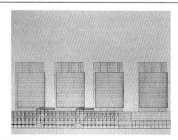	*Partner in charge:* A. Eugene Kohn *Partner in charge, design:* William Pedersen *Senior designer:* Anthony Pellecchia *Client:* Olympia and York Development, Limited	*Exterior:* Stone, metal, reflective glass *G.S.F.:* 6 million (4 towers) *No. of floors:* 50

Project/Date		Project Team	Building Information

GENERAL RE HEADQUARTERS, SCHEME 1
Office Building
Stamford, Connecticut
1981

Partner in charge: A. Eugene Kohn
Partner in charge, design: Wiliam Pedersen
Senior designer: William Louie
Client: General Re

Structure: Steel/concrete
Exterior: Limestone, brick, reflective glass, terra cotta, copper
G.S.F.: 1.17 million
No. of floors: 6.

LINCOLN WEST
Residential Tower
New York, New York
1981

Partner in charge: A. Eugene Kohn
Partner in charge, design: William Pedersen
Senior designer: Mark Strauss
Client: B. A. Capital

Exterior: Limestone, granite, glass
G.S.F.: 400,000
No. of floors: 40

TABOR CENTER
Office Building
Denver, Colorado
1981/85

Partner in charge: A. Eugene Kohn
Associate Partner in charge, design: Lee Polisano
Senior designer: Anthony Pellecchia
Project manager: Lee Polisano
Associate Architect: R.N.L., Denver; Urban Design Group, Denver
Client: Williams Realty Co.

Structure: Cast-in-place concrete tube wall, steel frame
Exterior: Architectural concrete, granite, stainless-steel bolts, tinted glass
Interior: Architectural concrete, granite, stainless steel
G.S.F.: 1.54 million
No. of floors: 40/32

KOHN PEDERSEN FOX OFFICES
New York, New York
1981

Partner in charge: William Pedersen
Partner in charge, design: William Pedersen
Senior designer: Alexander Ward
Project manager: Randy Gerner

Interior: Painted wood, gypsum board, vinyl tile, sandblasted glass

---

KOHN PEDERSEN FOX OFFICE
Conference Table and Desks
New York, New York
1981

Partner in charge: William Pedersen
Partner in charge, design: William Pedersen

Interior: Wood, marble, stainless steel, mother-of-pearl

HBO, RENOVATION
Office Building
New York, New York
1981

Partner in charge: A. Eugene Kohn
Partner in charge, design: Arthur May
Senior designer: Sudhir Jambhekar
Project manager: William Schweber
Associate Architect: Kohn Pedersen Fox Conway Associates, Inc.
Client: Home Box Office, Inc.

Exterior: Glass curtain wall
Interior: Marble, terrazzo, drywall
G.S.F.: 330,000
No. of floors: 15

Project/Date		Project Team	Building Information

300 WEST MONROE STREET
Office Building
Chicago, Illinois
1981

Partner in charge: A Eugene Kohn
Partner in charge, design: William Pedersen
Senior designer: David Leventhal
Project manager: Creighton Jones
Job Captain: J. Edward Outen
Project architect: Paul Rosen
Associate Architect: A. Epstein & Sons
Chicago, Illinois
Client: Cadillac Fairview Corporation, Ltd.

Structure: Steel
Exterior: Granite, metal, glass
Interior: Granite, metal, glass
G.S.F.: 1.36 million
No. of floors: 51

PARK CENTRE
Hotel and Office Complex
Calgary, Alberta, Canada
1982

Partner in charge: A. Eugene Kohn
Partner in charge, design: Arthur May
Senior designer: Geraldine Pontius
Project planner: Mark Strauss
Associate Architect: The Chandler Kennedy Architectural Group, Calgary, Canada
Client: Cadillac Fairview Corporation, Ltd.

Structure: Steel
Exterior: Granite, reflective glass
Interior: Granite, travertine
G.S.F.: 2.5 million
No. of floors: Hotel: 15
Offices: 55

BANK OF THE SOUTHWEST, COMPETITION
Office Building
Houston, Texas
1982

Partner in charge: A. Eugene Kohn
Partner in charge, design: William Pedersen
Senior designer: Sudhir Jambhekar
Client: Century Development Corporation

Structure: Composite tube
Exterior: Granite, tinted glass, white-painted steel
Interior: Finished in various stones
G.S.F.: 2.0 million
No. of floors: 94

GENERAL RE HEADQUARTERS, SCHEME II
Office Building
Stamford, Connecticut
1982/85

Partner in charge: Sheldon Fox
Partner in charge, design: William Louie
Senior designer: Chao-Ming Wu
Project manager: Creighton Jones
Job Captain: Deborah Booher
Client: General Re Corporation

Structure: Parking levels: Cast-in-place and "filigree" concrete
Upper levels: steel frame
Exterior: Granite, reflective glass, aluminum frames
Interior: Marble, granite, mahogany
G.S.F.: 1.17 million
No. of floors: 6

THE PROCTOR & GAMBLE GENERAL OFFICES COMPLEX
Cincinnati, Ohio
1982/85

Partner in charge: A. Eugene Kohn
Partner in charge, design: William Pedersen
Partner in charge, planning: Patricia Conway
Partner in charge, mgt.: Robert Cioppa
Senior designer: Alexander Ward
Project manager: Lee Polisano, Timothy Hartley
Job Captain: Benedict Curatolo
Designer of Public Spaces: Craig Nealy
Client: Procter & Gamble

Structure: Concrete pan joist and frame system
Exterior: Granite, limestone, marble, double-glazed and reflective glass, aluminum frames, stainless steel
Interior: Marble, granite, travertine, terrazzo, stainless-steel, trim, mahogany
G.S.F.: 823,000
No. of floors: 17

Project/Date		Project Team	Building Information

UNIVERSITY PERFORMING ARTS CENTER
Bucknell University
Lewisburg, Pennsylvania
1982

Partner in charge: A. Eugene Kohn
Partner in charge, design: William Pedersen
Senior designer: David Leventhal
Project manager: William Schweber
Job Captain: Charles Alexander
Client: Bucknell University

Structure: Steel frame
Exterior: Brick, limestone
G.S.F.: Scheme A: 63,000
Scheme B: 43,000
No. of floors: 2

GROUPE BOUYGUES CORPORATE HEADQUARTERS, COMPETITION
St. Quentin-en-Yvelines, France
1982

Partner in charge: A. Eugene Kohn
Partner in charge, design: William Pedersen
Senior designer: Gary Handel, Chao-Ming Wu
Client: Groupe Bouygues

Structure: Precast concrete
Exterior: Precast concrete, granite, tinted glass
Interior: Granite, marble, precast concrete
G.S.F.: 700,000
No. of floors: 5

---

75 FEDERAL STREET
Office Building
Boston, Massachusetts
1982

Partner in charge: A. Eugene Kohn
Partner in charge, design: William Pedersen
Senior designer: Sudhir Jambhekar
Client: Miller-Klutznick-Davis-Gray

Structure: Steel tube
Exterior: Granite, limestone, tinted glass
G.S.F.: 1.2 million
No. of floors: 41

SINGAPORE URBAN REDEVELOPMENT LAND PARCEL 8, COMPETITION
Office Building, Stock Exchange
Singapore
1982

Partner in charge: A. Eugene Kohn
Partner in charge, design: William Louie
Senior designer: Shin Onishi
Client: Pontiac Lands, Limited

Structure: Concrete frame
Exterior: Granite, marble, aluminum, tinted glass
Interior: Marble, granite
G.S.F.: 440,000
No. of floors: Office: 28
Stock exchange: 5

---

36 WEST 66TH STREET
Residential Tower; Feasibility Study
New York, New York
1982

Partner in charge: A. Eugene Kohn
Partner in charge, design: Arthur May
Senior designer: Richard Clarke
Project planner: Mark Strauss
Client: Reliance Development Co.

Structure: Steel
Exterior: Brick, limestone
G.S.F.: 146,000
No. of floors: 38

ABC STUDIO 23/24
New York, New York
1982/84

Partner in charge: Sheldon Fox
Associate Partner in charge, design: Robert Evans
Senior designer: Paul Pichardo
Project manager: Jan Gleysteen
Job Captain: Walter Chabla
Client: ABC

Structure: Steel, concrete
Exterior: Brick, metal panels, louvers, glass block, painted steel
Interior: Quarry tile, wood, aluminum trim
G.S.F.: 135,000
No. of floors: 7

Project/Date		Project Team	Building Information

THIRD NATIONAL BANK
Nashville, Tennessee
1982/85

Partner in charge: A. Eugene Kohn
Partner in charge, design: Arthur May
Senior designer: Dean Chavooshian
Project manager: Demetrios Pantazis
Client: Third National Bank
The Murphree Company
The Equitable Life Assurance Society of the United States

Structure: Steel, concrete
Exterior: Granite, architectural concrete, marble, copper, brick
Interior: Granite, marble
G.S.F.: 600,000
No. of floors: 31

---

900 NORTH MICHIGAN AVENUE
Mixed-Use Building
Chicago, Illinois
1983/88

Partner in charge: A. Eugene Kohn
Partner in charge, design: William Pedersen
Senior designer: Sudhir Jambhekar
Associate Architect: Perkins & Will, Chicago, Illinois
Client: Urban Investment & Development Co.

Structure: Lower floors: reinforced concrete
Hotel and residential floors: steel
Exterior: Limestone with granite accent
Interior: Retail mall: marble/terrazzo, painted wall surface with stainless-steel trim
Office lobby: granite and marble
G.S.F.: 2.1 million
No. of floors: 66

---

125 EAST 57TH STREET
Mixed-Use Office and Retail
New York, New York
1983/86

Partner in charge: A. Eugene Kohn
Partner in charge, design: William Pedersen
Senior designer: Gary Handel
Job Captain: Laurie Stavrand
Client: Madison Equities

Structure: Structural steel
Exterior: Granite, reflective glass
Interior: Marble, granite, bronze, stainless steel
G.S.F.: 424,000
No. of floors: 31

PENN'S LANDING
Mixed-Use Complex
Philadelphia, Pennsylvania
1983

Partner in charge: A. Eugene Kohn
Partner in charge, design: Arthur May
Client: The Reliance Group

Exterior: Brick, granite
G.S.F.: 1,004,600
No. of floors: 24

---

600 WHITE PLAINS ROAD
Office Building
Tarrytown, New York
1983

Partner in charge: Sheldon Fox
Partner in charge, design: Arthur May
Senior designer: Jerri Smith
Project manager: Demetrios Pantazis
Client: Peter Sharp & Company

Exterior: Granite, glass
G.S.F.: 340,000
No. of floors: 6

ARBOR CIRCLE
Office Building
Parsippany, New Jersey
1983/86

Partner in charge: A. Eugene Kohn
Partner in charge, design: William Louie
Senior designer: Robert Busler, Christopher Keeney
Project manager: Gary Stluka
Job Captain: Robert Busler
Client: Prudential Insurance Company of America

Structure: Steel frame
Exterior: Reflective glass, aluminum mullions, precast concrete
Interior: Terrazzo, marble, glass block
G.S.F.: 790,000
No. of floors: 4

Project/Date		Project Team	Building Information

COURT HOUSE PLAZA, COMPETITION
Mixed-Use Complex
Arlington, Virginia
1984/87

Partner in charge: A. Eugene Kohn
Partner in charge, design: Arthur May
Senior designer: Richard Clarke
Project planner: Mark Strauss
Associate Architect: C.H.K. Associates, Silver Spring, Maryland
Client: The Charles Smith Company, The Artery Organization

Structure: Concrete
Exterior: Precast concrete, brick, limestone, glass
Interior: Marble, granite
G.S.F.: 1.8 million
No. of floors: 4–23

NATIONAL BANK OF COMMERCE
Office Building
San Antonio, Texas
1984

Partner in charge: A. Eugene Kohn
Partner in charge, design: Arthur May
Senior designer: Dean Chavooshian
Project planner: Mark Strauss
Client: The Murphree Company

Exterior: Precast concrete, limestone, granite
G.S.F.: 580,000
No. of floors: 32

CNG TOWER
Corporate Office Complex
Pittsburgh, Pennsylvania
1984/87

Partner in charge: A. Eugene Kohn
Partner in charge, design: William Pedersen
Senior designer: Robert Evans
Project planner: Mark Strauss
Project manager: Creighton Jones
Job Captain: Paul Deibert
Client: Lincoln Property Co.

Structure: Steel, concrete
Exterior: Granite, reflective glass, aluminum, stainless-steel trim
Interior: Marble, stainless steel
G.S.F.: 700,000
No. of floors: 32

ONE O'HARE CENTER
Office Building
Rosemont, Illinois
1984/86

Partner in charge: A. Eugene Kohn
Partner in charge, design: William Louie
Senior designer: Thomas Navin
Project manager: Jan Gleysteen
Job Captain: Eileen Weingarten
Client: One O'Hare Center Limited Partnership

Structure: Steel frame
Exterior: Reflective glass, aluminum frames, stainless-steel trim and decoration, granite, marble
Interior: Marble, granite, mahogany, stainless-steel and bronze trim
G.S.F.: 380,000
No. of floors: 12

ABC PHASE II
Office, Studio Building
New York, New York
1984/86

Partner in charge: Sheldon Fox
Partner in charge, design: Arthur May
Senior designer: Judith Di Maio
Project manager: Miron Sigal
Job Captain: James Outen
Client: ABC

Structure: Steel
Exterior: Brick, granite, reflective glass
Interior: Aluminum, marble
G.S.F.: 250,000
No. of floors: 14

1000 WILSHIRE BOULEVARD
Office Building
Los Angeles, California
1984/86

Partner in charge: A. Eugene Kohn
Partner in charge, design: Arthur May
Senior designer: John Lucas
Project manager: Michael Kostow
Associate Architect: Langdon, Wilson, Mumper Architects Los Angeles, California
Client: The Reliance Development Group

Structure: Steel frame
Exterior: Granite, tinted and reflective glass
Interior: Marble, granite
G.S.F.: 490,000
No. of floors: 21

Project/Date		Project Team	Building Information
180 EAST 70TH STREET Residential Building New York, New York 1984/86		*Partner in charge:* A. Eugene Kohn *Partner in charge, design:* Arthur May *Senior designer:* Jody Sayler *Project manager:* Gary Stluka *Job Captain:* Russell Patterson *Client:* Trafalgar House Real Estate, Inc.	*Structure:* Concrete flat slub *Exterior:* Granite, limestone, brick, marble, copper *Interior:* Mahogany, marble, bronze *G.S.F.:* 166,000 *No. of floors:* 31
MELLON BANK CENTER Office Building Philadelphia, Pennsylvania 1984/86		*Partner in charge:* A. Eugene Kohn *Partner in charge, design:* William Louie *Senior designer:* Peter Schubert *Project manager:* Myron Sigal *Client:* Richart I. Rubin/Equitable Life Assurance Society of the United States	*Structure:* Steel frame *Exterior:* Granite, marble, reflective glass, aluminum frames, stainless-steel trim *Interior:* Marble, granite, stainless steel, bronze trim *G.S.F.:* 1.29 million *No. of floors:* 56
383 MADISON AVENUE Office Building New York, New York 1984/89		*Partner in charge:* A. Eugene Kohn *Partner in charge, design:* William Pedersen *Partner in charge, mgt.:* Robert Cioppa *Senior designers:* Judith Di Maio, Robert Henry *Job Captain:* Bun-Wah Nip *Client:* First Boston Realty and Development Corporation	*Structure:* Steel frame *Exterior:* Granite, glass *Interior:* Marble, granite *G.S.F.:* 1.6 million *No. of floors:* 71
1111 BRICKELL PLAZA Office Building Miami, Florida 1984/89		*Partner in charge:* A. Eugne Kohn *Partner in charge, design:* William Louie *Senior designer:* Chao-Ming Wu *Project manager:* Lee Polisano *Client:* Realco International and W. R. Associates	*Structure:* Cast-in-place concrete core, steel frame *Exterior:* Sandstone, marble, granite, terra-cotta trim, reflective glass, aluminum frames *Interior:* Marble, terrazzo, sandstone, granite, stainless steel, bronze trim *G.S.F.:* 1.45 million *No. of floors:* 31
TWO LOGAN SQUARE Office Building Philadelphia, Pennsylvania 1984/87		*Partner in charge:* A. Eugene Kohn *Partner in charger, design:* Arthur May *Senior designer:* Dean Chavooshian *Project manager:* Myron Sigal *Job Captain:* Paul Pichardo *Client:* Urban Investment Development Association/Two Logan Square Associates	*Structure:* Steel frame *Exterior:* Granite, reflective glass *Interior:* Marble *G.S.F.:* 765,000 *No. of floors:* 35
HYATT REGENCY Greenwich, Connecticut 1984/86		*Partner in charge:* Sheldon Fox *Partner in charge, design:* Arthur May *Senior designer:* Geraldine Pontius *Project planner:* Geraldine Pontius *Project manager:* Charles Alexander *Job Captain:* Michael Greene *Client:* Hyatt Development Corporation	*Structure:* Steel, concrete *Exterior:* Precast concrete, brick, copper, wood *Interior:* Steel, glass, precast concrete, marble *G.S.F.:* 312,000 *No. of floors:* 4

Project/Date		Project Team	Building Information
HESS CENTER Office Building; Feasibility Study Secaucus, New Jersey 1984		*Partner in charge:* A. Eugene Kohn *Partner in charge, design:* Arthur May *Senior designer:* Jerri Smith *Project planner:* Mark Strauss *Client:* Amerada Hess Corporation	*Exterior:* Granite, tinted and reflective glass, precut *Interior:* Marble, granite *G.S.F.:* 830,000 *No. of floors:* 25
GARRISON CHANNEL PLACE Mixed-Use Redevelopment Tampa, Florida 1984/88		*Partner in charge:* A. Eugene Kohn *Partner in charge, design:* William Louie *Senior designer:* Paul Gates *Project planner:* Mark Strauss *Project manager:* Gary Stluka *Client:* Major Realty/Prudential Insurance Co.	*Structure:* Cast-in-place concrete core, steel frame *Exterior:* Sandstone, granite, marble, terra-cotta and stainless-steel trim, concrete, reflective glass, aluminum frames *Interior:* Terrazzo, marble, sandstone, terra-cotta and stainless-steel trim *G.S.F.:* 6.93 million *No. of floors:* 34
POST OFFICE, COMPETITION New York, New York 1984		*Partner in charge:* Arthur May	*G.S.F.:* 922, 500 *No. of floors:* 28
LINCOLN CENTER, COMPETITION New York, New York 1984		*Partner in charge:* Arthur May	*G.S.F.:* 650,000 *No. of floors:* 41
NEW YORK TRADE MART New York, New York 1984/89		*Partner in charge:* A. Eugene Kohn *Partner in charge, design:* William Pedersen *Partner in charge, mgt.:* Robert Cioppa *Senior designer:* Alexander Ward *Project manager:* Gary Stluka *Client:* Trammell Crow Company/Tishman Speyer Properties/The Equitable Life Assurance Society of the United States	*Exterior:* Granite, limestone, terra-cotta, terne-coat stainless steel *G.S.F.:* 2.4 million *No. of floors:* 20
PRUDENTIAL-HILTON TOWER Office Building New York, New York 1984/88		*Partner in charge:* A. Eugene Kohn *Partner in charge, design:* William Louie *Senior designer:* Michael Gabellini *Project manager:* Lee Polisano *Job Captain:* Greg Waugh *Client:* The Prudential Insurance Company/The Hilton Hotel Corporation	*Structure:* Steel frame *Exterior:* Reflective glass, aluminum frames, granite, marble, stainless steel *Interior:* Granite, marble, stainless-steel and bronze trim, mahogany, ebony *G.S.F.:* 750,000 *No. of floors:* 34

Project/Date		Project Team	Building Information
101 FEDERAL STREET Office Building Boston, Massachusetts 1984/87		*Partner in charge:* Sheldon Fox *Partner in charge, design:* William Pedersen *Senior designer:* Craig Nealy/ Christopher Keeny *Project manager:* Gregory Clement *Job Captain:* Anna Pieczara-Blanchfield *Client:* Franklin Federal Partners/ Himmel/MKDG/H. N. Gohn Associates, Inc.	*Structure:* Post-tensioned concrete to 11th floor, steel above *Exterior:* Limestone, granite, marble, reflective glass *Interior:* Marble, terrazzo *G.S.F.:* 680,000 *No. of floors:* 31
70 EAST 55TH STREET Office Building New York, New York 1984/86		*Partner in charge:* A. Eugene Kohn *Partner in charge, design:* William Pedersen *Senior designer:* David Leventhal *Project manager:* Myron Sigal *Job Captain:* Bun-Wah Nip *Client:* Heron International Limited/Fidelity Service Corporation/Stategem Realty	*Structure:* Concrete *Exterior:* Granite, brick, metal, tinted glass *Interior:* Marble, stainless steel *G.S.F.:* 139,000 *No. of floors:* 26
LINCOLN PROPERTIES CULTURAL DISTRICT Mixed-Use Complex Dallas, Texas 1984/87		*Partner in charge:* A. Eugene Kohn *Partner in charge, design:* William Pedersen *Partner in charge, mgt.:* Robert Cioppa *Senior designer:* Gary Handel *Project planner:* Craig Nealy *Job Captain:* Walter Chabla *Associate Architect:* Harwood K. Smith, Dallas, Texas *Client:* Lincoln Properties Company Service Corporation/ Stategem Realty	*Structure:* Cast-in-place concrete *Exterior:* Granite, reflective glass *Interior:* Granite, marble, bronze, stainless steel *G.S.F.:* 4.2 million *No. of floors:* 50
AMERICAN FLETCHER NATIONAL BANK Office Building Indianapolis, Indiana 1984		*Partner in charge:* A. Eugene Kohn *Partner in charge, design:* Arthur May *Senior designer:* John Lucas *Project planner:* Mark Strauss *Client:* Lincoln Properties American Fletcher National Bank	*Structure:* Concrete *Exterior:* Limestone, granite, glass *G.S.F.:* 800,000 *No. of floors:* 51
LINCOLN CENTER MINNEAPOLIS Office Building Minneapolis, Minnesota 1984/87		*Partner in charge:* A. Eugene Kohn *Partner in charge, design:* William Pedersen *Partner in charge, mgt.:* Robert Cioppa *Senior designer:* Richard Del Monte *Project manager:* Robert Barbach *Job Captain:* Dow Jarrett *Client:* Lincoln Properties	*Structure:* Reinforced concrete *Exterior:* Granite, concrete, marble, reflective glass *Interior:* Granite, marble, stainless steel *G.S.F.:* 1.5 million *No. of floors:* 31
STANFORD UNIVERSITY GRADUATE SCHOOL OF BUSINESS EXPANSION Palo Alto, California 1984/87		*Partner in charge:* A. Eugene Kohn *Partner in charge, design:* William Pedersen *Partner in charge, mgt.:* Robert Cioppa *Senior designer:* Megan Walker *Project manager:* William Schweber *Associate Architect:* Stone Marraccini Patterson, San Francisco, California *Client:* Stanford University Graduate School of Business	*Structure:* Steel *Exterior:* Kasota stone *Interior:* Drywall *G.S.F.:* 64,000 *No. of floors:* 3

Project/Date		*Project Team*	*Building Information*

500 E STREET S.W.
Office Building
Washington, D. C.
1984/87

Partner in charge: A. Eugene Kohn
Associate Partner in charge, design: Robert Evans
Senior designer: Jerri Smith
Project manager: Demetrios Pantazis
Job Captain: Martin Kapell
Client: School Street Associates, Boston Properties, and First City Properties

Structure: Reinforced concrete
Exterior: Granite, precast concrete, reflective glass, aluminum frame, metal panels
Interior: Stone, wood
G.S.F.: 384,000
No. of floors: 9

ATLANTA PALLADIUM
Mixed-Use Complex
Atlanta, Georgia
1985/87

Partner in charge: A. Eugene Kohn
Partner in charge, design: Arthur May
Senior designer: Jann Wolfe
Associate Architect: Smallwood, Reynolds, Stewart, Stewart & Associates, Inc., Atlanta, Georgia
Client: Metro Development Corporation

Structure: Concrete
Exterior: Precast concrete, marble, tinted and reflective glass
Interior: Marble, wood columns, panels, plaster ceiling
G.S.F.: 1.6 million
No. of floors: 18

---

712 FIFTH AVENUE
Mixed-Use Tower
New York, New York
1985/87

Partner in charge: A. Eugene Kohn
Partner in charge, design: William Pedersen
Senior designer: David Diamond
Project manager: Glenn Garrison
Job Captain: Deborah Booher
Client: Steadsol Fifth Associates

Structure: Concrete
Exterior: Limestone, marble, bronze
Interior: Marble, decorative metal, bronze
G.S.F.: 490,000
No. of floors: 51

GATEWAY CENTER
Feasibility Study
Boston, Massachusetts
1985

Partner in charge: A. Eugene Kohn
Partner in charge, design: William Pedersen
Senior designer: Craig Nealy
Project planner: Mark Strauss
Associate Architect: Helmuth, Obata & Kassabaum, Inc., Kansas City, Missouri
Client: H. N. Gorin Associates, Inc.

Structure: Steel
Exterior: Reflective glass, brick, limestone
Interior: Granite, stainless steel, glass
G.S.F.: 5.0 million
No. of floors: 48

COLISEUM SITE, COMPETITION
New York, New York
1985

Partner in charge: Arthur May

G.S.F.: 2.8 million
No. of floors: 80 (twin tower)

---

300 EAST 64TH STREET
Residential Building
New York, New York
1985/87

Partner in charge: A. Eugene Kohn
Partner in charge, design: Arthur May
Senior designer: Robert Busler
Project manager: Gary Stluka
Client: Trafalgar House Real Estate, Inc.

Structure: Concrete
Exterior: Granite, limestone, brick
Interior: Wood, marble
G.S.F.: 61,000
No. of floors: 24

Project/Date		Project Team	Building Information
BLOCK FIVE Office Building Seattle, Washington 1985/88		*Partner in charge:* Robert Cioppa *Partner in charge, design:* William Pedersen *Senior designer:* Sudhir Jambhekar *Job Captain:* Susan Davis-McCarter *Associate Architect:* The McKinley Architects P.C., Seattle, Washington *Client:* Wright Runstud & Company	*Structure:* Steel *Exterior:* Limestone, granite, reflective-glass curtain wall *Interior:* Finished in various stones, woodwork *G.S.F.:* 1.5 million *No. of floors:* 55
SHEARSON LEHMAN BROTHERS PLAZA Office Building New York, New York 1985/88		*Partner in charge:* Robert Cioppa *Partner in charge, design:* William Louie *Senior designer:* Thomas Navin *Project manager:* Gary Stluka *Client:* Shearson Lehman Brothers, Inc.	*Structure:* Steel frame *Exterior:* Granite, marble, nonreflective glass in granite walls, reflective glass, aluminum frames *Interior:* Terrazzo, marble, granite, stainless-steel and bronze trim *G.S.F.:* 1.6 million *No. of floors:* 38
125 SUMMER STREET Office Building Boston, Massachusetts 1985/88		*Partner in charge:* Sheldon Fox *Partner in charge, design:* Arthur May *Senior designer:* John Lucas *Project manager:* Glenn Garrison *Client:* Perry/Jaymont Venture	*Structure:* Concrete *Exterior:* Granite, glass *G.S.F.:* 1.0 million *No. of floors:* 45
FIDELITY BUILDING Corporate Headquarters Boston, Massachusetts 1985		*Partner in charge:* A. Eugene Kohn *Partner in charge, design:* William Pedersen *Partner in charge, mgt.:* Robert Cioppa *Senior designer:* David Leventhal *Client:* Fidelity Investments	*Structure:* Low rise: concrete Tower: steel frame *G.S.F.:* 900,000 *No. of floors:* 43
225 WEST WACKER DRIVE Office Building Chicago, Illinois 1985		*Partner in charge:* A. Eugene Kohn *Partner in charge, design:* William Pedersen *Senior designer:* Gary Handel *Client:* The Palmer Group, Ltd., Developers	*Structure:* Concrete *Exterior:* Granite, low-reflective glass *Interior:* Granite, marble *G.S.F.:* 700,000 *No. of floors:* 27
TAYLOR-WOODROW PROJECT Office Building and Hotel; Feasibility Study San Francisco, California 1985		*Partner in charge:* A. Eugene Kohn *Partner in charge, design:* William Pedersen *Senior designer:* John Lucas *Project planner:* Mark Strauss *Associate Architect:* Tower Architects, San Francisco, California *Client:* Taylor-Woodrow of California	*Structure:* Concrete *Exterior:* Limestone, granite, reflective glass *G.S.F.:* Office: 300,000 Hotel: 250,000 *No. of floors:* Office: 26 Hotel: 35

Project/Date		Project Team	Building Information

SOUTH FERRY, COMPETITION
Office Building, Ferry Terminal, Public Library
New York, New York
1985

Partner in charge: A. Eugene Kohn
Partner in charge, design: William Pedersen
Senior designer: Paul King
Associate Architect: Cooper, Eckstut Associates, New York, New York
Client: South Ferry Associates/ Continental Development Group, Inc.

Structure: Steel, perimeter tube, concrete caissons
Exterior: Granite, glass, metal trim
Interior: Marble, decorative metal, glass
G.S.F.: 1.5 million
No. of floors: 51

PARIS FRONT DE SEINE
Office Tower
Paris, France
1985

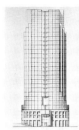

Partner in charge: A. Eugene Kohn
Partner in charge, design: William Louie
Senior designer: Chao-Ming Wu
Client: Norbert Phal S.A.

Structure: Steel frame
Exterior: Low-reflective glass, aluminum panels, limestone, travertine
Interior: Granite, French limestone, stainless steel
G.S.F.: 350,000
No. of floors: 27

CARLSON CENTER, MASTER PLAN
Mixed-Use Complex
Minneapolis, Minnesota
1985

Partner in charge: A. Eugene Kohn
Partner in charge, design: William Louie
Senior designer: Chao-Ming Wu
Client: Carlson Companies, Inc.

G.S.F.: 1.4 million
No. of floors: 3–7

SUFFOLK COUNTY COURTHOUSE, COMPETITION
Islip, New York
1985

Partner in charge: A. Eugene Kohn
Partner in charge, design: Arthur May
Partner in charge, mgt.: Robert Cioppa
Senior designer: Paul Katz
Client: Suffolk County

Structure: Concrete, steel frame
Exterior: Brick, limestone, granite
Interior: Terrazzo, marble, wood, bronze, stainless steel
G.S.F.: 823,000
No. of floors: 12

UNITED STATES EMBASSY
Nicosia, Cyprus
1986/1988

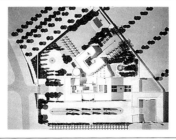

Partner in charge: A. Eugene Kohn
Partner in charge, design: William Pedersen
Senior designer: Paul King
Project manager: Lee Polisano
Client: U.S. Dept. of State, Office of Foreign Buildings Operations

G.S.F.: 75,000
No. of floors: 1–3

CANARY WHARF TOWER
London, England
1986/1993

Partner-in-charge: A. Eugene Kohn
Partner-in-charge, design: William Pedersen
Partner-in-charge, management: Robert Cioppa
Senior designer: Craig Nealy
Client: The Canary Wharf Development Co. Ltd.

Structure: Composite stell and concrete frame system.
Exterior: Brushed metal mullion with tinted system with tinted vision glass and metal-and-stone infill panels.
G.S.F.: 2,600,000 gsf.
Number of floors: 47.

A. Eugene Kohn was born in Philadelphia, Pennsylvania, in 1930. He received a Bachelor of Architecture degree in 1953 and a Master of Architecture degree in 1957, both from the University of Pennsylvania, where he was a Theopolis Parson Chandler graduate fellow. Mr. Kohn is a former lieutenant commander of the United States Navy.

Prior to forming Kohn Pedersen Fox Associates PC, Mr. Kohn was president and partner of John Carl Warnecke and Associates (1967–76); design director of Welton Becket Associates New York (1965–67); and senior designer for Vincent G. Kling Associates in Philadelphia, Pennsylvania (1960–65), where his work received two American Institute of Architects National Honors awards.

Mr. Kohn has been practicing architecture for thirty years, is registered in twenty-eight states, and is a member of the NCARB. He is a Fellow of the American Institute of Architects, the Royal Institute of British Architects, a member of the New York Building Congress, the Urban Land Institute, and the Municipal Art Society of New York. He also serves on the Boards of Directors of the Architectural League of New York and the Chicago City Ballet. He is on the Board of Overseers of the University of Pennsylvania's Graduate School of Fine Arts, and the Advisory Boards of the Wharton Real Estate Center and for the Master of Science Degree in Real Estate Development at the Columbia University's Graduate School of Architecture and Planning.

Mr. Kohn has lectured widely and has served on numerous design-award juries. He has served as a member of the Architectural Record Round Table and has been visiting critic at both the University of Pennsylvania (1984) and the University of California–Los Angeles (1983). He has had several articles published, including "Energy-related Growth," which appeared in *Urban Design* magazine.

William Pedersen was born in St. Paul, Minnesota, in 1938. He received a Bachelor of Architecture degree from the University of Minnesota in 1961 and was a recipient of the school's Gargoyle Club Prize. In 1963, he received a Master of Architecture degree from the Massachusetts Institute of Technology, where in 1963 he was a Whitney Fellow. In 1965, he won the Rome Prize in Architecture and studied for two years at the American Academy of Rome.

Prior to joining in the formation of Kohn Pedersen Fox, Mr. Pedersen was vice-president of John Carl Warnecke and Associates (1971–76); an associate with I. M. Pei and Partners (1967–71); and a designer with Eduardo Catalano (1964–65) and Pietro Belluschi (1963).

In 1982, *Newsweek* magazine ("The New American High Rise," 8 November 1982) recognized Mr. Pedersen as a major influence in the evolution of the tall office building in America today. Mr. Pedersen has had several articles published, including "Considerations for Urban Architecture and the Tall Building," in *Southwest Center: The Houston Competition* (Rizzoli International, 1983) and "Architecture and Praxis: A Self-Analysis of the Essential Criteria for the Urban Skyscraper," in *The New Art Examiner* (June, 1983, Vol. 10). He has also been interviewed for *American Architecture Now II* (Rizzoli International, 1985).

Mr. Pedersen frequently lectures and serves on academic and professional juries and symposia. He has held the Eero Saarinen Chair at Yale University (1986), and has also been a visiting critic at Harvard University (1984), Columbia University (1983), and the Rhode Island School of Design (1982). Mr. Pedersen is a member of the American Institute of Architects, the Architectural League, the New York State Association of Architects, the Society of Architectural Historians, and he is a Fellow of the American Academy in Rome. Mr. Pedersen has received numerous A.I.A. design awards, including the 1984 A.I.A. National Honor Award for 333 Wacker Drive, Chicago, Illinois. His most recent honor, which he shares with partner Arthur May, is the 1985 Arnold W. Brunner Memorial Prize in Architecture, awarded by the American Academy and the Institute of Arts and Letters.

Sheldon Fox was born in New York City in 1930. He received a Bachelor of Architecture degree in 1953 from the University of Pennsylvania where he graduated with honors, and from 1953 to 1955 he served as a first lieutenant in the the United States Army.

Mr. Fox has been practicing architecture for thirty years and is registered in twelve states. He is an active member of the New York Building Congress, for which he has served as director, the American Institute of Architects, and the Architectural League of New York. Mr. Fox is active in civic affairs and has served as chairman of the Design Review board in Stamford, Conn. and as a director of the Lighthouse Business Council. Mr. Fox has lectured on architectural management and serves on the A.I.A. Practice Management Committee and Large Firm Roundtable.

Prior to joining in the formation of Kohn Pedersen Fox, Mr. Fox was senior vice-president of John Carl Warnecke and Associates (1972–76) and a partner in Kahn and Jacobs, Architects (1955–72).

Patricia Conway was born in Reading, Pennsylvania, in 1937. She received a Bachelor of Arts degree in English literature from New York University Washington Square College in 1959 and, in 1964, a Master of Arts in English literature from the New York University Graduate School of Arts and Science, where she was a Lenley Scholar. Ms. Conway began her career as a design journalist and critic. She was an associate editor of *Industrial Design Magazine* (1964–66) and a free-lance writer (1966–72) for the *Washington Post Potomac Magazine, Design Quarterly, The Washingtonian, Design and Environment, Nation's Cities,* and *Print.* Ms. Conway coauthored *Ornamentalism: The New Decorativeness in Architecture and Design* (Clarkson N. Potter, 1982), an American Book Award recipient. Ms. Conway lectures frequently in the United States and England and has curated several major design exhibitions.

In 1972, Ms. Conway received a Master of Science degree in Urban Planning from the Columbia University School of Architecture, where she was a Mellon Scholar and a William Kinne Fellows Traveling Fellow. She is currently a Loeb Fellow at Harvard University.

Prior to joining in the formation of Kohn Pedersen Fox, she was associate director of planning for John Carl Warnecke and Associates (1972–76). Ms. Conway is also president of the firm's interiors division, Kohn Pedersen Fox Conway Associates, Inc.

Arthur May was born in New York City in 1940. He received a Bachelor of Architecture degree in 1963 from Rensselaer Polytechnic Institute and, in 1964, a Master of Architecture degree from the University of Pennsylvania, where he studied under Louis Kahn. He received the Rickets Prize for Scholastic Achievement and the Thesis Prize in 1963. In 1975, Mr. May won the Rome Prize in Architecture and is a Fellow of the American Academy in Rome.

Prior to joining Kohn Pedersen Fox Associates, Mr. May was a vice-president with John Carl Warnecke and Associates (1972–75) and worked with I. M. Pei and Partners (1964–69).

Mr. May has been a visiting professor at the University of Pennsylvania (1984) and at the University of California, Los Angeles (1983). He is a member of the American Institute of Architects, the NCARB, and the New York State Association of Architects.

Mr. May has won several design awards. With his partner, William Pedersen, Mr. May was awarded the 1985 Arnold W. Brunner Memorial Prize in Architecture by the American Academy and the Institute of Arts and Letters. In 1984, he received the New York Chapter of the American Institute of Architects Distinguished Architecture Award for the Hercules building. The Hercules atrium won an award in 1984 from *Architecture Magazine* and, in 1967, Mr. May was the recipient of a *Progressive Architecture* design award.

William C. Louie was born in New York City in 1942.
Mr. Louie began working as an architect in 1961, and he
received a Bachelor of Science in Architecture degree
from City College of New York in 1974. Prior to joining
Kohn Pedersen Fox, Mr. Louie was senior associate with
John Carl Warnecke and Associates (1969–77). Mr. Louie
is a member of the American Institute of Architects and
the New York State Association of Architects. Mr. Louie's
awards include the 1984 PCI Award for Goldome Bank
for Savings Headquarters; 1986 PCI Award for Arbor
Circle; and the 1986 NYS AIA Merit Award for General
Re Corporate Headquarters.

Robert L. Cioppa was born in Mount Vernon, New York,
in 1942. Mr. Cioppa was a liberal arts honors student at
Boston College before receiving his Bachelor of
Architecture degree from Pratt Institute in 1967. In
1983, Mr. Cioppa graduated from the Stanford
University Graduate School of Business Executive
Program. Prior to joining Kohn Pedersen Fox in 1977,
Mr. Cioppa was an associate with John Carl Warnecke
and Associates. In 1967, Mr. Cioppa was the recipient of
the New York Society of Architects Alpha Ro Chi Medal.

KOHN PEDERSEN FOX CONWAY PARTNERS

Randolph H. Gerner, A.I.A.
Bachelor of Architecture, The City College of New York, 1975
Master of Architecture, Honors, University of Pennsylvania, 1979

Judy Swanson
Bachelor of Arts, Stetson University, 1966
Bachelor of Fine Arts, Interior Design, Pratt Institute, 1969

Miguel Valcarcel, A.I.A.
Bachelor of Science in Architecture, Cum Laude, The City College of the University of New York, 1976
Bachelor of Architecture, The City College of the University of New York, 1977

KOHN PEDERSEN FOX
ASSOCIATE PARTNERS

J. Dean Chavooshian, A.I.A.
Bachelor of Arts in Theology, American University, 1972
Master of Architecture, Virginia Polytechnic Institute, 1977

Robert W. Evans, A.I.A.
Bachelor of Arts and Architecture, Rice University, 1971
Rome Prize in Architecture, 1972

Gary E. Handel, A.I.A.
Bachelor of Architecture, Cornell University College of Architecture, 1979
Progressive Architecture Design Award, 1982

Sudhir S. Jambhekar, A.I.A.
Bachelor of Architecture, University of Bombay, 1964
Master of Science, Architecture, and Urban Design, Columbia University School of Architecture, 1979

David M. Leventhal, A.I.A.
Bachelor of Arts, Harvard University, 1974
Master of Architecture, Harvard University Graduate School of Design, 1979

John M. Lucas, A.I.A.
Bachelor of Arts, Yale College, 1963
Master of Architecture, University of Pennsylvania, 1967

Lee A. Polisano, A.I.A.
Bachelor of Arts, LaSalle College, 1974
Master of Architecture, Virginia Polytechnic Institute, 1977

William I. Schweber, A.I.A.
Bachelor of Architecture, Massachusetts Institute of Technology, 1960

Myron S. Sigal, A.I.A.
Associate in Building Design and Construction, Pratt Institute, 1964

Gary Stluka, A.I.A.
Bachelor of Architecture, University of Illinois at Champaign-Urbana, 1973
Plym Travelling Fellow, 1981

Mark E. Strauss, A.I.A./A.P.A.
Bachelor of Architecture, Cornell University College of Architecture, 1976
Master of Urban Planning, The City College of New York, 1977

Alexander M. Ward, A.I.A.
Bachelor of Arts, Summa Cum Laude, Princeton University, 1975
Master of Architecture, Harvard University Graduate School of Design, 1979

Chao-Ming Wu, A.I.A.
Bachelor of Arts, Summa Cum Laude, Harvard University, 1976
Master of Architecture, Highest Honors, Harvard University Graduate School of Design, 1980

KOHN PEDERSEN FOX CONWAY
COLLABORATORS, 1976–1986

Judith A. Baginski
Rolando Campbell
Rodolfo Castillo
Charles A. Dodge
Miriana I. Doneva
Teri Figliuzzi
Robin Fritzsche
Nancy Funkhauser
Randolph H. Gerner
Steven R. Groves
Marsha D. Keskinen
Theodora Kosar
Richard N. Kronick
Amy Langer
Helene J. Lickdyke
Betty Liu
Anne L. Manning
Elizabeth K. Maruggio
Stephen M. Mihailos
Patricia Milgrim
Erica B. Millar
Margaret M. Neubauer
Ruxandra Panaitescu
Keith Frome Rosen
Paul J. Rosen
Seth H. Rosenthal
Ruby Schacker
Christine Sudduth
Diana Turner
Judy Lynn Swanson
Diane Turner
Miguel Valcarcel
Elizabeth C. Wheeler
Jarvis Wong
Andrea Zinn

KOHN PEDERSON FOX
COLLABORATORS, 1976–1986

Margaret Albanese
Howard Albert
Giancarlo Alhadeff
Charles Alexander
Dimitri Alexandrakis
Robert Allen
Hiroyuki Aoshima
Alan Aronoff
Traci Aranoff
Theresa Atkin
Steven Bach
Paval Balla
Vladimir Balla
Christopher Bardt
Robert Barbach
Maura Barbour
Anthony Barnaba
Elias Batinjaneh
Terry Bell
Ann Benz
David Bergmann
Alexander Bergo
Beth Bethen
Nathan Bibliowicz
Clarinda Bisceglia
Dvora Blay
Gale Blocker
Joan Blumenfeld
Gale Blocker
Deborah Booher
James Borchard
Roberta Boston-Ross
Robert Bostwick
Stephanie Bradie
Glenn Brode
Barry Bronfman
Bridget Brown
Stephen Buck
Gae Buckley
Jacob Buksbaum
Andrus Burr
Robert Busler
Stephen Byrns
James Cali
Delva Cameron
Judy Cammer
Carmine Cappadona
Walter Chabla
Benny Chan
Katherine Chappell
Peter Ching

Du Choi
Tae K. Choi
Tak-Tim Choi
Michael Chren
Richard Clarke
Gregory Clement
Yolanda Cole
Jeanne Constantin
Karen Cook
Dawn Couch
Rustom Cowasjee
Angela Crawford
Roger Crowley
John Crellin
Ben Curatolo
Elizabeth Daly
Beverly Davis
Susan Davis-McCarter
Karen Dauler
Kathryn Dean
Raul de Carvalho
Crane DeCamp
Paul Deibert
Annabel Delgado
Richard DelMonte
Anthony Desnick
Joseph Devlin
Mary DeVries
David Diamond
James Dicker
Judith DiMaio
Joseph DiMonda
Peter Dixon
Velma Dortch
Christopher Egan
Salima Farid
Jean Farrell
Curtiss Fentress
Kathleen Ferrara
Benjamin Firestine
Veronica Fischer
Kevin Flanagan
Michael Forstl
Alicia Foussats
Dania Francis
Arthur Freed
Barbara Friedman
John Michael Gabellini
Glenn Garrison
Paul Gates
Anthony Gelia

Leslie Grill
Jan Gleysteen
Laurence Goldberg
Frank Goode
Michael Gordon
Jan Gorlach
Alexander Gorlin
Genevieve Gormley
Michael Greene
Barbara Guarrera
Ernest Guenzburger
Gail Guevara
Charles Gustina
Armando Gutierrez
Jonathan Halper
Cleveland Harp
John Harris
Timothy Hartley
Susanne Hein
Anne Hendricks
Robert Henry
Horst Hermann
Natalie Hlavna
Angeline Ho
Julie Holm
Alison Holt
Thomas Holzmann
Monique Houston
David Howard
Herman Howard
Virginia Incremona
Margaret Jacobs
Raul Jara
Dow Jarrett
James Johnson
H. Creighton Jones
James Jorganson
Robert Kahn
James Kalsbeek
Michael Kao
Martin Kapell
David Kaplan
Angie Katselianos
Paul Katz
Marsha Kaufman
Cheryl Kaufmann
Christopher Keeny
Lucien Keldany
Sharon Kennedy
Celina Kersh
Laura Kesten

Geraldine Kierse
Heegom Kim
Myoung Kim
Paul King
Sulan Kolatan
Terry Kornblum
Arthur Korenstein
Michael Kostow
Kunio Kudo
Jeffery Kusmick
Joseph Kusnick
Gail La Cava
Robert Landsman
Janis Learner
Fred Lebart
Vincent Lee
Samuel Lewis
Gale Limansky
Frank Lombardo
Leslie Lu
Raymond McCaskill
Carrol McCutchen
Ann McDonald
William McGilvray
Kathryn McGraw
Michael Mallardi
Suzanne Martinson
Leon Meeks
Peter Menderson
Carlos Menendez
Hugh Mercer
Willis Messiah
Jose Monge
Gail Morrell
Jane Murphy
Paul Naecker
Saradendu Narayan
Thomas Navin
Craig Nealy
Lisa Negri
Elaine Newman
Jeffrey Ng
Bun-Wah Nip
Shin Ohnishi
Patrick O'Malley
James Outen
Christo Paitakis
William Palmore
Demetrios Pantazis
James Papoutsis
Aaron Parker

Judy Parker
Russell Patterson
Anthony Pellecchia
Robin Pendleton
Josephine Perpall
Gordon Peterson
Catherine Phal-Colavecchio
Paul Pichardo
Anna Pieczara
Josephine Piro
Andrew Pollack
Geraldine Pontius
Manuel Quijano
Toni Racana
Anne Reeve
Katherine Retelas
Rita Reynolds
Russell Riccardi
Charlene Richards
Ilona Rider
Donna Robertson
Marjorie Rodney
Victor Rodriguez
Harold Rolls
Kenneth Rose
Scott Rudenstein
John Sabolchak
Joel Sanders
Keiko Sasaki
Jody Sayler
August Schaefer
Charles Schmitt
Peter Schubert
Alan Schwabenland
Laura Schwartz
Alexander Seniuk
E. Enayat Seraj
Thomas Shafer
Audrey Shen
Andrea Simitch
Gillian Skeen
John Smart
Charles Smith
Dawn Smith
Jerri Smith
Warren Smith
Ann Soochet
Richard Sowinski
William Spade
Laurie Stavrand
Susan Steakin

Ilene Steingut
Sonia Strachan
Peter Tao
LuAnne Tepes
John Thomas
Mark Thometz
Charlotte Thomson
Anthony Tsirantonakis
Stephen Valentine
Andrew Vines
James von Klemperer
Megan Walker
Gregory Waugh
Jane Webster
Greta Weil
Eileen Weingarten
Elaine Wolfe
Jann Wolfe
Christopher Wynn
Vladislav Zacek
Leah Zennario
Fredric Zonsius

SELECTED BIBLIOGRAPHY

General

Anderson, Grace M. "Kohn Pedersen Fox: External Forces Shape Multiform Towers." *Architectural Record,* June 1981, pp. 81–91.

"Architecture as a Corporate Asset." *Business Week,* 4 October 1984.

Conway, Patricia. "The Corporation as Modern Medici." *Leaders Magazine,* April/May/June 1983, p. 136.

Conway, Patricia, and Jensen, Robert. *Ornamentalism.* Clarkson N. Potter, 1982.

Conway, Patricia, and Kohn, A. Eugene. "Energy-related Growth." *Urban Design,* Fall 1977, p. 25.

Dixon, John Morris. "Projects." *Progressive Architecture,* October 1983, pp. 84–91.

Futugawa, Yukio. "Kohn Pedersen Fox." *GA Document,* no. 12, January 1985, pp. 114–27.

Giovannini, Joseph. "High-rises That Recapture the Spirit of Skyscrapers." *Los Angeles Herald Examiner,* 1 March 1982, sec. B, pp. 1–2.

Goldberger, Paul. *The Skyscraper.* New York: Alfred A. Knopf, 1981.

———. "Romantic Modernism Is Now at the Cutting Edge of Design." *New York Times,* 8 July 1984, sec. 2, p. 23.

*———. "Achitecture That Pays Off Handsomely." *New York Times,* 16 March 1986, magazine section, p.48.

Guenther, Robert. "Architect Team Gains Fame for Design and Salesmanship." *Wall Street Journal,* 13 June 1984, p. 31.

Huxtable, Ada Louise. *The Tall Building Artistically Reconsidered: The Search for a Skyscraper Style.* New York: Pantheon Books, 1984.

Kohn, A. Eugene. "Architecture Interior and Industrial Design." *Leaders Magazine,* April/May/June 1983, p. 119.

"Due Opere di Kohn Pedersen Fox." *L'Industria della Costrutzioni,* March 1984, pp. 54–65.

"KPF Classical Controversial." *Progressive Architecture,* July 1985, p. 73.

"Magic in the Exterior Skin." *Space Design,* November 1984, pp. 31–49.

"Recent Works of Kohn Pedersen Fox." *Toshi-Jutaku,* March 1984, pp. 56–92.

"Tour de Bureaux—Immeuble de Bureaux." *L'Architecture d'Aujourd'hui,* October 1983, p. VII.

"Well-tailored Stone." *Architectural Record,* June 1985, pp. 162–69.

ABC Buildings

"ABC Production Center." *A + U Magazine,* July 1982, pp. 85–91.

"Chapter Awards Program." *Oculus* (New York A.I.A. Chapter), vol. 46, no. 9, May 1985, p. 10.

Goldberger, Paul. "ABC's New Buildings: A Lesson in Placating Fearful Neighbors." *New York Times,* 16 July 1979, p. C12.

Yee, Roger. "Mixed Use for an Urban Neighborhood." *Architectural Record,* January 1981, pp. 65–71.

Amoco

"Buildings in the News: Hexagonal Tower Resolves Conflicting Street Grids." *Architectural Record,* October 1978, p. 41.

"Downtown Denver Keeps Going Up and Up with Amoco Energy. An Interview with Architect Gene Kohn Brings Some Denver-style Philosophy from New York." *Denver Business World,* 9 October 1978.

Ebisch, Robert. "Response to Location." *Building Design & Construction,* October 1980.

Haselbush, Willard. "Business World: New Denver Skyscraper to Feature 'Covered Plaza'." *Denver Post,* 23 December 1978, p. 39.

AT&T Long Lines Eastern Regional Headquarters

Anderson, Grace. "A Lofty Galleria Skylights Suburban Offices." *Architectural Record,* November 1981, pp. 88–95.

"AT&T Long Lines Eastern Regional Headquarters." *Baumeister,* September 1982.

"AT&T Long Lines Eastern Regional Headquarters." *L'Industria delle Costruzioni,* October 1982, p. 46.

Yee, Roger. "AT&T's Galleria in Virginia." *Corporate Design Magazine,* January 1982, pp. 95–97.

AT&T Long Lines

Block 5, Seattle, Washington

"Classic Tower for Downtown Seattle." *Seattle Daily Journal of Commerce,* 26 July 1985, p. 1.

Petrich, Caroline. "Romance on Third Avenue." *Arcade: The Northwest Journal for Architecture and Design,* vol. 5, no. 3, August/September 1985, pp. 1, 12.

CNG Tower

Todd, Wallace, and Wallace, David. "The Catalyst: An Innovative Mixed-use Development." *Institute for Urban Design Project Monograph,* September 1984.

101 Federal Street, Boston
Goldberger, Paul. "Urban Building Trends Lend Boston an Odd Mix." *New York Times*, 6 June 1985.

125 East 57th Street, New York
Oser, S. Alan. "Split-lot Lexington Project Melds Conflicting Themes." *New York Times*, 14 October 1984, p. R7.

Garrison Channel Plan
Garrison, Renee. "Making Mountains Out of Buildings Is Part of the Plan." *Tampa Tribune*, 28 July 1985, Home and Design sec., p. 1.

General Re Headquarters
Alofsin, Anthony, and Bloomfield, Julia. "Architettura U.S.A. Trenta Piani di Creatività." *L'Uomo Vogue*, June 1983, pp. 176–83.
Goldberger, Paul. "Stamford's Renewal: Sun Belt in Connecticut." *New York Times*, 11 March 1985, pp. A1, B4.

The Goldome Bank for Savings Headquarters
Longdon, Phillip. "Letters from Buffalo: City Recyling Its Rich Heritage." *Preservation News*, September 1981, pp. 8–9.
Newmark, Herbert L. "Goldome Bank: A Shining Example of Design Matching Program." *Facilities Design & Management*, November 1983, pp. 64–69.

Hercules
"Buildings in the News: A Stone and Glass Corporate Headquarters in Wilmington." *Architectural Record*, January 1981, p. 47.
"Due Opere di Kohn Pedersen Fox." *L'Industria delle Costruzioni*, March 1984, pp. 54–65.
Futagawa, Yukio. "Kohn Pedersen Fox." *GA Document*, no. 12, January 1985, pp. 114–27.
"Hercules Incorporated Headquarters." *Baumeister*, October 1984, pp. 45–49.
"Hercules Headquarters." *Building Stone Magazine*, September/October 1984, pp. 42–44.
"Kohn Pedersen Fox Associates." *A + U Magazine*, May 1984, pp. 37–50.
.... "Kw/PF." *World Construction and Engineering*, March 1985, pp. 36–53.
Melnick, Scott. "Glass Meets Granite in Corporate Headquarters." *Building Design & Construction*, February 1984, pp. 94–98.

Miller, Nory. "Thinking Tall." *Progressive Architecture*, December 1980, p. 48.
"Soaring Space with a Civic Purpose." *Architecture Magazine*, February 1984, pp. 78–83.

Houston Office Tower—Block 265
Klebow, Nora. "Contextual Functionalism—The Work of Kohn Pedersen Fox." *Crit Magazine*, Fall 1983, pp. 14–17.
Kohn, A. Eugene. "Architecture Interior & Industrial Design." *Leaders Magazine*, April/May/June 1983, p. 119.

Kincaid Tower
"Setbacks Reduce Mass in Small-scaled Downtown." *Architectural Record*, July 1978, p. 41.

One Logan Square
Anderson, Grace. "In Philadelphia's Tradition." *Architectural Record*, February 1985, pp. 142–49.
"One Logan Square." *Building Stone Magazine*, January/February 1983, pp. 14–15.
"One Logan Square." *Building Stone Magazine*, November/December 1984, pp. 18–20.

383 Madison Avenue
"First Boston's New York Tower." *Property News International*, 27 June 1985.
Knevitt, Charles. "Three buildings bidding to scrape the highest sky over New York." *The London Times*, 11 June 1985.
Rastorfer, Darl. "William J. Le Messurier's super-tall structures: architectural engineering." *Architectural Record*, February 1985, pp. 151–57.

900 North Michigan
"New Chicago Tower's Design Hints at Old Skyscrapers." *Building Design Journal*, November 1984, p. 5.

Park Centre
Futugawa, Yukio, "Kohn Pedersen Fox," *GA Document*, no.12, January 1985, pp. 114–27.

Procter & Gamble World Headquarters
Boles, Daralice and Murphy, Jim. "Cincinnati Centerpiece," *Progressive Architecture*, October 1985, pp. 71–87.
Goldberger, Paul. "A Homage to the Skyscraper." *New York Times*, 18 April 1982, Architecture View, p. 20.
Klebow, Nora. "Contextual Functionalism—The Work of Kohn Pedersen Fox." *Crit Magazine*, Fall 1983, pp. 14–17.
"Kohn Pedersen Fox Associates." *World Construction & Engineering*, March 1985, pp. 44–49.
Merkel, Jayne. "The Procter & Gamble Headquarters Building." *Dialogue*, Nos. 5–6, 1985, pp. 16–20.
"Recent High-rise Building in the U.S.A." *A + U Magazine*, October 1982, pp. 98–106.
Rosen, Steven. "P&G Plans Garden Everyone Can Enjoy." *Cincinnati Enquirer*, 16 April 1983, pp. 6–11.
Schnipper, Scott. "P&G's Earthly Garden Rooted in Fertile Research." *Facilities Design & Management*, September 1985, pp. 62–70.
Solomon, Julie B. "P&G Makes an Architectural Statement." *Wall Street Journal*, 10 June 1985, Leisure and Arts sec.

Projects X,Y
"Les Nouveaux Gratte-ciel Américains . . . Suite." *L'Architecture d'Aujourd'hui*, September 1982, pp. XIV–XV.

Rocky Mountain Energy
"Architecture Defers to Majestic Surroundings." *Architectural Record*, April 1983, pp. 126–29.
Korman, Richard. "Rocky Mountain Energy Wins a Race Against Time." *Facilities Design & Management*, January 1983, pp. 46–53.

Southwest Center Houston Competition
Arnell, Peter, and Bickford, Ted, eds. *Southwest Center: The Houston Competition*. New York: Rizzoli International Publications, 1983.
Holmes, Ann. "82-Story Design for Houston Tower." *Houston Chronicle*, 12 October 1982, sec. 4, p. 5.
"Wuthering Heights—Bank of the Southwest Competition." *Domus*, February 1983, p. 12–13.

Tabor Center
"Denver Distilled." *Architectural Record*, September 1985, pp. 127–35.
Futagawa, Yukio. "Kohn Pedersen Fox." *GA Document*, no. 12, January 1985, pp. 114–27.

Opsata, Margaret. "The Recipe for Urban Mixed Use." *Building Design Journal*, October 1983, pp. 12–14.
"Recent High-rise Buildings in the U.S.A." *A + U Magazine*, October 1982, pp. 102–105.

333 Wacker Drive
Alofsin, Anthony, and Bloomfield, Julia. "Architettura U.S.A. Trenta Piani di Creativita." *L'Uomo Vogue*, June 1983, pp. 176–83.
Conway, Patricia, and Jensen, Robert. *Ornamentalism*. Clarkson N. Potter, 1982.
"Due Opere di Kohn Pedersen Fox." *L'Industria della Costruzioni*, March 1984, pp. 54–65.
Futagawa, Yukio. "Kohn Pedersen Fox." *GA Document*, no. 9, February 1984, pp. 84–89.
Gapp, Paul. "Outside Architects Have Their Designs on Chicago." *Chicago Tribune*, 10 July 1983.
———. "A Gutsy New Yorker and His Taut, Green Giant on the River." *Chicago Tribune*, 23 October 1983, Arts sec., p. 13.
Goldberger, Paul. "Chicago Has a New Profile." *New York Times*, 8 May 1983.
Greenspan, David A. "333 Wacker Drive." *Inland Architect*, October 1983, pp. 10–15.
Greer, Nora Richter. "A Complex Response to an Unusual Site." *Architecture Magazine*, May 1984, pp. 186–93.
Irace, Fulvio. "Romanticism and Reintegration." *Domus*, September 1984, pp. 2–7.
Klebow, Nora. "Contextual Functionalism—The Work of Kohn Pedersen Fox." *Crit Magazine*, Fall 1983, pp. 14–17.
"Kohn Pedersen Fox Associates." *A + U Magazine*, May 1984, pp. 37–50.
"Les Nouveaux Gratte-ciel Américains . . . Suite." *L'Architecture d'Aujourd'hui*, September 1982, pp. XIV–XV.
Pedersen, William. "Bill Pedersen on Urban Architecture." *Compass* (Equitable Real Estate), Fall 1984, pp. 18–20.
"The Sky's the Limit." *Newsweek*, 8 November 1982, pp. 66–73.
Wright, Gordon. "Unusual Framing Accommodates Fan-shaped Plan." *Building Design & Construction*, June 1983, pp. 96–99.

1000 Wilshire Boulevard
DeWolf, Evelyn. "Post Modern Office Tower Planned." *Los Angeles Times*, 21 October 1984, p. 1.

AWARDS

1987 AIA Honors Award for Proctor and Gamble General Offices Complex, Cincinnati, Ohio, by the National AIA.

1986 PCI Award for Arbor circle, Parsippany, New Jersey, by the Pre-stressed Concrete Institute.

1986 NYS AIA Merit Award for General Re Corporate Headquarters, Stamford, Connecticut, by the American Institute of Architects, New York State Chapter.

1984 PCI Award for Goldome Bank for Savings, Buffalo, New York, by the Pre-stressed Concrete Institute.

1986 Citation for the Groupe Bouygues Corporate Headquarters project, Versailles, France, by the New York Chapter of the American Institute of Architects.

1985 Award for Design Excellence for One Logan Square and WABC-TV Studio 23/24, by the American Institute of Architects, New York State Chapter.

1985 Professional Excellence in Urban Design for Tabor Center, Denver, Colorado, by the College of Design and Planning, University of Colorado, Denver, Colorado.

1985 Distinguished Architecture Award for WABC-TV Studio 23/24, New York, New York, by the New York Chapter of the American Institute of Architects.

Regional Award for Architectural Concrete for Tabor Center, Denver, Colorado, by the American Concrete Institute.

1984 Award for Significant Contribution to the Construction Industry for the Usage of Architectural Concrete for Tabor Center, Denver, Colorado, by Engineering News Record Magazine.

Award for Excellence in New Construction for Eight Penn Center, Philadelphia, Pennsylvania, by the Old Philadelphia Redevelopment Corporation, 1983.

Silver Medal Design Award for One Logan Square, Philadelphia, Pennsylvania, by the Philadelphia Chapter of the American Institute of Architects, 1982.

Architectural Merit Award for Eight Penn Center, Philadelphia, Pennsylvania, by the Philadelphia Chapter of the American Institute of Architects, 1982.

Interior Award for AT&T Long Lines Eastern Regional Headquarters, Oakton, Virginia, by the Philadelphia Chapter of the American Institute of Architects, 1982.

Excellence in Design Honor Award for the Rocky Mountain Energy Company Headquarters, Broomfield, Colorado, by the Western Mountain Region American Institute of Architects, 1981.

Excellence in Design Honor Award for Kincaid Towers, Lexington, Kentucky, by the Kentucky Society of Architects, 1981.

Architectural Record 1980 Record Interiors for the executive-floor lobby and reception area at AT&T Company/195 Broadway Corporation, 1980.

1984 Distinguished Architecture Award for Hercules Incorporated Headquarters, Wilmington, Delaware, by the New York Chapter of the American Institute of Architects.

Award for Excellence in New Construction for One Logan Square, Philadelphia, Pennsylvania, by the Old Philadelphia Redevelopment Corporation, 1984.

AIA Honors Awards 1984 for 333 Wacker Drive, Chicago, Illinois, by the National American Institute of Architects.

Architecture Magazine Interior Architecture Award for Hercules Incorporated Headquarters, Wilmington, Delaware, 1984.

Gold Institute Award for AT&T Long Lines Eastern Regional Headquarters, Oakton, Virginia, 1983.

Architectural Merit Award for One Logan Square, Philadelphia, Pennsylvania, by the Pennsylvania Society of Architects, 1983.

1983 Award for Excellence in Architecture for ABC Washington News Bureau, Washington, D.C., by the Washington Chapter of the American Institute of Architects.

Urban Design Award for Excellence in Renovation and Preservation for the ABC/Armory Studio at 56 West 66th Street in New York City, 1978.

P/A Awards Program for Recognition of Merit for Design for Kincaid Towers, Lexington, Kentucky, 1978.

EXHIBITIONS

GA International 87. Tokyo, Japan. April 4–May 10, 1987

Exposition "Lieux? de Travail". Centre Geroges Pompidou, Centre de Creation, Industrielle CCI. Paris, France. June 1986, October 1986.

Craft in Architecture. The New York State Association of Architects/The American Institute of Architects Annual Convention. New York, New York. October 1985.

The Works of Kohn Pedersen Fox. Royal Institute of British Architects. London, England. June–July 1985.

Exhibition of Work by Newly Elected Members and Recipients of Awards. Arnold W. Brunner Memorial Prize in Architecture, American Academy and Institute of Arts and Letters. New York, New York. May–June 1985.

1985 Distinguished Architecture Awards Exhibit. The New York City Chapter of the American Institute of Architects. Municipal Art Society, Urban Center, New York, New York. May–June 1985.

Lost and Won Competitions. American Institute of Architects. San Francisco, California. 1985.

Selected Works. The Baltimore Chapter of the American Institute of Architects. Baltimore, Maryland. March–April 1985.

Architex 85. Barbican Exhibition Center. London, England. May 1985.

Buildings in Progress Since Midtown Zoning. Municipal Art Society, Urban Center, New York, New York. January–February 1985.

American Institute of Architects Annual Members Exhibit. The Philadelphia Chapter of the American Institute of Architects. Philadelphia, Pennsylvania. 1983.

CREDITS

Photography

Peter Aaron/ESTO: p.94–3,4; p.97–4.

Hedrich Blessing: p.130–1.

Dan Cornish: p.31–2; p.153–2; p.154–1; p.155–6.

Elliot Fine: p.24–1.

Judd Haggard: p.278.

Horner: p.65–2; p.66–1,2; p.69–2,3,4,5; p.81–2; p.82–1,2; p.83–3; p.85–2; p.87–6; p.109–2,3; p.112–1; p.113–3; p.115–2; p.116–1,2; p.117–5,6,7,8; p.139–4; p.141–2; p.142–1; p.149–2; p.151–6; p.169–2; p.170–1,2; p.171–3; p.187–3; p.191–3; p.197–2,3; p.201–7,8; p.213–2; p.217–3; p.229–2; p.252–1; p.253–3; p.285–1,2.

Wolfgang Hoyt/ESTO: p.14–4,5; p.17–2; p.27–2; p.28–3,4.

Timothy Hursley: p.89–2.

Barbara Karant: p.33–3; p.37–2,3; p.44–1; p.45–2; p.96–1,2,3.

Chun Lai: p.59–2; p.163–2; p.166–1,2; p.167–5; p.179–5,6.

Norman McGrath: p.31–3; p.32–1,2; p.33–4,5; p.51–2; p.52–1,3; p.53–4,5,6; p.56–1; p.57–2,3,4,5; p.314.

Gregory Murphy: p.39–2; p.43–4; p.46–1; p.47–2; p.48–1; p.49–2.

Jock Pottle: cover; p.21–2; p.29–5; p.36–1; p.52–2; p.60–1; p.61–2,3; p.71–2,3; p.72–1,2; p.73–3,4,5; p.92–1,2; p.93–3,4; p.94–1,2; p.97–5,6; p.99–5; p.101–3; p.103–2,3; p.105–4,5; p.119–2; p.120–1,2; p.121–3,4; p.122–1; p.129–2; p.130–1,2,5; p.131–6; p.135–2,3; p.145–2; p.146–1; p.147–2,3; p.155–2,3,4,5; p.175–2; p.178–1; p.179–7; p.181–2; p.182–1,2; p.183–3,4; p.185–4; p.193–2; p.195–4,5; p.199–7,8; p.205–5,6; p.207–2; p.208–1; p.209–2; p.211–4,5; p.216–2; p.219–2; p.221–3,4; p.225–2; p.228–1; p.229–3; p.231–2; p.234–2; p.235–3; p.237–2; p.240–1; p.241–2,3; p.249–2; p.255–2; p.267–2; p.271–2; p.282–1; p.283–2; p.285–3; p.316; p.318; back cover.

Ezra Stoller/ESTO: p.23–3,4,5,6; p.24–2; p.25–3,4,5.

Judith Turner: title page; p.95–5,6,7,8; p.100–1,2; p.313; p.315; p.317; p.319–1,2; p.320; p.321.

Renderings

Lebbeus Woods; p.76–1; p.138–1,2,3; p.142–2; p.190–1,2; p.203–2; p.258–1.

ACKNOWLEDGEMENTS

Special thanks to A. Eugene Kohn for his unyielding faith and cooperation. Our thanks also go to William Pedersen, Kenneth Frampton, and Robert A. M. Stern for their support and guidance in the preparation of this monograph. We extend our gratitude to Dennis Abramson, Patricia Conway, Peter Dixon, Warren A. James, Gregory Katz, Gail La Cava, Carrol McCutchen, Ilona Rider, and Alexander Ward for their general help and goodwill.

The Editors